Visual Quic

WordPerfect
for
Windows

Paul Webster
Carrie Webster

Peachpit Press

WordPerfect for Windows: Visual QuickStart Guide
Paul Webster
Carrie Webster

Peachpit Press, Inc.
2414 Sixth Street
Berkeley, CA 94710
(510) 548-4393
(510) 548-5991 (fax)

Notice of Liability:

The information in this book is distributed on an "as is" basis, without warranty. While every precaution has been taken in the preparation of this book, neither the author nor Webster & Associates shall have any liability to any person or entity with respect to any liability, loss, or damage caused or alleged to be caused directly or indirectly by the instructions contained in this book or by the computer software and hardware products described therein.

Trademarks:

Throughout this book, trademarked names are used. Rather than put a trademark symbol in every occurrence of a trademarked name, we are using the names only in an editorial fashion and to the benefit of the trademark owner, with no intention of infringement of the trademark. Where those designations appear in this book, the designations have been printed in initial caps.

ISBN: 0-938151-94-0

Printed and bound in the United States of America

Why a Visual QuickStart?

Virtually no one actually reads computer books; rather, people typically refer to them. This series of **Visual QuickStart Guides** has made that reference easier thanks to a new approach to learning computer applications.

While conventional computer books lean towards providing extensive textual explanations, a **Visual QuickStart Guide** takes a far more visual approach—pictures literally show you what to do, and the text is limited to clear, concise commentary. Learning becomes easier, because a **Visual QuickStart Guide** familiarizes you with the look and feel of your software. Learning also becomes faster, since there are no long-winded passages to comb through.

It's a new approach to computer learning, but it's all solidly based on experience: Webster & Associates have logged thousands of hours of classroom computer training, and have written several books on desktop publishing topics.

Chapter 1 provides a general introduction to WordPerfect 5.1 for Windows and discusses the screen components.

Chapters 2 through **13** graphically overview the major WordPerfect 5.1 for Windows features. These chapters are easy to reference and, with the extensive use of screen shots, allow concepts to be quickly grasped.

Appendix A displays all the major dialog boxes and how they are accessed.

Acknowledgments

The authors wish to acknowledge the assistance of Tony Webster, Lesleigh Simms, Roger Stott, and Philippa Yelland in the writing and editing of this book.

Contents

WordPerfect for Windows

The Screen

WordPerfect for Windows uses the graphic nature of the Windows interface. You will see how your document looks and, as you edit it, most changes you make will be visible instantly. With the *Button Bar* and *Ruler* displayed on screen, WordPerfect offers a range of powerful editing and text manipulation features that help to simplify and speed document preparation.

Figure 1. The WordPerfect screen is shown below. On start-up, your screen may include only the *Menu Bar* and *Status Bar,* as both the *Button Bar* and *Ruler* are displayed only if they have been selected previously. All major features of the WordPerfect screen are described in this chapter.

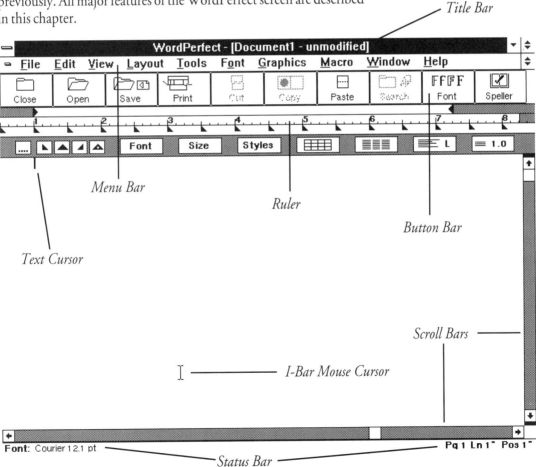

Title Bar

Menu Bar

Ruler

Button Bar

Text Cursor

Scroll Bars

I-Bar Mouse Cursor

Status Bar

THE SCREEN COMPONENTS

THE STATUS BAR

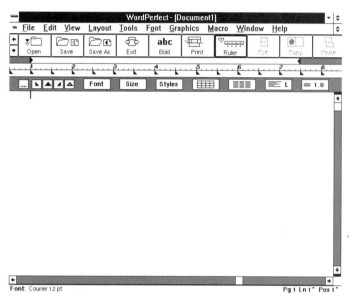

Figure 2. Whenever you open WordPerfect, you will see a *Status Bar* at the bottom of the screen. As you begin to use WordPerfect, you will notice this bar changing. It is reflecting what you are doing in your document. Before you have made any changes in WordPerfect, the left of the *Status Bar* tells you the default font and size. The right of the *Status Bar* indicates the page number where the cursor is resting and the position of the cursor on that page. *Ln* signifies the cursor line location and *Pos* stands for the horizontal position of the cursor on that line. The default setting is 1 inch for each of these options, which denotes a 1 inch top and left margin.

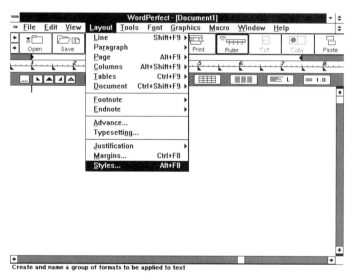

Figure 3. After selecting a menu with the mouse, the information on the left side of the *Status Bar* changes. It indicates to you the particular function of the selected menu or command.

THE TITLE BAR

Figure 4. The *Title Bar* is common to all Windows Applications. It indicates the program name and the title of the current document as well as its path. If you have not yet saved the current document, the *Title Bar* will read **Document 1**. It will also say **unmodified** until you make changes.

Figure 5. The *Title Bar* also contains (a) the *Control Menu Box* and (b) the *Maximize* and *Minimize* buttons. Clicking once on the *Control Menu Box* activates the *Windows Control* menu and from the menu it is possible to exit from the program, minimize or maximize the current window, or activate the Windows *Task List* dialog box.

The single down-arrow of the *Minimize* button (1) will minimize the program window to an icon at the bottom left of the screen. This icon is double-clicked to reactivate the window. Clicking on the *Maximize* button (2) causes WordPerfect to fill the entire screen; the *Maximize* button then changes to the *Resize* button (3). Clicking on the *Resize* button returns the screen to its previous size.

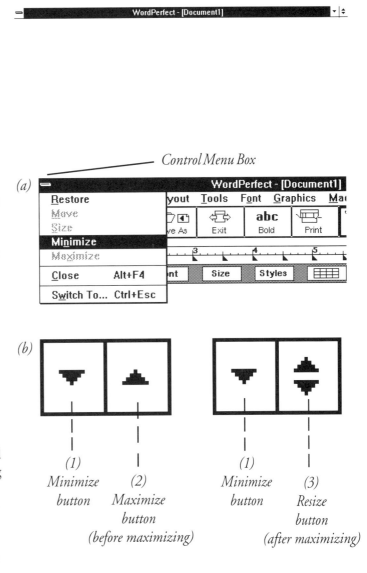

Control Menu Box

THE MENU BAR

File Edit View Layout Tools Font Graphics Macro Window Help

Figure 6. The *Menu Bar* runs along the top of the screen below the *Title Bar.* If your mouse is clicked or held down on a menu option, a list of further options or commands will be displayed under this menu. Menus are common to all Windows applications. The WordPerfect *Menu Bar* also contains a *Minimize/Maximize* button and a *Control Menu Box* that apply to this document only.

You have two ways of displaying the WordPerfect menus. The first is the default setting, in which all menu commands are visible. However, if you select the *Short Menus* option from the **View** menu, some commands are no longer available.

(a)

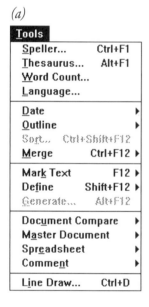

(b)

Figure 7. The **Tools** menu is displayed with all commands available (a). In (b) the same menu is shown after the *Short Menus* option has been selected. The range of commands shown has been reduced to the bare essentials.

THE SCROLL BARS

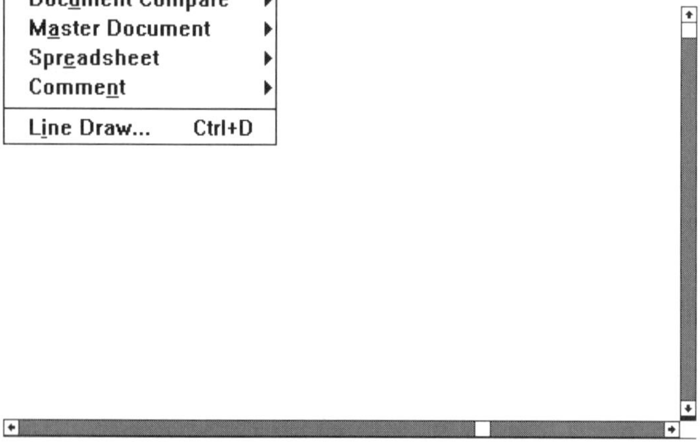

Figure 8. The *Scroll Bars* are used with the mouse to move quickly around your page. The gray area of the *Scroll Bar* can be clicked on to move up, down, or across in large steps. To move in smaller steps, click on the arrows at either end of the *Scroll Bars.* To move around in arbitrary steps, hold the mouse down on the white square in the *Scroll Bar,* move it to the desired position, and release the mouse. When the white square is at the very top of the vertical *Scroll Bar,* it indicates you are at the top of the page.

Figure 9. The vertical *Scroll Bar* is on by default but the horizontal *Scroll Bar* may not be displayed. If you want the horizontal *Scroll Bar* to appear every time you enter WordPerfect, select the *Display* command in the *Preferences* sub-menu from the **File** menu. In the *Scroll Bar* section of the *Display Settings* dialog box, click on the *Display Horizontal Scroll Bar* option.

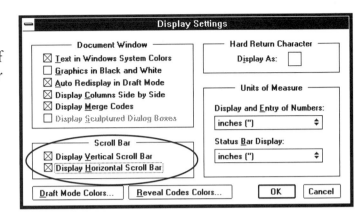

THE RULER

Figure 10. The *Ruler* in WordPerfect is activated by selecting the *Ruler* command from the **View** menu. It is a very useful feature and provides quick and easy access to a variety of options and commands for formatting your document. Selecting the *Ruler* command in the **View** menu, while the *Ruler* is displayed, will de-activate the *Ruler*.

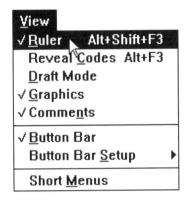

Figure 11. After selecting the *Ruler* command, you will see the *Ruler* appear toward the top of the screen below the *Menu Bar*.

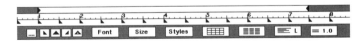

Figure 12. Along the very top of the *Ruler* are the margin indicators or guides. These guides display the current left and right text margins. The white area between the two inward-facing arrows indicates the area in which text will be positioned.

Current left and right margin indicators

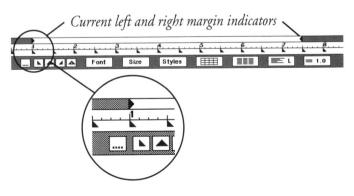

MARGINS

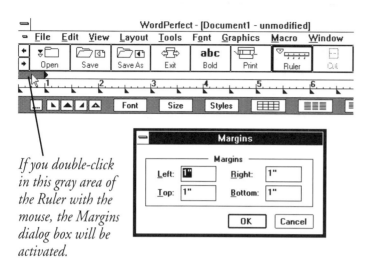

If you double-click in this gray area of the Ruler with the mouse, the Margins dialog box will be activated.

Figure 13. By double-clicking on the gray area to the west of the left margin marker or to the east of the right margin marker, you will activate the *Margins* dialog box. Here you can change the current margin settings by keying in a new number for each option.

For more information on the *Margins* dialog box see Chapter 3 — **Page Formatting.**

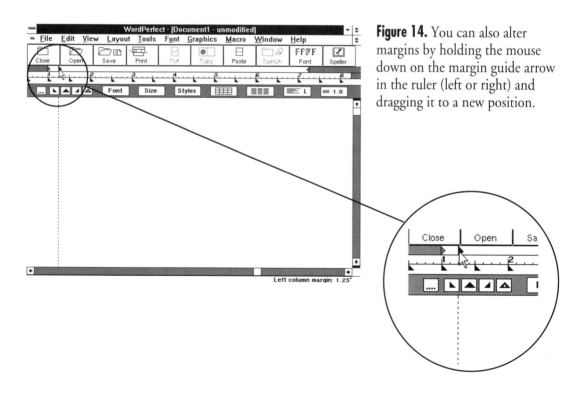

Figure 14. You can also alter margins by holding the mouse down on the margin guide arrow in the ruler (left or right) and dragging it to a new position.

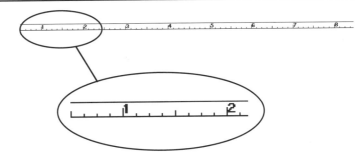

Figure 15. Below the margin guides is the actual *Ruler* itself. The unit of measurement for the *Ruler* is set in the *Display Settings* dialog box (Figure 9) which is obtained from the *Display* command in the *Preferences* sub-menu in the **File** menu. (For more information see Chapter 5 — **Setting Preferences**.) This *Ruler* is useful in establishing the current margin settings (just above the *Ruler*), and the current tab settings (just below the *Ruler*).

TABS

Figure 16. Underneath the actual *Ruler* are the tab markers. These triangular-shaped markers denote each tab stop—that is, how far the text is going to move when the Tab key is hit.

By default, tabs are set at every 0.5 inches.

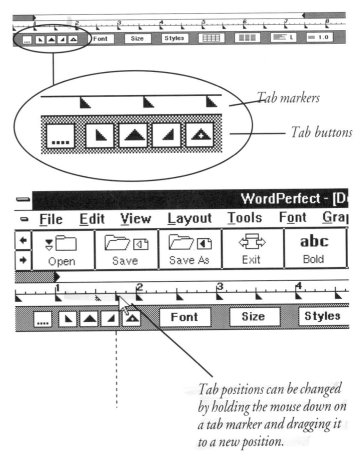

Tab markers

Tab buttons

Figure 17. The tab markers not only denote each tab stop, but they also allow you to alter tab positions. This is done by holding down the mouse on a triangular marker and dragging it to a new position on the *Ruler*. Tabs may be also added and deleted with the mouse. To delete a tab marker from the *Ruler*, simply drag it below the *Ruler* and release the mouse.

Tab positions can be changed by holding the mouse down on a tab marker and dragging it to a new position.

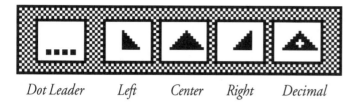

Dot Leader   *Left*   *Center*   *Right*   *Decimal*

Figure 18. To add a tab to the *Ruler,* hold the mouse down on one of the *Tab* buttons (whichever type of tab you want) and drag it to the *Ruler.* Wherever you release your mouse, the new tab will appear. For more information on tabs, see Chapter 3 — **Page Formatting.**

FONT BUTTON

Figure 19. The *Font* button, to the right of the *Tab* buttons, allows you to apply fonts to text quickly. Hold your mouse down on this button and run it down the menu to select the required font. Figures 20 to 22 show how to add fonts to this list.

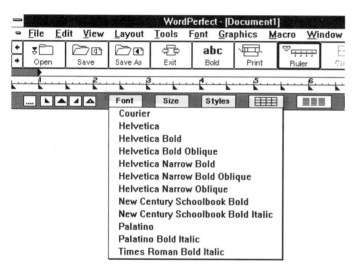

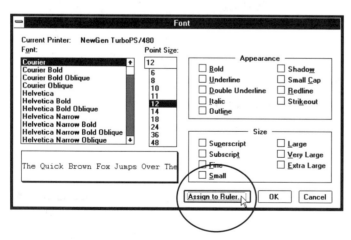

Figure 20. To fill this list with all your available fonts, or just the ones you want, activate the *Font* command from the **Font** menu. In the *Font* dialog box that appears, click on the *Assign to Ruler* command. Double-clicking on the *Font* button will also activate the *Font* dialog box.

Figure 21. You are now given the opportunity of adding or clearing fonts to or from this list while in the *Ruler Fonts Menu* dialog box. Select the font on the left and click on the *Add* button. Alternatively, double-click on the font at left. Either method will enter the required font in the *Fonts on Ruler* list box on the right. Click on *OK* twice to return to the screen.

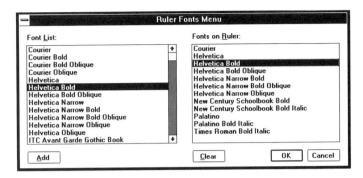

Figure 22. Once you have added all the necessary fonts, they will then appear in the *Font* list from the *Ruler.* You can now apply them to your text by holding the mouse down on the *Font* button and selecting the required typeface from the list.

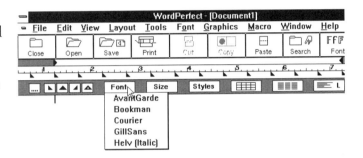

SIZE

Figure 23. The *Size* button in the *Ruler* lets you change the size of text quickly and easily by selecting a new size from the list of sizes available. Double-clicking on the *Size* button will activate the *Font* dialog box.

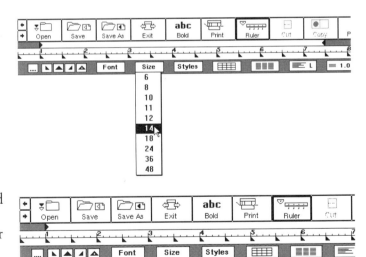

STYLES

Figure 24. When the mouse is held down on the *Styles* button, any styles that have been created in, or came with, WordPerfect can be turned on by selecting the style name from the list. Double-clicking on the *Styles* button will activate the *Styles* dialog box. For more information on styles, see Chapter 9 — **Styles & Outlines.**

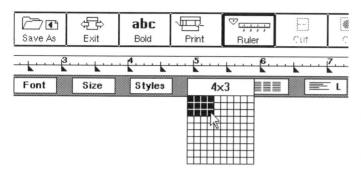

TABLES

Figure 25. The *Table* button (the grid button to the right of the *Styles* button) provides a visual means of creating tables. When the mouse is held down on this button, a small grid appears. As you drag the mouse over this grid, it becomes highlighted, and a table size appears above it. This represents how big your table will be in columns by rows.

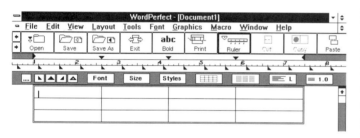

Figure 26. Once you release the mouse, a table will appear on your page at the size specified at the top of the grid. Double-clicking on the *Tables* button will activate the *Create Table* dialog box. For more information on tables, see Chapter 8 — **Creating Tables.**

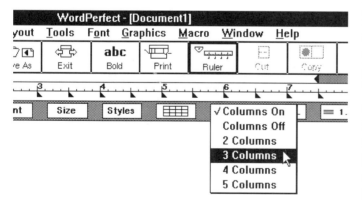

COLUMNS

Figure 27. The *Columns* button (next to the *Tables* button) provides a quick way of creating multiple column documents. When you hold down the mouse on the *Columns* button, the menu that appears allows you to turn the columns on or off, or select from two to five columns. The new column setting will begin from the cursor position onwards.

Figure 28. If you double-click on the *Columns* button, you will get the *Define Columns* dialog box. Here you have more control over the sizing of the columns and the spacing between them. For more information on columns, see Chapter 3 — **Page Formatting**.

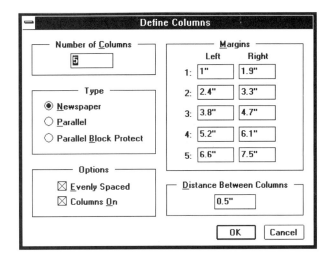

JUSTIFICATION

Figure 29. The *Justification* button (to the right of the *Columns* button) provides a quick way of changing text justification. The options available in this menu are *Left, Right, Center,* and *Full.* Justification can occur from the cursor position onwards, or only to a selected paragraph or paragraphs.

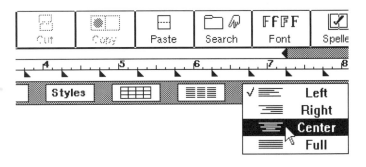

Figure 30. Once you have selected one of the options from the *Justification* menu, the first letter of this option will appear in the button. You do not have to activate the menu to see what style of justification is active.

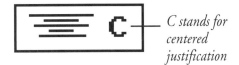

C stands for centered justification

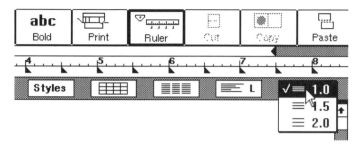

LINE SPACING

Figure 31. The *Line Spacing* button provides a quick way of changing line spacing. When you hold the mouse down on this button, the options available are 1.0, 1.5 and 2.0. This affects the amount of space you have between each line of selected text, or all lines that appear after the cursor.

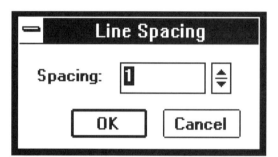

Figure 32. If you double-click on the *Line Spacing* button, the *Line Spacing* dialog box appears. Here you can enter line spacing amounts not available in the *Ruler*.

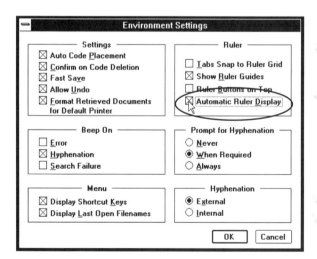

Figure 33. If you wish the *Ruler* to appear every time you start WordPerfect, this can be chosen in the *Environment Settings* dialog box. This dialog box is activated from the *Environment* command in the *Preferences* sub-menu from the **File** menu. Select the *Automatic Ruler Display* option in this dialog box to ensure that the *Ruler* will appear by default every time you start WordPerfect.

THE BUTTON BAR

Figure 34. To activate or de-activate the *Button Bar* on the WordPerfect screen, select the *Button Bar* command from the **View** menu. The WordPerfect *Button Bar* is a visual means by which commands and functions can be selected, without moving through menus or dialog boxes or using shortcut keys. Default Button Bars are provided with WordPerfect. You can design and name your own, however, gaining quick and easy access to the commands you use most often.

Figure 35. The *Button Bar,* by default, is situated at the top of your screen, below the *Menu Bar* and above the *Ruler.* These buttons can now be used in conjunction with the mouse to select a command. Each button, by default, contains a picture and a command name, representing a function or command from the WordPerfect menus.

For example, the second button shown above represents the *Open* command from the **File** menu. Clicking on this button is the equivalent of directly selecting the *Open* command from the **File** menu.

EDITING THE BUTTON BAR

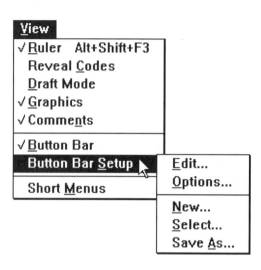

Figure 36. The options for editing existing *Button Bars,* as well as creating your own, are available from the *Button Bar Setup* command sub-menu from the **View** menu.

The first option available in the *Button Bar Setup* sub-menu of Figure 36 is the *Edit* option.

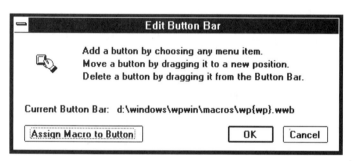

Figure 37. Selecting the *Edit* option from the *Button Bar Setup* sub-menu will activate the *Edit Button Bar* dialog box.

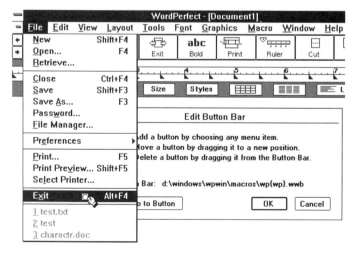

Figure 38. It is now possible to add more command buttons to a *Button Bar* by choosing them from a menu, as though you are selecting the command normally. Once you have selected a command from a menu, it appears in the *Button Bar* you are editing.

Figure 39. With the *Edit Button Bar* dialog box active, it is also possible to alter the current order of the buttons in the *Button Bar*. This is done by holding the mouse down on the button you would like moved, then dragging the mouse and releasing it in a new position on the *Button Bar*.

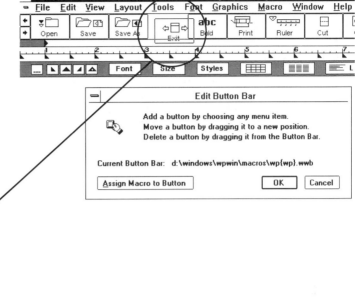

Figure 40. The *Exit Button* moved in Figure 39 has now swapped positions with the *Bold* button.

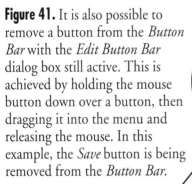

Figure 41. It is also possible to remove a button from the *Button Bar* with the *Edit Button Bar* dialog box still active. This is achieved by holding the mouse button down over a button, then dragging it into the menu and releasing the mouse. In this example, the *Save* button is being removed from the *Button Bar*.

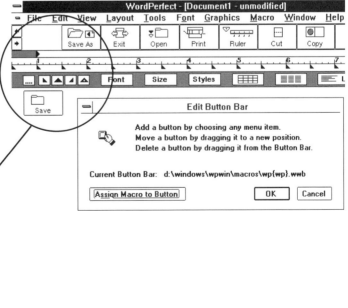

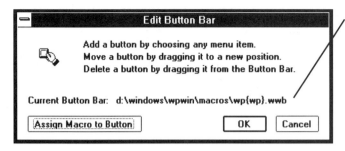

Figure 42. The *Edit Button Bar* dialog box also displays the directory in which the current *Button Bar* file is saved.

BUTTON BAR OPTIONS

The *Options* command in the Figure 36 *Button Bar Setup* sub-menu affects the appearance of the *Button Bar*. Selecting it causes the Figure 43 dialog box to appear.

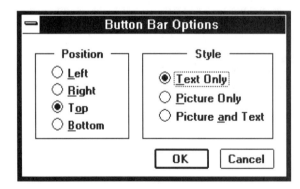

Figure 43. The selections within the *Position* section of the *Button Bar Options* dialog box affect where the *Button Bar* sits on the page. The default position is at the top of the screen. To change its position to appear on the left, right or bottom of the screen, you select the relevant choice under the *Position* option.

Figure 44. Note how each button in the *Button Bar* of Figure 1 contains both a picture and some text. The selections under the *Style* option in the *Button Bar Options* dialog box of Figure 43 alter the contents of each button. If you select the *Text Only* option and click on *OK*, you will see the effect of this selection in the following figure.

| Save | Save As | Exit | Open | Print |

Figure 45. The *Button Bar* now contains only text, rather than pictures and text. Selecting the *Text Only* option reduces the amount of screen space taken up by the *Button Bar*.

CREATING A BUTTON BAR

Selecting the *New* command in the *Button Bar Setup* sub-menu of Figure 36 activates the *Edit Button Bar* dialog box of Figure 46.

Figure 46. This dialog box now gives you the ability to create your own *Button Bar* and fill it with your favorite commands. After selecting the *New* command, the current *Button Bar* is deleted in preparation for the one you are about to create.

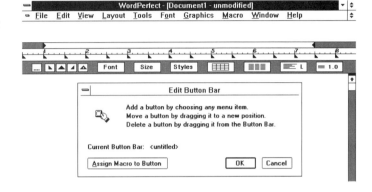

Figure 47. You are now free to add your own commands to the *Button Bar*. This is done by selecting commands from menus, exactly as if you were using these commands. In this case, however, they will just be added to the *Button Bar*. Note that the mouse pointer changes shape to indicate that you are selecting commands just in order to create buttons.

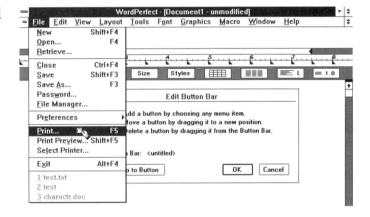

Figure 48. The *Print* command from the **File** menu, selected in Figure 47, has now been added to the new *Button Bar*.

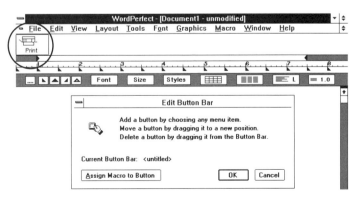

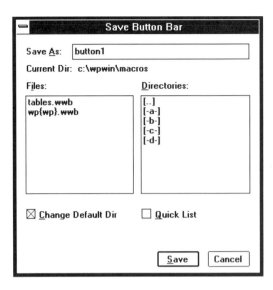

Figure 49. Once you have finished adding commands to the *Button Bar,* click on OK in the Figure 48 dialog box and you will be prompted to save the file through the *Save Button Bar* dialog box shown here. All you need do at this stage is simply enter a name for this file. For this example we have put in the name *Button1.* No extension has to be added to this file. Once the name has been entered, click on the *Save* button to save the file to disk.

The *Button Bar* you created remains active, as well as now existing as a file on disk, with perhaps other *Button Bar* files. Different *Button Bar* files can be used by different people, for different purposes.

SELECTING A BUTTON BAR

If you wish to load a totally different *Button Bar* file, choose the *Select* command from the *Button Bar Setup* sub-menu of Figure 36.

Figure 50. From the *Select Button Bar* dialog box, you can choose any *Button Bar* files that have been previously saved. This is done by locating the directory in which *Button Bar* files have been saved, then either double-clicking on the name of the file in the list, or by highlighting it once with the mouse and clicking on *Select.* The previous *Button Bar* disappears, and the new *Button Bar* is loaded.

Three *Button Bars* are available for selection in this figure.

The *Save As* command in the *Button Bar Setup* sub-menu of Figure 36 lets you rename the current *Button Bar.*

Figure 51. The new name is keyed into the *Save As* text box. The *Save As* option is used if you want to modify an existing *Button Bar* slightly. This option makes a copy of the currently displayed *Button Bar,* which you are then free to change without affecting the original version. This is an optional way of creating a new *Button Bar.*

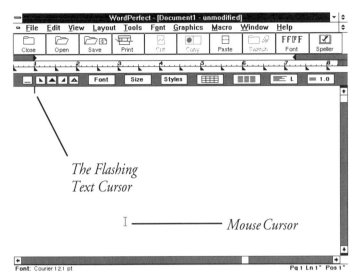

The Flashing
Text Cursor

I —————— Mouse Cursor

THE CURSOR

Figure 52. The *Text Cursor* is the flashing bar that sits on the page. It can be inserted into text with the mouse and moved around with the cursor keys. Wherever this cursor is situated, new text will appear when you start typing. The *Backspace* key on your keyboard will remove the character before the *Cursor*, while the *Delete* key removes the character at the *Cursor*. The *Status Bar* also tells you the line and position of the cursor.

The *Mouse Cursor* is shown as an "I-beam" icon on the screen.

EDITING TEXT

WordPerfect documents can be edited and formatted in various ways. This chapter looks at simple editing and formatting of text, while Chapter 3 looks at more complex page and paragraph formatting.

TYPEOVER MODE

By default, WordPerfect works in *Insert* mode. This means any text keyed into the middle of existing text will force that existing text to move to the right. This is the normal method of word processor operation.

Figure 1. If you press the *Insert* key on your keyboard, you will activate *Typeover* mode, which is revealed in the *Status Bar*. New text will no longer move to the right as it is inserted into the current text. The new text will appear directly over the existing text. Turn *Typeover* mode off by pressing the *Insert* key again.

Note: When using Typeover mode, you cannot type over codes. If the text that you are typing over encounters a code, the code remains and the text is simply inserted at this point. (For an explanation of codes see the Reveal Codes section starting at Figure 12 of this chapter.)

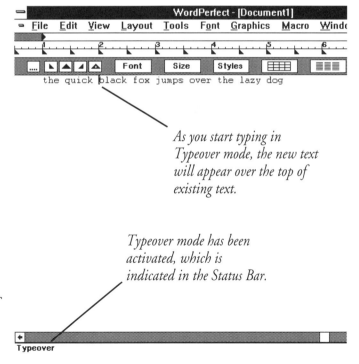

As you start typing in Typeover mode, the new text will appear over the top of existing text.

Typeover mode has been activated, which is indicated in the Status Bar.

EDITING KEYS

The *Backspace* and *Delete* keys on your keyboard are used for simple text editing in your document. The *Backspace* key moves the cursor one space to the left, removing characters as it goes. The *Delete* key removes the characters to the right of the cursor. The cursor remains stationary, deleting text to the right, which moves toward the cursor.

UNDO AND UNDELETE

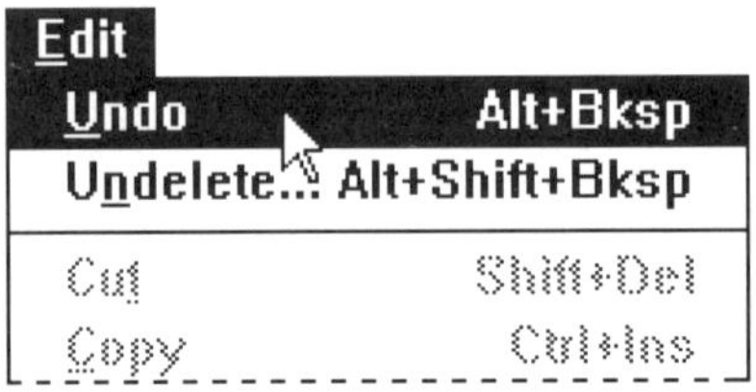

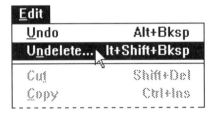

Figure 2. The *Undo* command from the **Edit** menu will reverse the last editing change you have made. When dealing with text, it will undo your most recent text editing operation.

Figure 3. The *Undelete* command works in a slightly different way. Selecting the *Undelete* command from the **Edit** menu activates the *Undelete* dialog box.

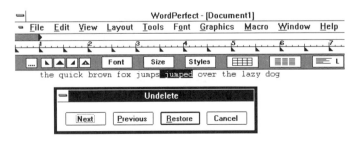

Figure 4. With the *Undelete* dialog box active, you have the ability to display the last three deletions you made, and restore the appropriate one. In this example the selected word (jumped) was previously deleted and is now reappearing after selecting the *Undelete* command.

MOVING THE CURSOR AROUND THE SCREEN

This is done in a number of ways. With the new graphic interface of WordPerfect for Windows you may find it a lot easier to use the mouse. To reposition the text cursor with the mouse, simply click the left button of the mouse in the new position, and the cursor will appear there.

Use the *Scroll Bars* to move to parts of your document that are not currently in view.

USING THE KEYBOARD

Figure 5. The directional arrows and the Home and End keys on your keyboard can be used to move the mouse around the screen. Using these keys, in conjunction with the Ctrl and Alt keys, will also move the cursor by words, paragraphs, or whole lines at a time.

Home
Page Up
End
Page Down

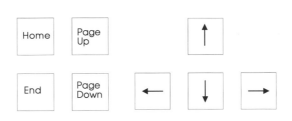

SELECTING TEXT

Selecting text in WordPerfect is necessary for such editing functions as cutting and copying, and also for formatting text (changing font, size, indenting, tabs, etc.). There are a number of ways you can select text.

Figure 6. One selection method is to position the cursor at the beginning of the text to be

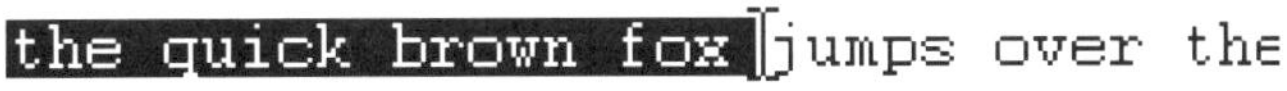

the quick brown fox jumps over the

```
Research indicates that the upsurge in purc
stems from a trend towards the traditional.
actual music has been found to be beneficia
well-being
```

With the flashing cursor at the beginning of the text, press the Shift key and hold it down. Move the mouse to the end of the block and click it. All text between the two points will be selected.

```
Research indicates that the upsurge in purc
stems from a trend towards the traditional.
actual music has been found to be beneficia
well-being.
```

Double-click to select words

```
Research indicates that the upsurge in purc
stems from a trend towards the traditional.
actual music has been found to be beneficia
well-being.
```

Triple-click to select sentences

```
Research indicates that the upsurge in purc
stems from a trend towards the traditional.
actual music has been found to be beneficia
well-being.
```

Quadruple-click to select paragraphs

```
Research indicates that the upsurge in purc
stems from a trend towards the traditional.
actual music has been found to be beneficia
well-being.
```

selected, hold the mouse down, drag it to the end of the text block, and release the mouse. As you move the mouse along, the text to the left of the I-beam will be selected. All selected text is highlighted in reverse video.

Figure 7. Another way of selecting text is to insert the cursor at the beginning of the text, hold the Shift key down, and click the mouse once at the end of the text block you wish to select. Everything between these two points will be selected.

Figure 8. Clicking with the mouse button can also be used to select words, sentences, and paragraphs. Double-click to select a word, triple-click to select a sentence, and quadruple-click to select a paragraph.

Holding down the Shift key will allow you to select all text between the cursor and the mouse pointer.

Figure 9. Text can also be selected through the *Select* sub-menu from the **Edit** menu. You have the option here of selecting either the *Sentence* or the *Paragraph* in which the cursor is located currently.

Another quick way of selecting text is to press F8 at the cursor position where you want the selection to start. The next key you press will become the outer boundary of the selection, so pressing F8 then the "." key will select all text to the end of the sentence.

CUT, COPY, PASTE, APPEND

Figure 10. The *Cut* command from the **Edit** menu removes selected text or a graphic from the document and puts it in the Windows Clipboard. It will remain there until you use the *Cut* or *Copy* command again.

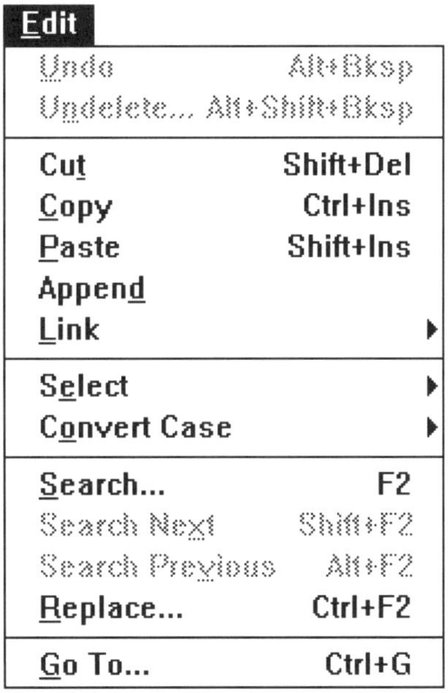

The *Copy* command from the **Edit** menu makes a copy of the selected text or graphic and puts it in the Windows Clipboard. The same rules apply here that apply with the *Cut* command; only the selected object remains in the document.

The *Paste* command will insert, from the Windows Clipboard, whatever was previously cut or copied. This will appear at the current cursor position.

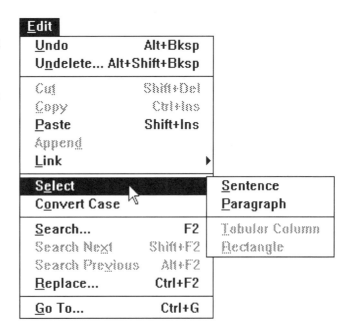

The *Append* command lets you add text or graphics to what is already in the Clipboard. The appended information remains in the Clipboard until something else is cut or copied.

CONVERT CASE

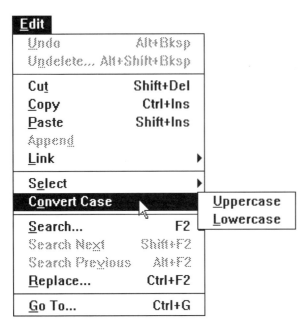

Figure 11. The *Convert Case* command from the **Edit** menu lets you convert selected text to either all uppercase or all lowercase characters. The letter "I" will remain in capitals when it appears in text by itself, and when it appears before an apostrophe.

If you want the first letter of the first sentence to remain in capitals, when you are converting the rest of the text to lowercase you must include the punctuation mark of the previous sentence in the selection.

REVEAL CODES

Figure 12. Formatting codes are inserted into your document every time an attribute is applied to text or to the page. These codes are not visible in normal working mode, but if you activate the *Reveal Codes* screen, you can view these codes. To turn on this screen, select the *Reveal Codes* command from the **View** menu.

Figure 13. This is how the *Reveal Codes* screen looks with a formatted document open. The codes appear in brackets and refer to the different commands they represent.

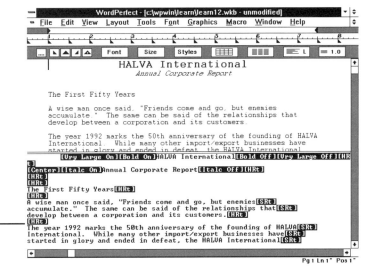

Reveal codes screen ————————

Figure 14. Some commands, such as bold, have a *[Bold On]* and a *[Bold Off]* code, with the bold text appearing between the two codes. These are called *paired codes*.

[Bold On]HALVA International[Bold Off]

Figure 15. There are two ways of applying *paired codes*. The first way is to select the text you want affected and choose the required command. Note that when text is selected, a temporary *[Select]* code is inserted and the words *Select On* appear on the left-hand side of the *Status Bar*.

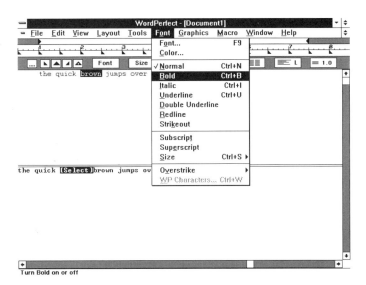

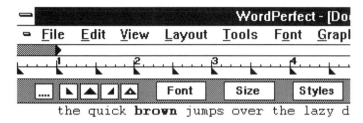

the quick **brown** jumps over the lazy d

Figure 16. After selecting the *Bold* command from the **Font** menu (Figure 15), the selected text becomes bold and *[Bold On]* and *[Bold Off]* codes are inserted in the document.

Alternatively, you can turn the *Bold* command on (by selecting it from the **Font** menu or by pressing Ctrl+B), while keying in the text, and then turn it off again once you have keyed in the text you require bold. To turn it off again, select the command from the menu again, or move the cursor past the *[Bold Off]* command in the *Reveal Codes* screen using the right arrow key on the keyboard. Selecting the *Normal* command from the **Font** menu will also turn the *Bold* command off.

he quick [Bold On]brown[Bold Off] jumps ov

[Vry Large On][Bold On]HALVA International[Bold Off][Vry Large Off]

Figure 17. Multiple sets of *paired codes* can be applied to text in the same fashion as a single code. Here the *Very Large* and *Bold* commands have been applied to the selected text. Note the *[On]* and *[Off]* commands that appear on both sides of the text.

Some codes, known as *open codes*, do not have an *On* and an *Off* code. These codes will affect the text from where they begin, until they come across a different version of the same code.

Figure 18. The *Font* command, for example, is an *open code* and will affect all text from the cursor, until the end of the document, or until it is superseded by another font code. In this example, the font Bookman Demi has affected the text until it finds the Helvetica Narrow code. The Helvetica Narrow code will now apply to the rest of the document (or until another font code is used).

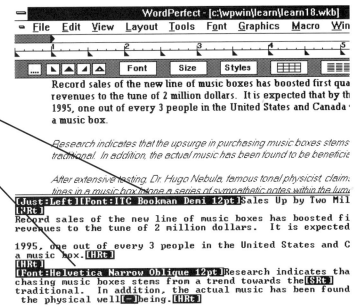

Figure 19. Each time you apply a command to either the text or the page layout, a code is inserted either at the position of the cursor or at the beginning of the page or paragraph. Where a code is inserted depends on whether you have turned on *Auto Code Placement* in the *Environment Settings* dialog box and by the type of code. The *Auto Code Placement* option is on by default and will affect the following commands in several ways:

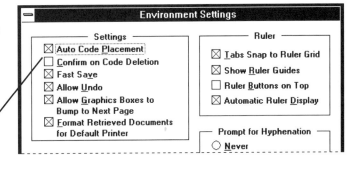

Some of the commands that will move their codes to the beginning of the paragraph in which the cursor is inserted are: *Columns, Margins (left and right), Paragraph Numbering,* and *Tab Set.*

The commands that will move their codes to the beginning of the page in which the cursor is located are: *Margins (top and bottom), Page (Center), Page Numbering, Page Size,* and *Suppress.*

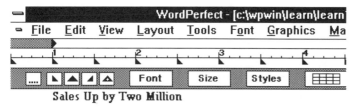

Figure 20. Codes can be deleted from the *Reveal Codes* screen by clicking on them with the mouse to select them, and then pressing the Delete key. In this example, the Bookman Demi 12 pt code was selected. After pressing the Delete key, the code will disappear.

Codes are usually deleted when you want to change an existing attribute in your document.

(a)

`[L/R Mar:1.5",1.5"]the quick brown jumps ov`

Select and delete this code

(b)

Margins

Margins

Left: `2"`   Right: `2"`

Top: `1"`   Bottom: `1"`

OK   Cancel

(c)

`[L/R Mar:2",2"]the quick brown jumps ove`

Figure 21. If you have set up your margins already, for example, and you wanted to change them, it is advisable first to select and delete the current margin code (a). Then establish the new margin setting in the *Margins* dialog box of (b). The new margin code will now replace the old one as in (c).

Once a code is deleted, the attribute it represented will also be deleted from the document. With a *paired code,* you can delete either the *On* or the *Off* code.

Deleting unwanted codes is important because these codes may have an undesirable affect on your document.

Figure 22. If you have the *Confirm on Code Deletion* option on in the *Environment Settings* dialog box (see Figure 19), you are given a warning if you are about to delete a code accidentally. This will work only if the *Reveal Codes* screen is not active.

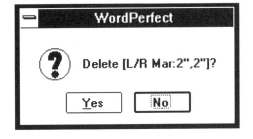

Figure 23. Other objects such as tables and graphics also have corresponding codes that can be deleted in *Reveal Codes*.

```
[Fig Box:1;bord-2.wpg;][Tbl Def:I;3,1.06",1.13",1.13"]
[Row][Cell][Cell][Cell]
[Row][Cell][Cell][Cell][Tbl Off]
```

The Fig Box:1; code is a graphic code, which is followed by the name of the graphic. The remaining codes in this sample are for a table.

Figure 24. *Reveal Codes* are also activated by holding the mouse down on the black section below the vertical *Scroll Bar* and dragging the mouse up to where you want the *Reveal Codes* Screen to begin. Once you release the mouse, *Reveal Codes* are activated.

The *Reveal Codes* screen can be resized at any time to suit your requirements.

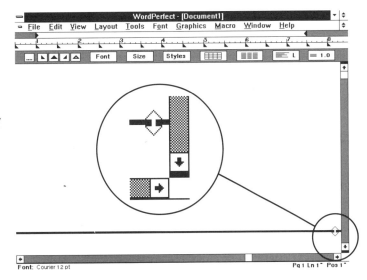

Figure 25. *Reveal Codes* are turned off by selecting the *Reveal Codes* command from the **View** menu.

They can also be turned off by dragging the window back down to the bottom of the screen.

THE FONT MENU

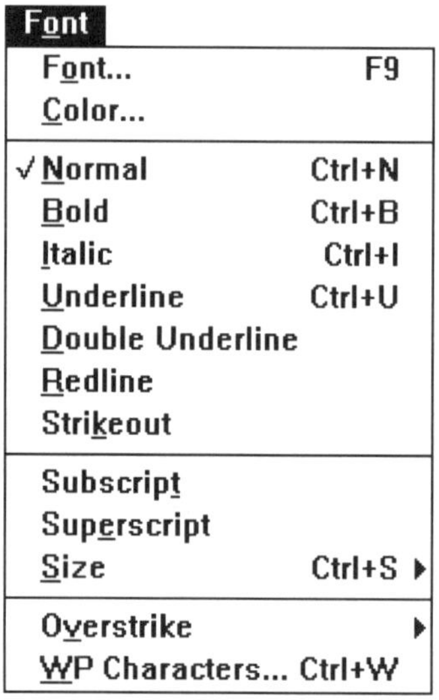

Figure 26. The different options available in the **Font** menu are mainly concerned with the formatting of text.

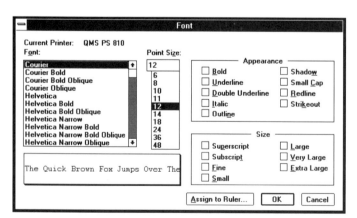

Figure 27. The first available option in the **Font** menu is the *Font* command, which activates the *Font* dialog box. Here you can select a new typeface from the *Font* list, and a new size for the text from the *Point Size* list. Any changes you make in the *Font* and *Point Size* lists will affect selected text, or if none is selected, all text from the cursor onwards.

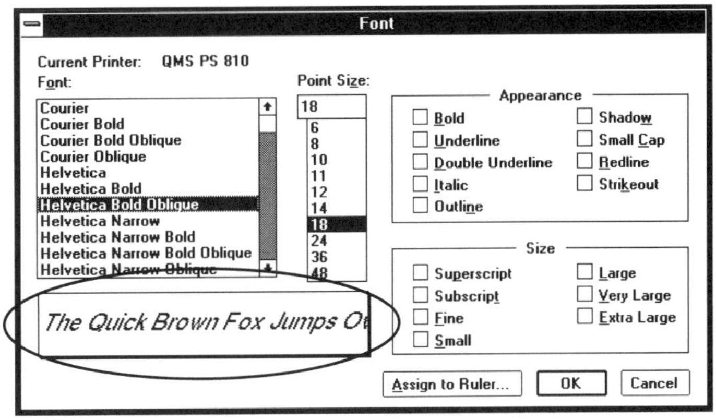

Figure 28. The text in the frame below the *Font* list will change to reflect the options selected in the *Font* dialog box.

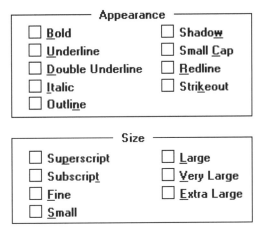

Figure 29. The options in the *Appearance* and *Size* sections of the *Font* dialog box will affect selected text. Alternatively, you can turn one of these options on while typing, and then turn it off again, once you have affected the required section of text.

Most of the options in the *Appearance* section are self-explanatory and you can see their effect through the example text in this dialog box. The *Redline* option is generally used to highlight any text added to a document, so that it stands out from the rest of the text. The *Strikeout* option places a line through the relevant text. It is used to highlight text that should be deleted from a document.

The *Size* options will affect the size of text in relation to the current point size. *Size* settings are percentages of the current font. For example, percentages might be: *Fine* 60%, *Small* 80%, *Large* 120%, *Very Large* 150%. Current size settings may be viewed or altered in the *Print Settings* dialog box activated by selecting the *Print* command from the *Preferences* sub-menu in the **File** menu.

For information on the *Assign To Ruler* option, see Chapter 1 — **WordPerfect for Windows.**

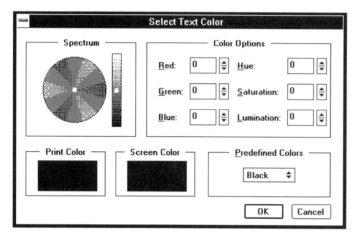

Figure 30. The *Color* command from the **Font** menu of Figure 26 activates the *Select Text Color* dialog box. Here you can change the color of text in your document. Changes made in this dialog box will affect text from the cursor onwards or just selected text.

The *Predefined Colors* pop-up list contains a number of colors already established that you can apply to text. It is also possible to create your own colors in the *Spectrum* and *Color Options* sections of this dialog box.

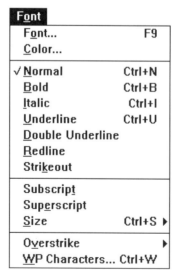

Figure 31. The *Normal, Bold, Italic, Underline, Double Underline, Redline, Strikeout, Subscript, Superscript,* and *Size* options in the **Font** menu are the same options available from the *Font* dialog box (Figure 27). The *Normal* option turns off all text attributes. You can apply these options to text without first activating the *Font* dialog box. In addition, there are control key shortcuts for most frequently used options.

Figure 32. To create *Overstrike* characters, select the *Create* command from the *Overstrike* sub-menu in the **Font** menu (a); this activates the *Create/Edit Overstrike* dialog box shown in (b). Here you designate characters that WordPerfect will place on top of one other, by simply keying them into the text frame and clicking on *OK*.

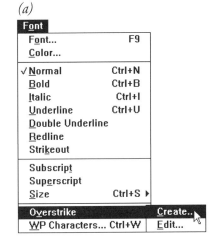

(a)

(b)

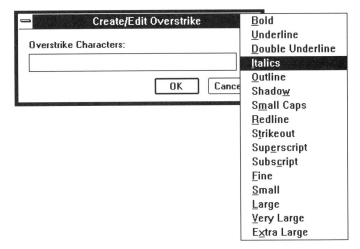

Figure 33. The left-facing arrow in the *Create/Edit Overstrike* dialog box activates a sub-menu that lets you apply certain attributes to your overstrike character.

The *Edit* option in the *Overstrike* sub-menu of Figure 32(a) searches for the overstrike character before the cursor, and displays it in the dialog box allowing you to make any changes, as required.

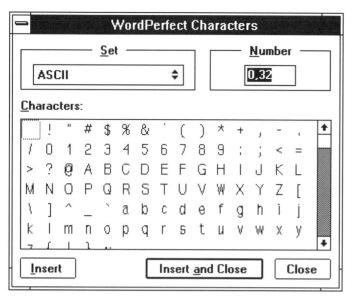

Figure 34. The *WP Characters* command from the **Font** menu of Figure 26 activates the *WordPerfect Characters* dialog box. Here you can choose from more than 1500 characters from 12 character sets to insert in your document. The character can be selected from the character frame, or the number (combination) can be keyed into the *Number* text box.

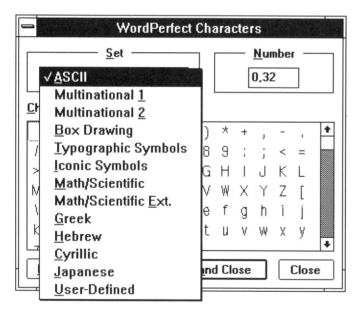

Figure 35. The *Set* pop-up list contains a range of character sets that will display in the *Characters* frame of Figure 34.

SEARCH AND REPLACE

Figure 36. The *Search* command from the **Edit** menu activates the *Search* dialog box of Figure 37.

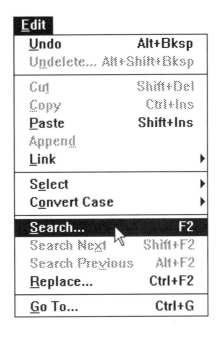

Figure 37. The options in the *Search* dialog box allow you to search for certain items in your document. In the *Search For* text frame, enter the text you wish to find in the current document.

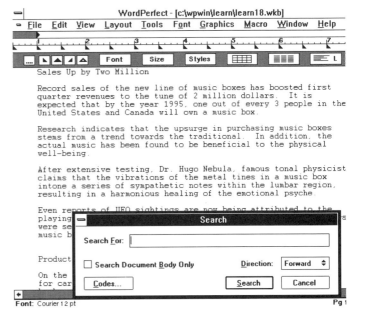

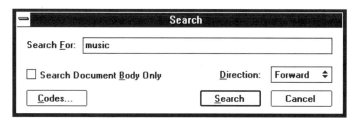

Figure 38. In this case we have inserted a word that we want found in our document. After keying in the *Search For* text, click on the *Search* button.

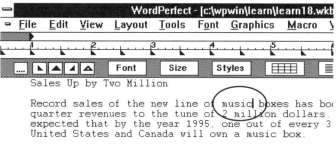

Figure 39. Once WordPerfect has located the word, the *Search* dialog box disappears and the flashing text cursor is placed immediately after the word. It is now possible to edit the word, delete it, add text at this point, or make any other changes.

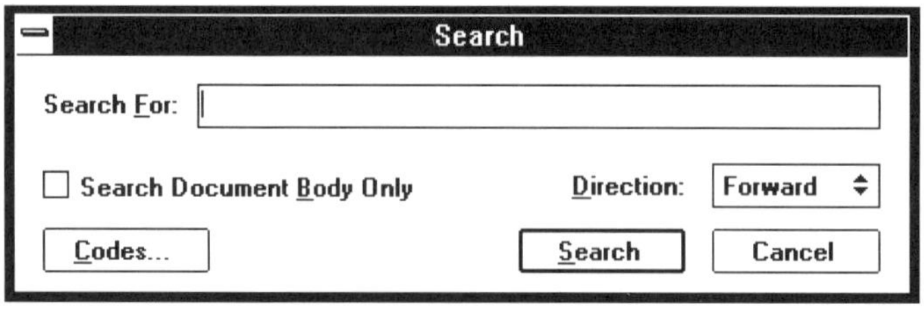

Figure 40. The *Search Document Body Only* option in the *Search* dialog box ensures WordPerfect will search only the main document, skipping text that occurs in the form of headers, footers, footnotes, text boxes, and so on.

The *Direction* pop-up list in the *Search* dialog box lets you decide whether the search will move *Forward* or *Backward* in the document. If your cursor is at the bottom of the document, for example, then you would choose the *Backward* option.

Figure 41. The *Codes* button in the *Search* dialog box activates this *Codes* dialog box. Selecting a code from the *Search Codes* list, and clicking on the *Insert* button, will place the selected code in the *Search For* text box in the *Search* dialog box. This lets you search and locate specific codes in the current document.

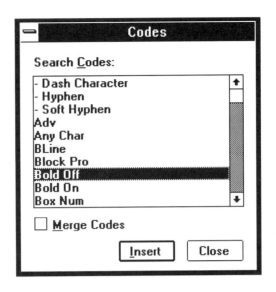

Figure 42. Once you have used the *Search* command, the *Search Next* command in the **Edit** menu becomes available (compare this **Edit** menu with the one in Figure 36). Selecting the *Search Next* command from the **Edit** menu will place the cursor after the next occurrence of the word for which you searched previously. In this case it was the word "music."

The *Search Previous* command will move the cursor so that it is immediately after the previous occurrence of the word for which you last searched.

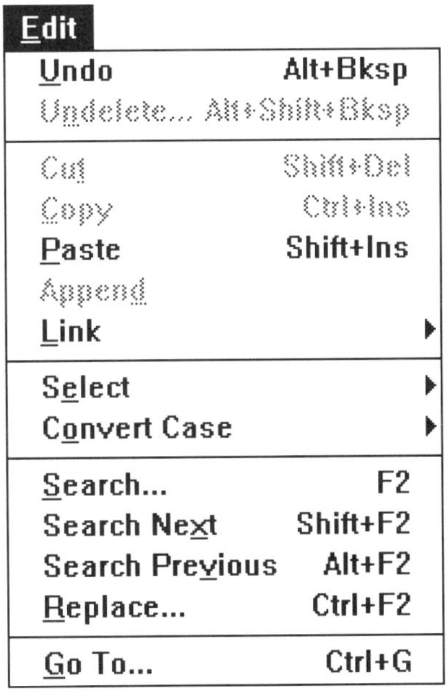

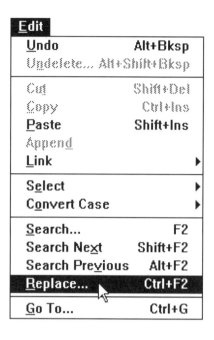

Figure 43. The *Replace* command in the **Edit** menu activates the *Search and Replace* dialog box of Figure 44.

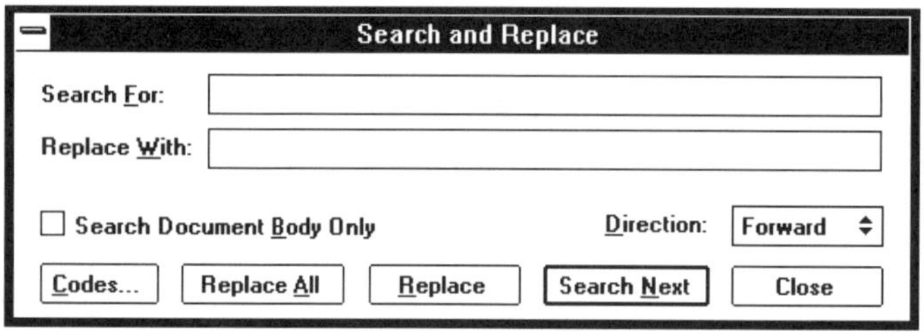

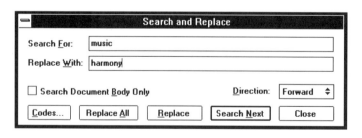

Figure 44. The *Search and Replace* dialog box lets you search for a word, as in the *Search* dialog box, but the options in this dialog box also let you replace the word.

Figure 45. After keying the necessary text into the *Search For* and *Replace With* text boxes, you click on the *Search Next* button.

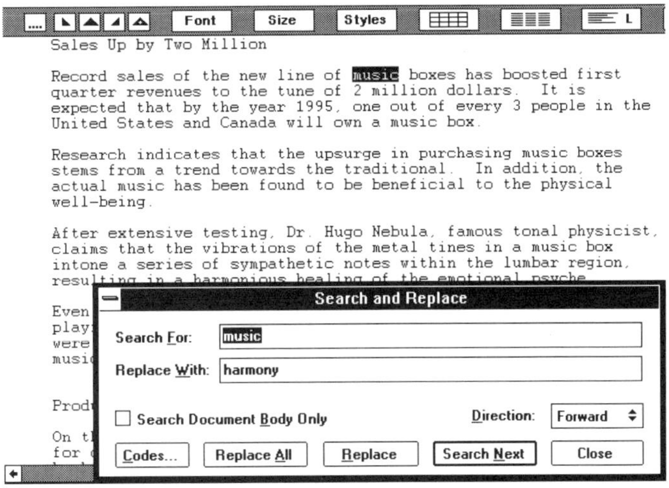

Figure 46. When WordPerfect finds the word inserted in the *Search For* text box, it is highlighted in the document.

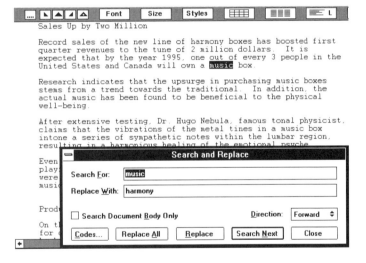

Figure 47. After clicking on the *Replace* button, the selected word in the document is replaced with the word in the *Replace With* text box, and the next occurrence of the word in the document is highlighted.

The *Search Next* button in the *Search and Replace* dialog box will find the next occurrence of the word in the *Search For* text box and highlight it in the document. Again, the *Replace* button is used if you want to replace the word. Or, click on the *Search Next* button to move on.

The *Replace All* option will scan the whole document for all occurrences of the word in the *Search For* text box and replace them all with the word in the *Replace With* text box.

The *Direction, Search Document Body Only,* and *Codes* options in the *Search and Replace* dialog box perform the same functions as they do in the *Search* dialog box (see Figures 40 and 41).

PAGE FORMATTING 3

THE LAYOUT MENU

Most page formatting features in WordPerfect are contained in the **Layout** menu. The term page formatting, in this case, includes *Page Size*, *Margins*, and *Columns*, as well as features such as *Tabs*, *Indents*, *Justification*, *Footnotes*, *Endnotes*, and *Typesetting*. The *Styles* command is discussed in Chapter 9 — **Styles & Outlines**.

Figure 1. The Layout menu.

LINE

The first option in the **Layout** menu is the *Line* option. Selecting this command will activate the *Line* sub-menu of Figure 2.

Layout	
<u>L</u>ine	Shift+F9 ▶
Pa<u>r</u>agraph	▶
<u>P</u>age	Alt+F9 ▶
<u>C</u>olumns	Alt+Shift+F9 ▶
<u>T</u>ables	Ctrl+F9 ▶
<u>D</u>ocument	Ctrl+Shift+F9 ▶
<u>F</u>ootnote	▶
<u>E</u>ndnote	▶
<u>A</u>dvance...	
Typesettin<u>g</u>...	
<u>J</u>ustification	▶
<u>M</u>argins...	Ctrl+F8
<u>S</u>tyles...	Alt+F8

TAB SET

Figure 2. The first command in the *Line* sub-menu from the **Layout** menu is the *Tab Set* option. Selecting this will activate the *Tab Set* dialog box of Figure 3. This is an alternative method of setting up tabs to that of using the Ruler, as described in Chapter 1 — WordPerfect for Windows.

Layout		
<u>L</u>ine	Shift+F9	<u>T</u>ab Set...
Pa<u>r</u>agraph		<u>S</u>pacing...
<u>P</u>age	Alt+F9	<u>H</u>eight...
<u>C</u>olumns	Alt+Shift+F9	<u>N</u>umbering...
<u>T</u>ables	Ctrl+F9	Hyp<u>h</u>enation...
<u>D</u>ocument	Ctrl+Shift+F9	<u>C</u>enter Shift+F7
<u>F</u>ootnote		<u>F</u>lush Right Alt+F7
<u>E</u>ndnote		Special C<u>o</u>des...

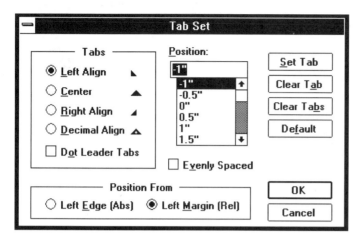

Figure 3. Once the *Tab Set* dialog box has been activated, you can place various tab types along the *Ruler* accurately.

Note: The changes you make in the Tab Set dialog box will come into affect from the cursor onwards.

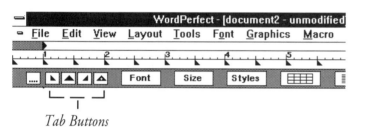

Tab Buttons

Figure 4. The *Tab Set* dialog box is also activated by double-clicking on one of the *Tab* buttons in the Ruler.

Figure 5. The first section of the *Tab Set* dialog box shows the *Tabs* options. *Left Align* forces the text to start after the tab, similar to a left margin. *Center* centers the text on the tab, with equal amounts of text on either side of the tab. *Right Align* forces text to move to the left of the tab position. The *Decimal Align* option aligns decimal points at the tab position, which is useful for entering columns of numbers. The *Dot Leader Tabs* option places a row of dots between the previous tab location (or left margin) and the text at the next tab position.

Figure 6. The *Position* box in the *Tab Set* dialog box is where you key in the tab position when you wish to add a tab. An alternative to keying in a position in this box is to select a position from the list box below. Once you select a figure from this list, it will appear in the *Position* text box. Using the *Tabs* section of Figure 5, you can then change the type of tab, if required. Alternatively, you can clear the tab using the Figure 7 options.

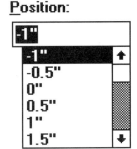

Figure 7. The *Set Tab* button is used to add a new tab position or change an existing one. In the latter case, select a position from the list under the *Position* text box and click on the required *Tabs* alignment from Figure 5; then select the *Set Tab* option for the changes to come into effect.

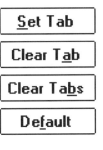

The *Clear Tab* option will remove an unwanted tab. After selecting the tab from the list of positions, click on the *Clear Tab* button and it will be deleted.

The *Clear Tabs* button will remove all tab stop positions, while the *Default* button will return the tab positions to the default setting of one every half inch.

Figure 8. The *Evenly Spaced* option, when checked, lets you set tabs at evenly spaced intervals. To do this, key in the position of the first tab in the *Position* text box and then key in the amount of space required between each tab in the *Repeat Every* box.

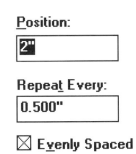

Figure 9. The *Position From* options give you the choice of starting tabs from the edge of the page or the left margin. The *Left Edge* option will start tabs from the edge of the page no matter what margins you have set (absolute tabs). The *Left Margin* option will start tab settings from the left margin (relative tabs). In this latter case, tab positions will move if you change the left margin setting.

LINE SPACING

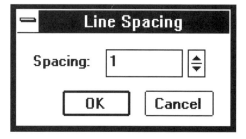

Figure 10. The second command in the *Line* sub-menu of the **Layout** menu (Figure 2) is the *Spacing* command. This will activate the *Line Spacing* dialog box. In this box, you can increase or decrease the inter-line spacing of text in your document. This option will affect selected text or all text from the cursor onwards.

Line spacing line spacing line spacing

Line spacing line spacing line spacing

Line spacing line spacing line spacing

Line spacing line spacing line spacing

Line spacing line spacing line spacing

Line spacing line spacing line spacing

Line spacing line spacing line spacing

Line spacing line spacing line spacing

Line spacing line spacing line spacing
Line spacing line spacing line spacing
Line spacing line spacing line spacing
Line spacing line spacing line spacing
Line spacing line spacing line spacing
Line spacing line spacing line spacing
Line spacing line spacing line spacing
Line spacing line spacing line spacing

Figure 11. If you change the spacing to 2, for example, the selected text will become double-spaced. WordPerfect will accept fractional line spacing, such as 1.75.

Line Spacing set at 1

Line Spacing set at 2

HEIGHT

Figure 12. The third command in the *Line* sub-menu of Figure 2 is the *Height* command. This command will activate the *Line Height* dialog box, which allows you to adjust the text measurement from baseline to baseline. The distance between baselines, by default, is determined by the point size of the current text. Select the *Fixed* option if you wish to key in your own measurement. This measurement will remain constant even if you change the point size of the text. The *Auto* option is the default setting and the one you will use normally. The changes you make in this dialog box will affect selected text or all text from the cursor position onwards.

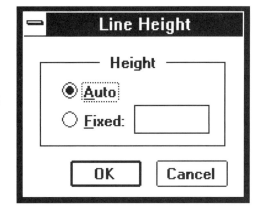

NUMBERING

Figure 13. This command from the *Line* sub-menu shown in Figure 2 turns automatic line numbering on or off. If you have this command activated, WordPerfect will place line numbers next to each line of the document, of either selected text, or the cursor position onwards.

Figure 14. The *Numbering* feature does not appear in the document window, but you can view it in the *Print Preview* screen.

```
1   Record sales of the new line of music boxes has boosted fir
2   quarter revenues to the tune of 2 million dollars.  It is
3   expected that by the year 1995, one out of every 3 people i
4   United States and Canada will own a music box.
5
6   Research indicates that the upsurge in purchasing music box
7   stems from a trend towards the traditional.  In addition, t
8   actual music has been found to be beneficial to the physica
9   well-being.
10
11  After extensive testing, Dr. Hugo Nebula, famous tonal phys
12  claims that the vibrations of the metal tines in a music bo
13  intone a series of sympathetic notes within the lumbar regi
14  resulting in a harmonious healing of the emotional psyche.
```

HYPHENATION

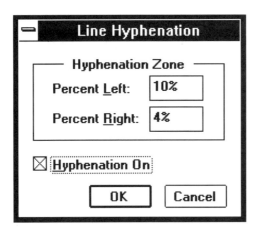

Figure 15. The *Line Hyphenation* dialog box is activated by selecting the *Hyphenation* command from the *Line* sub-menu in the **Layout** menu. To turn *Hyphenation* on, simply click in the *Hyphenation On* check box. This will affect text from the location of the cursor onwards. (If you have turned on the *Auto Code Placement* option in the *Environment Settings* dialog box, the Hyphenation code will be placed at the beginning of the paragraph in which the cursor is located.)

The *Hyphenation Zone* determines when WordPerfect will hyphenate a word. If a word falls within this zone, and *Hyphenation On* is checked, the word will be hyphenated. The options in the *Hyphenation Zone* can be modified if required, but the default settings will generally suffice.

CENTER AND FLUSH RIGHT

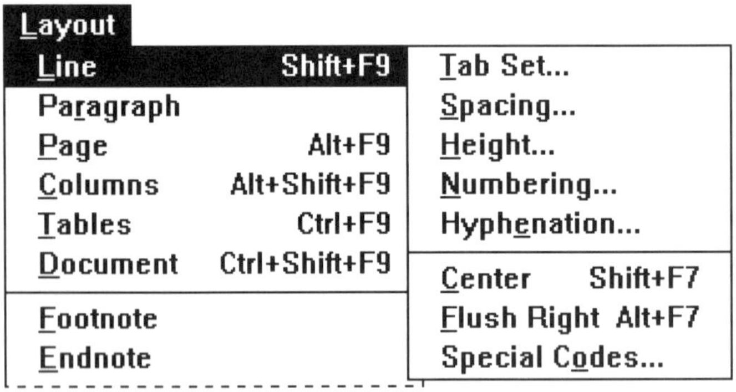

Figure 16. The *Center* command in the *Line* sub-menu will center-justify a line of text at a time. The cursor must be located at the beginning of the first word of the text to be centered. The *Flush Right* command right justifies a line of text. These two commands are used for single lines of text and are turned off when a hard return is inserted. To center or right align larger blocks of text, use the *Justification* options at the bottom of the **Layout** menu.

SPECIAL CODES

Figure 17. The *Special Codes* command in the *Line* sub-menu of Figures 2 and 16 activates the *Insert Special Codes* dialog box. *Special Codes* are inserted into a document for ease of formatting. The code you select in this dialog box will be inserted into the document at the cursor location, once you click on the *Insert* button.

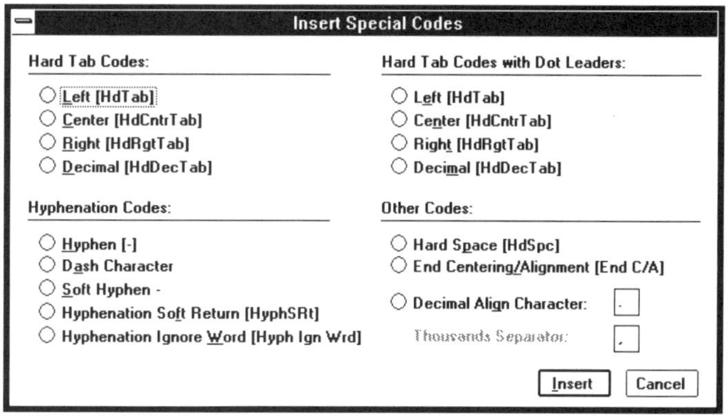

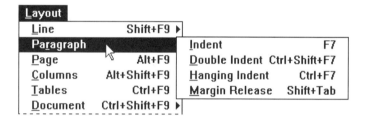

PARAGRAPH

Figure 18. The *Paragraph* command in the **Layout** menu will activate this sub-menu for use with paragraphs only. When selecting these commands, first place the cursor in front of the paragraph you wish to adjust.

INDENT

Figure 19. This command indents the full paragraph to the first tab position on the *Ruler*. You can adjust this distance by changing the tab settings. For multiple indents, select the command as many times as necessary. The first paragraph in this example has been indented to the first tab stop.

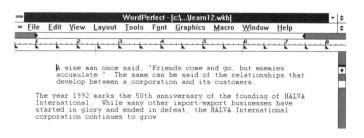

DOUBLE INDENT

Figure 20. This command indents the text from both the left and right margins by one tab stop.

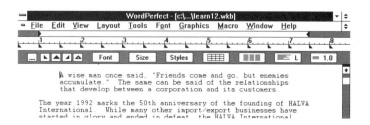

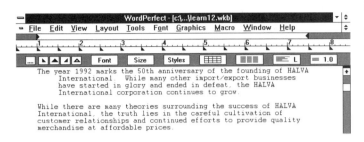

HANGING INDENT

Figure 21. This command keeps the first line of the paragraph in its original position and indents the rest of the paragraph to the next tab stop.

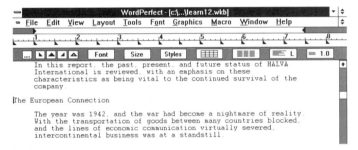

MARGIN RELEASE

Figure 22. When the cursor is at the beginning of the line, this command moves the line one tab stop to the left, even beyond the left margin. In this example, the line "The European Connection" was positioned using the *Margin Release* command.

PAGE

Figure 23. The *Page* sub-menu in the **Layout** menu contains commands that affect the page(s) of a document.

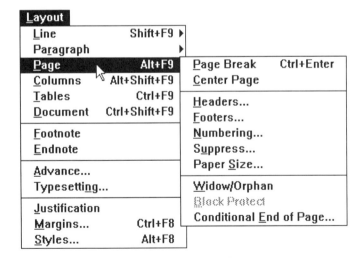

PAGE BREAK

The first option in the *Page* sub-menu is the *Page Break* command. Selecting this command inserts a page break in the document at the current cursor position.

WordPerfect automatically inserts a *soft* page break, which falls when text and/or graphics naturally reach the end of a page. The *Page Break* command gives you the option of manually determining where a page will end. This is known as a *hard* page break.

Figure 24. When you insert a *hard* page break, a double line will appear at the position of the text cursor.

A *soft* page break will only place one line across the page break position. The code for a *soft* page break in *Reveal Codes* is [SPg] while the *hard* page break will insert an [HPg] code.

CENTER PAGE

The *Center Page* command is the second option in the *Page* sub-menu (Figure 23) of the **Layout** menu.

Figure 25. The *Center Page* command centers text vertically in relation to the top and bottom margins. The result of this command can only be seen in the *Print Preview* screen. This figure shows before and after results of using the *Center Page* command. This command affects the current page only.

HEADERS AND FOOTERS

The next two commands in the *Page* sub-menu (Figure 23) are the *Headers* and *Footers* options. *Headers* and *Footers* insert information at the top and bottom of each page in your document. Headers appear at the top of the page and footers at the bottom. They are both created in the same way, so Figures 26 through 30 will only discuss the creation, editing, and placement, of headers.

```
Even reports of UFO sightings are now being at
playing of certain melodies on a music box.   W
were seen hovering last September over a cornf
music box was blamed.
```

```
Production Plans

On the drawing boards are music box watches, d
for cars, waterproof boxes for showers, ultra-
backpackers, and even a computerized music box
program your own tune.
```

Before   *After*

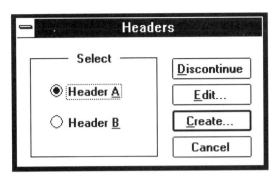

Figure 26. Select the *Headers* command from the *Page* sub-menu of Figure 23 to activate the *Headers* dialog box. In this dialog box, select the *Header A* option if you require only one piece of information at the top of the page. You may select the *Header B* option at a later stage if you wish to put two pieces of information on opposing sides at the top of a page.

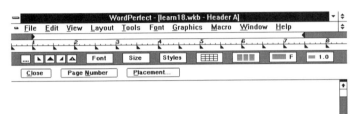

Figure 27. For this example, the setting was left on *Header A*. Next, click on the *Create* button to activate the *Header A* window.

(a)

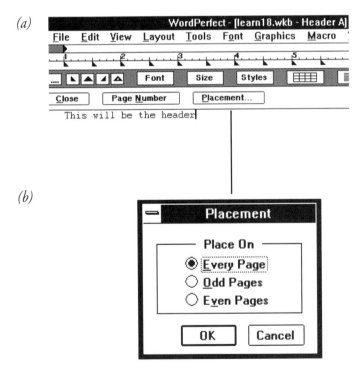

Figure 28(a). In the *Header A* window, key in the text you want as your header. This text can be formatted as you would normally format text in WordPerfect. The *Page Number* button inserts a ^B code in the header. The current page number will be printed automatically on each page.

(b)

Figure 28(b). The *Placement* button allows you to determine whether this header will appear on all pages, odd pages only, or even pages only. (This lets you create alternate headings.)

Once you have set up the header as required, click on the *Close* button in Figure 28(a) to return to the document.

Figure 29. Back in the document, the header can only be viewed on the *Print Preview* screen.

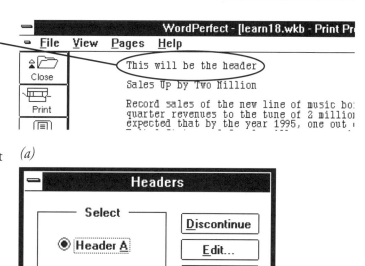

(a)

Figure 30(a). The *Edit* button in the *Headers* dialog box lets you edit an existing header. This is done in the same way that one is created, except that the existing header or footer will appear in the *Header* window. The *Discontinue* button, when clicked on, will discontinue the header or footer from the page that the cursor is currently on to the end of the document.

The position of headers and footers is at the top or bottom of the text area. They do not print in the margins.

SUPPRESS

Figure 30(b). The *Suppress* command in the *Page* sub-menu of the **Layout** menu will remove headers and footers from the page in which the cursor is positioned.

(b)

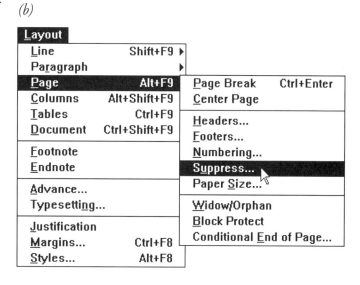

You can set up a new header or footer part-way through a document. This is done by placing the cursor on the page where you want to begin the new header and creating it in the method just described. A header or footer will continue in a document until either another header or footer is created or until a header/footer *Discontinue* code is encountered.

To remove a header/footer from a document, delete the code from the *Reveal Codes* screen.

NUMBERING

To insert page numbers, but not as part of a header or footer, use the *Numbering* command from the *Page* sub-menu of the **Layout** menu (Figure 23).

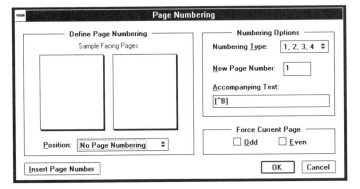

Figure 31. The *Numbering* command will activate the *Page Numbering* dialog box. The cursor must be on the page where you want page numbering to begin.

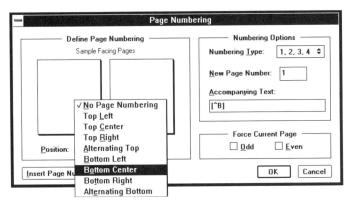

Figure 32. Hold the mouse down on the *Position* pop-up list under *Sample Facing Pages* to choose where your numbers will appear on the page.

The *Numbering Type* option in the *Numbering Options* section of the dialog box gives you three choices of numbering style.

The *New Page Number* option lets you key in a new starting page number.

The *Accompanying Text* option lets you determine what the symbol for page numbering will look like in the document. The default symbol for page numbering is the code ^B. You may, for example, add the word Page in front of this symbol, if you wish. The *Force Current Page* option lets you begin a certain page on either an odd or even page.

Clicking on the *Insert Page Number* button inserts a current page number at the cursor location. This is inserted as a code, allowing the inserted page number to change automatically if the current page number does.

Figure 33. The *Suppress* command in the *Page* sub-menu of Figure 30(b) activates the *Suppress* dialog box shown here. This lets you hide headers, footers, or page numbers on the page where the cursor is situated. The *Print Page Number at Bottom Center* option will print the page number in the bottom center of the page. This option will not be available if you have chosen to suppress page numbers.

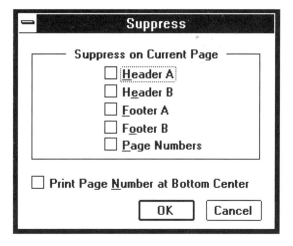

PAPER SIZE

The *Paper Size* command is the next command in the *Page* sub-menu of Figure 23. Selecting this command will activate the dialog box of Figure 34. This command is useful only if you have selected a WordPerfect printer driver. See Chapter 7 — **Printing** for more details on Windows and WordPerfect printer drivers.

Figure 34. The changes you make in the *Paper Size* dialog box will affect the document from the cursor position onwards. This dialog box also indicates the currently selected printer. To change the current paper size, choose another option from the list available and click on the *Select* button.

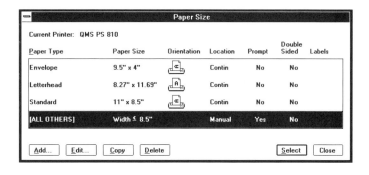

If you have a Windows printer driver selected, activating this command will show the current paper size only. See Figures 35 to 42 on how to add a new paper size definition to this dialog box.

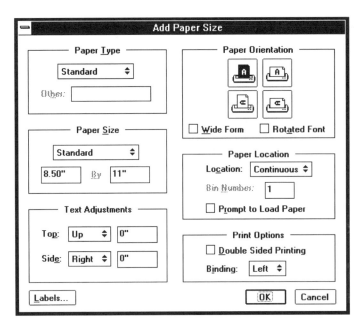

Figure 35. Click on the *Add* button in the *Paper Size* dialog box of Figure 34 to activate the *Add Paper Size* dialog box. This lets you add more options to the list of *Paper Types.*

See Figures 36 through 41 for further descriptions of this dialog box.

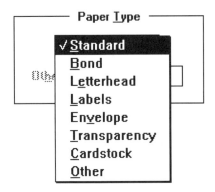

Figure 36. The *Paper Type* pop-up list lets you name the paper type. Select an option from the list, or select *Other* and give it your own name.

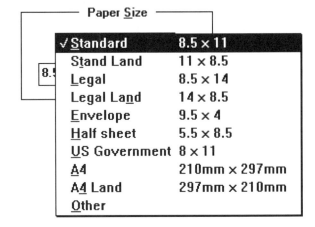

Figure 37. The *Paper Size* pop-up list lets you select a paper size from the options listed. Select *Other* to key in your own size.

Figure 38. The *Text Adjustments* options let you determine where on the page the text will be printed in relation to the top and/ or the side of the page. This option can be used if you are not happy with the current position, or if you plan to bind the document from the top or the side of the page.

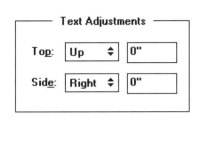

Figure 39. The *Paper Orientation* options let you specify which way the paper is being fed into the printer (portrait or landscape).

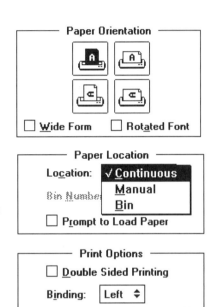

Figure 40. The *Paper Location* pop-up list determines how the paper is fed into the printer (continuously, manually, or which bin if a multi-bin printer).

The *Print Options* section lets you select double-sided printing if your printer has this capability. The *Binding* option lets you leave a space at the top or the left side of a page for binding purposes.

Figure 41. The *Labels* button at the bottom left of the *Add Paper Size* dialog box activates this *Edit Labels* dialog box. Here you can set up the options for printing labels.

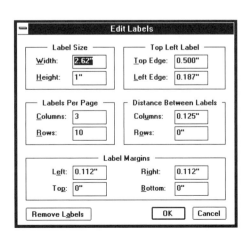

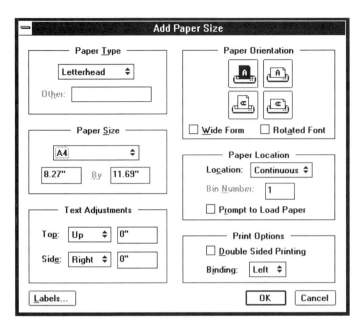

Figure 42. Once you have set up the paper size options in the *Add Paper Size* dialog box, click on the *OK* button.

Figure 43 reflects the new options inserted in this figure.

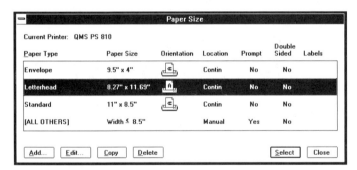

Figure 43. The new size option will appear in the list in the *Paper Size* dialog box. To make this new listed size the current paper size for the open document, make sure it is highlighted in the list, and click on the *Select* button. This will exit from the dialog box and take you back to your document.

The *Close* button will let you exit from the dialog box without activating the currently selected paper size.

If you wish to edit a paper size, highlight it in the list in the *Paper Size* dialog box, and click on the *Edit* button. This will activate the *Edit Paper Size* dialog box which is the same as the *Add Paper Size* dialog box of Figure 42.

The *Copy* option at the bottom of the *Paper Size* dialog box (Figure 43) lets you create another paper size based on an existing paper size, with slight changes. The original paper size will remain in the list of paper options in the *Paper Size* dialog box.

The *Delete* button in the *Paper Size* dialog box of Figure 43 allows you to delete a selected paper size from the list.

WIDOW/ORPHAN

Figure 44. Selecting the *Widow/ Orphan* options prevents single lines appearing at the top or bottom of the page away from the rest of the text. If you have the *Auto Code Placement* option on in the *Environment Settings* dialog box, then the *Widow/Orphan* code will appear at the beginning of the paragraph, in which the cursor is located, and will affect all following text.

Layout	
Line	Shift+F9 ▶
Paragraph	▶
Page	**Alt+F9**
Columns	Alt+Shift+F9
Tables	Ctrl+F9
Document	Ctrl+Shift+F9
Footnote	
Endnote	
Advance...	
Typesetting...	
Justification	
Margins...	Ctrl+F8
Styles...	Alt+F8

Page Break	Ctrl+Enter
Center Page	
Headers...	
Footers...	
Numbering...	
Suppress...	
Paper Size...	
Widow/Orphan	
Block Protect	
Conditional End of Page...	

BLOCK PROTECT

The *Block Protect* command ensures a selected block of text always remains on the same page, and is not separated by a page break.

CONDITIONAL END OF PAGE

The *Conditional End of Page* option keeps a number of lines together. Insert the cursor in the line above the lines you want to keep together and select this command. In the accompanying dialog box, key in the number of lines you wish to keep together.

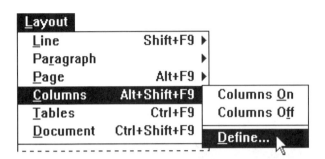

COLUMNS

Figure 45. There are two ways of defining columns. The first way is by selecting the *Columns/Define* command in the **Layout** menu. This activates the *Define Columns* dialog box of Figure 46.

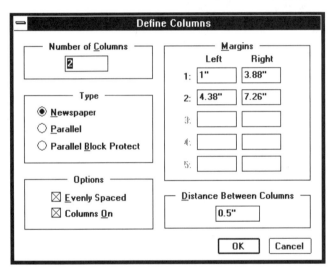

Figure 46. The first option in the *Define Columns* dialog box is the *Number of Columns* option. Key into this box the number of columns you desire.

The next option is the *Type* option. The *Newspaper* option is for columns that flow from the bottom of one column to the top of the next, such as a newspaper or newsletter.

The *Parallel* option is used for columns that run side by side. The text is grouped across the page in rows. Pressing Hard Page (Ctrl+Enter) will move the cursor to the next column. The *Parallel Block Protect* option is the same as *Parallel,* except that the rows stay together. If one column moves over the page the whole row of columns moves with it.

In the *Options* section, you have two choices:. *Evenly Spaced* and *Columns On.* With the *Evenly Spaced* option selected, WordPerfect determines the width of each column. Selecting the *Columns On* option ensures the settings in this dialog box are put into action after clicking on *OK.*

The next options are the *Margins* choices. A different setting can be used for each margin, allowing you to specify irregularly sized columns, if required. The last option available in the *Define Columns* dialog box is the *Distance Between Columns* option. This controls the spacing (gutters) between columns for *Evenly Spaced* columns.

Figure 47. The *Columns* button in the *Ruler* activates a sub-menu providing a quick selection alternative to the menu option. For more information on the *Ruler*, see Chapter 1 — **WordPerfect for Windows.**

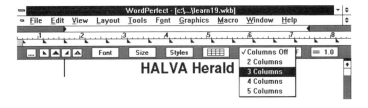

DOCUMENT

Figure 48. The first option available in the *Document* sub-menu is the *Summary* option. This is discussed in Chapter 5 — **Setting Preferences.**

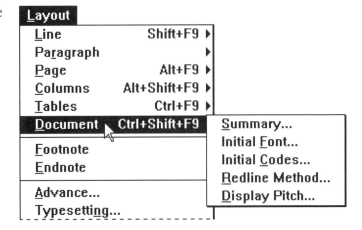

Figure 49. The *Initial Font* command in the *Document* sub-menu lets you change the default font and point size setting for the current document. Selecting this command activates the dialog box shown here. Choose the new font and size, and click on *OK*.

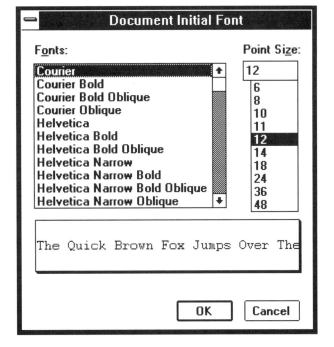

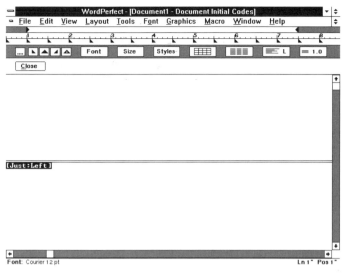

Figure 50. Selecting the *Initial Codes* option from the *Document* sub-menu of Figure 48 activates the *Document Initial Codes* window. In this window you set up text and page formatting attributes to become the default settings for the current document.

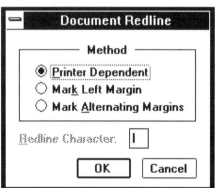

Figure 51. The *Redline Method* option in the *Document* sub-menu of Figure 48 activates the *Document Redline* dialog box. This provides a number of options to determine how the *Redline* feature (**Font** menu) will print.

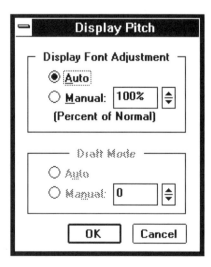

Figure 52. The *Display Pitch* option in the *Document* sub-menu of Figure 48 activates the *Display Pitch* dialog box. The settings in this dialog box affect the on-screen text appearance only.

The top half of this dialog box is used for *Normal Mode* operation. The bottom half adjusts settings for *Draft Mode*. Altering the *Display Pitch* settings may cause display problems on your screen. It is normally best to leave these settings unchanged.

FOOTNOTE/ENDNOTE

Figure 53. To insert a footnote in your document at the position of the cursor, select the *Create* command from the *Footnote* sub-menu in the **Layout** menu.

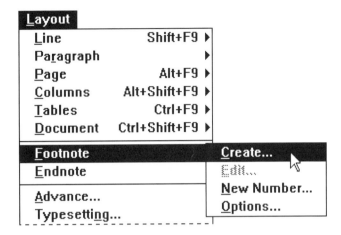

Figure 54. The action of Figure 53 activates the *Footnote* window. The footnote number is inserted here automatically and updated for each new footnote you create.

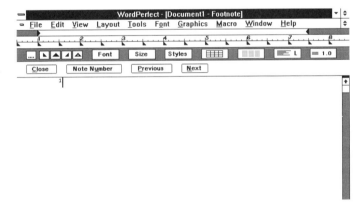

Figure 55. At this point, you key in the required footnote text and format it as you wish.

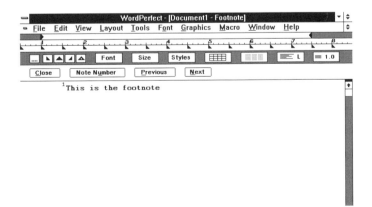

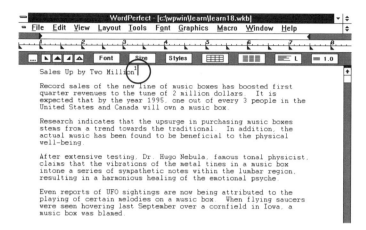

Figure 56. Close the *Footnote* window by clicking on the *Close* button of Figure 55. The footnote number will then appear in the text.

Figure 57. The actual footnote text can only be seen in the *Print Preview* screen, as shown here.

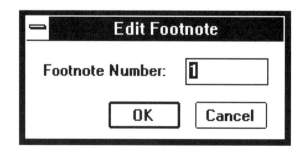

Figure 58. To edit a footnote, select the *Edit* command from the *Footnote* sub-menu of Figure 53. In the *Edit Footnote* dialog box that appears, key in the footnote number you wish to edit, and click on *OK*.

Footnotes can be deleted in the document window or in the *Reveal Codes* window.

Figure 59. The *Next* and *Previous* buttons in the *Footnote* window take you to the next or previous footnote you may have created.

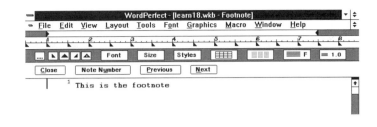

The *New Number* option in the *Footnote* sub-menu of Figure 53 lets you start a footnote with a new number of your choice.

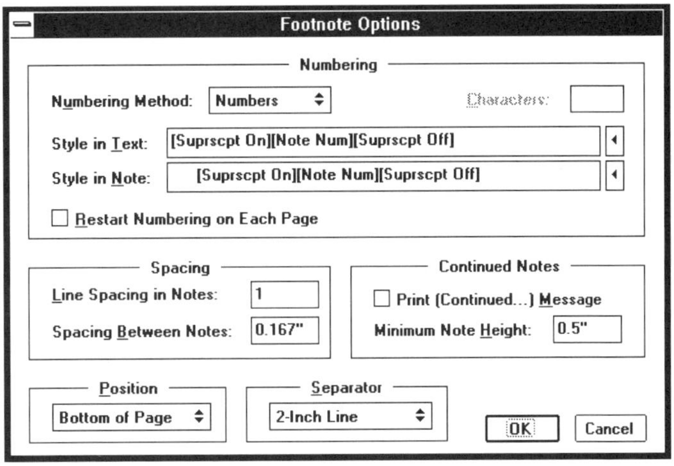

Figure 60. The *Options* command at the bottom of the *Footnote* sub-menu of Figure 53 activates the *Footnote Options* dialog box. This lets you change the style, format, and positioning of footnotes.

Endnotes are created in the same way as footnotes, only endnotes appear at the end of a document. To make endnotes appear before the end of a document, select the *Placement* command from the *Endnote* sub-menu in the **Layout** menu. The endnotes you have created will then appear at the cursor location.

ADVANCE

Figure 61. The *Advance* command in the **Layout** menu activates its own dialog box as shown here. In this box it is possible to specify a distance and direction you would like to re-position the cursor on the page. For instance, the *To Line* option advances the cursor a set distance from the top of the page. The effect of *Cursor* movement changes made with this option can be seen only in *Print Preview*.

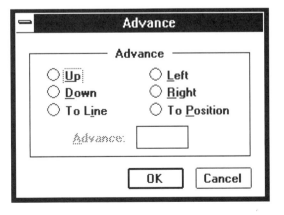

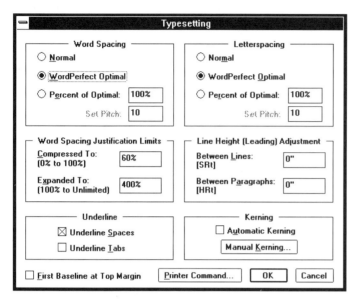

TYPESETTING

Figure 62. The options in the *Typesetting* dialog box, activated through the **Layout** command, control *Word Spacing* and *Letterspacing* in your document. *Word Spacing* adjusts spacing between words and *Letterspacing* adjusts spacing between letters.

The *Automatic Kerning* option, if selected, forces WordPerfect to adjust the spacing between specific letters. *Manual Kerning* allows you to manually adjust the spacing between letters. Kerning is generally used in large font situations, such as headings. The *Underline* options allow the underlining of spaces and tabs.

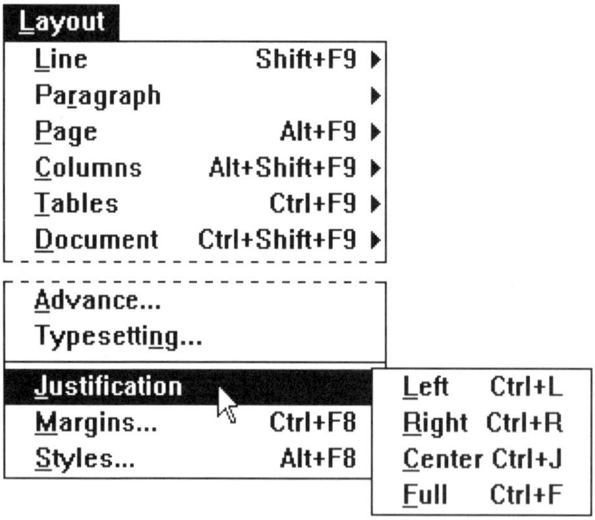

JUSTIFICATION

Figure 63. The *Justification* sub-menu in the **Layout** menu lets you alter the justification of selected text or all text from the cursor position onwards.

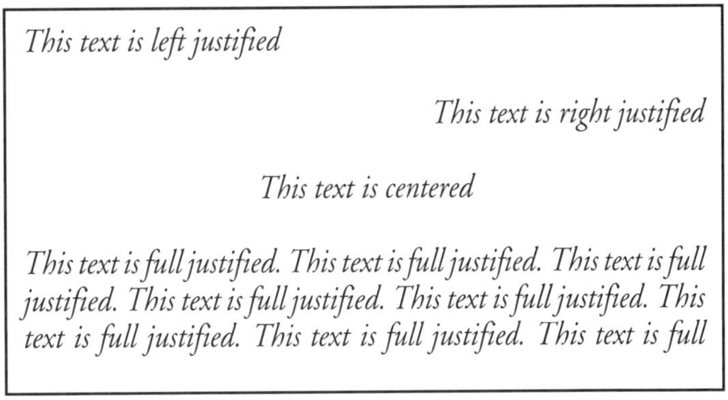

Figure 64. These examples show the four types of text justification available. The *Full* option wraps text onto the next line at the same position for each line, thus providing perfectly straight left and right margins.

This text is left justified

This text is right justified

This text is centered

This text is full justified. This text is full justified. This text is full justified. This text is full justified. This text is full justified. This text is full justified. This text is full justified. This text is full

MARGINS

Figure 65. You can modify margins in a number of ways. One method is to select the *Margins* command from the **Layout** menu, and modify the values within the *Margins* dialog box of Figure 66.

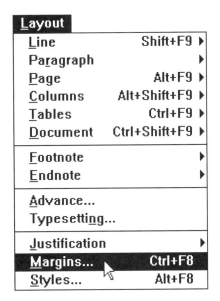

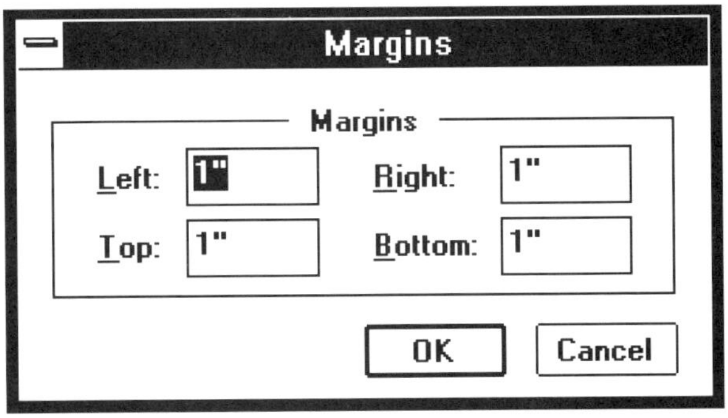

Figure 66. The changes made in the *Margins* dialog box will affect selected text, or text from the cursor onwards, until it comes across another margin code in the document.

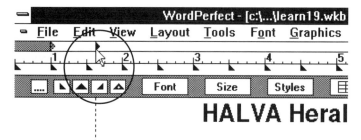

Figure 67. Another way to change margin settings, for the right and left margins, is to move the margin markers on the *Ruler* with the mouse.

See Chapter 1 — **WordPerfect for Windows** for more information on adjusting margins with the *Ruler.*

CREATING AND MANAGING FILES

4

WORDPERFECT FILES

Creating new files in WordPerfect is a simple process. WordPerfect also has many features that help in the managing of these files.

This chapter describes the various **File** menu commands associated with creating or managing new files. It also looks at manipulating multiple documents through the **Window** menu and how to work with *Quick Lists*.

Figure 1. The File menu.

NEW

The first option available in the **File** menu is the *New* command. On first starting WordPerfect, you will be in a new, empty, document. If you have not made any changes, the Title bar will read [*Document1 - unmodified*]. If you select the *New* command again, it will open a new document that will read [*Document2 - unmodified*]. *Document1* will still be open but not active.

At any time during the creation of a document, you can select the *New* command to start a new document (subject to a maximum of nine files open at once).

File	
New	Shift+F4
Open...	F4
Retrieve...	
Close	Ctrl+F4
Save	Shift+F3
Save As...	F3
Password...	
File Manager...	
Preferences	▶
Print...	F5
Print Preview...	Shift+F5
Select Printer...	
Exit	Alt+F4

OPEN

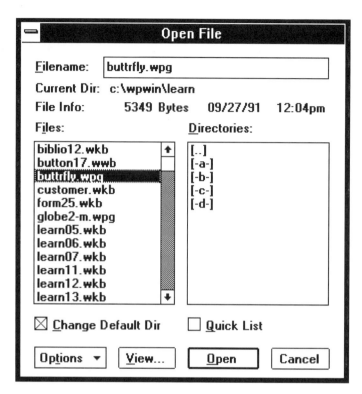

Figure 2. The *Open* command in the **File** menu of Figure 1 activates the *Open File* dialog box. From this dialog box, you can locate any previously saved WordPerfect files from the directories in which they were placed.

The *Filename* text box in this dialog box displays the name of the currently selected file in the *Files* list. Below the *Filename*, the *Current Dir* line indicates the currently open directory. The *File Info* line reveals the size of the selected file and when it was last modified.

The file and directory options can be changed by altering the selections in the *Files* and *Directories* list boxes. The *Change Default Dir* option, when checked, will make the directory displayed next to the *Current Dir* line the default directory, when you next choose to open or save a document.

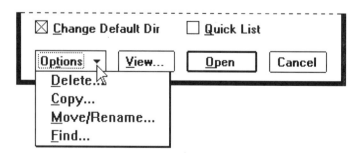

Figure 3a. The *Options* pop-up list at the bottom of the *Open File* dialog box lets you perform certain commands on a selected file in the *Files* list. The *Delete* option will remove the selected file. The *Copy* option activates the *Copy File* dialog box.

In the *Copy File* dialog box, you select another directory where you would like to make a copy of this file. The *Move/Rename* option lets you move the file to a different drive and/or directory or simply to rename the file while keeping it in the same directory. The *Find* option activates the *Find* dialog box, where you can search for files.

Figure 4. The *View* option at the bottom of the *Open File* dialog box displays a selected file in a separate window. This window contains scroll bars to view the full document, if required. Any WordPerfect text file can be viewed this way. Graphic files can also be viewed but not opened. Graphic files must be retrieved through the options in the **Graphics** menu.

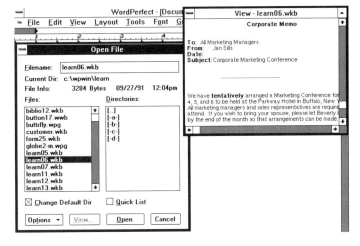

Once you have selected the file you wish to open, click on the *Open* button. Alternatively, double-clicking on the file name will also open it. The *Cancel* button will exit from the dialog box without opening a file.

Figure 5. After clicking on the *Open* button in the *Open File* dialog box, the selected file will appear in the current document window and its title will be reflected in the *Title Bar*. Until you make changes to the file, its *Title Bar* will also say *unmodified.*

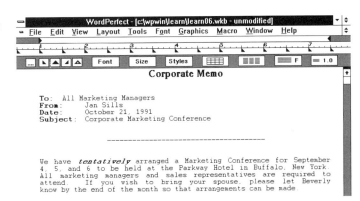

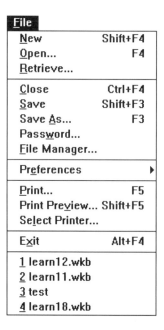

Figure 6. If you have the *Display Last Open Filenames* option selected in the *Environment Settings* dialog box (see Chapter 5 — **Setting Preferences**), then the last four recently opened documents will be listed at the bottom of the **File** menu. These files can then be opened by simply selecting the filename from this menu.

RETRIEVE

Figure 7. The *Retrieve* command in the **File** menu of Figure 1 activates the *Retrieve File* dialog box. The options available in this dialog box are exactly the same as in the *Open File* dialog box, only you click on the *Retrieve* button after selecting the file from the list of files.

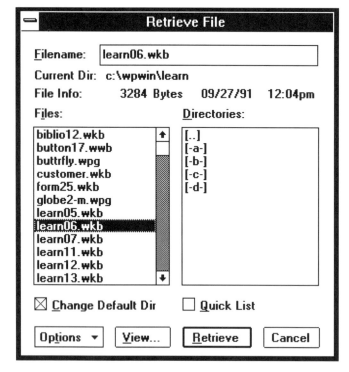

If you retrieve a file into a new document window, then the document *Title Bar* will take on the name of the file as it does when you open a file. If you retrieve a file into an existing named file, then you will first be asked if you want to insert the file into the current document. Then the newly retrieved file will appear in the current document at the position of the cursor. The name of the document will not change in this case.

CLOSE

Figure 8. The *Close* command from the **File** menu of Figure 1 will close the currently active document window without exiting from WordPerfect. If you have made any changes to the current document, then you will be asked if you want to save these changes. Clicking on the *Yes* option will save changes for an already-named document) or activate the *Save As* dialog box (for a new document). If you have another document open, it will become the active one. If there is no other document open, WordPerfect will revert to *Document 1 - unmodified.*

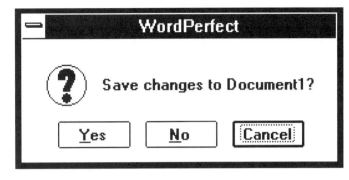

SAVE/SAVE AS

Figure 9. Selecting the *Save* or *Save As* command from the **File** menu for the first time in a WordPerfect document will activate the *Save As* dialog box. Here you are asked to name the document and decide where you want it saved. Choose the disk and directory, from the *Directories* list, in which you would like to save the file.

The filename is keyed into the *Save As* text box at the top of the dialog box. WordPerfect does not save files with an extension, so you may wish to name your own extension to assist in categorizing your files. An extension can be no more than three letters.

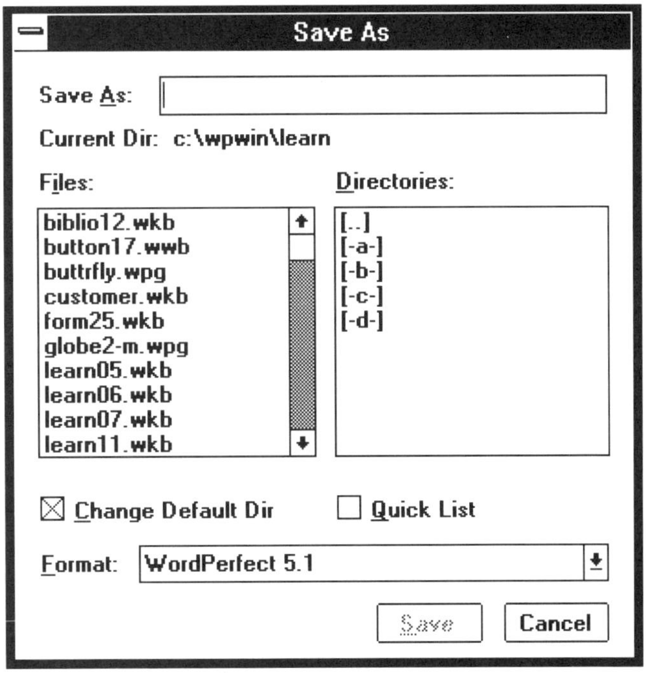

The *Change Default Dir* option, in the *Save As* dialog box, when checked, will change the default directory for saving files. The new default directory will be the one currently appearing on the *Current Dir* line toward the top of the dialog box.

The *Format* pop-up list, at the bottom of the *Save As* dialog box, allows you to save your WordPerfect document in a various different formats for use in other programs.

Once you have located the disk and directory you need, and named your file, click on the *Save* button. The new name for the file will appear in the document window *Title Bar*.

Choosing the *Save* command, for an already named file, will save to disk any changes made since the *Save* or *Save As* command was last used.

Choosing the *Save As* command, for an already named file, will also activate the *Save As* dialog box. This command allows you to make another copy of the file in the same or different directory.

PASSWORD

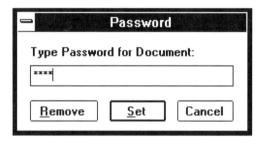

Figure 10. Selecting the *Password* command from the **File** menu activates the *Password* dialog box. In this dialog box, you can key in a password for the currently open document. When you key in the word, it will appear in the dialog box as multiple asterisk characters. Once you have keyed in the password, click on the *Set* button. You will then be asked to confirm the password by typing it in again.

Figure 11. When you need to re-open the file, you will be confronted with the *File Password Protected* dialog box. The file cannot be opened without entering the correct password.

Note: Use this feature with extreme care. If the password becomes lost, you will probably not be able to access your password-protected documents. Password protection will prevent others from accessing a document, but will not protect it from being deleted.

SWITCHING BETWEEN DOCUMENTS

Because WordPerfect allows more than one (up to nine) files to be opened at once, it is possible to move quickly between the currently open files. This feature enables information to be quickly and easily cut or copied and pasted between documents.

Each time you select the *New* command, or open another document without selecting the *Close* command, another document will become part of the list of open documents.

Figure 12. To view the list of all currently open files, activate the **Window** menu. In this example there are three documents open. The check mark next to the third document indicates that this is the currently active file. To make one of the other documents in this list active, simply select it from the list.

Window
<u>C</u>ascade
<u>T</u>ile
<u>1</u> c:\wpwin\learn\learn11.wkb - unmodified
<u>2</u> Document2 - unmodified
√ <u>3</u> c:\wpwin\learn\learn12.wkb - unmodified

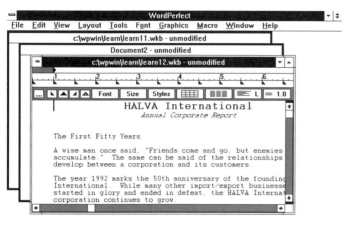

Figure 13. Selecting the *Cascade* command from the **Window** menu of Figure 12 will arrange the multiple open documents in an overlapping fashion, with the *Title Bar* of each document showing. The currently active document is the one at the front. Clicking on one of the document windows at the back will make that document window the currently active one.

Figure 14. The *Tile* command in the **Window** menu of Figure 12 will arrange the documents so that they can all be seen at once. Again, simply clicking on a document window will make that document the active one, denoted by a black *Title Bar*. In this figure, the bottom document is the active one. Any commands you select from the *Menu Bar* at the top of the screen will affect this document.

EXIT

Figure 15. The *Exit* command in the **File** menu will shut down WordPerfect. If you have not saved any open documents since making changes, you will be asked if you wish to save the changes for each document.

File	
New	Shift+F4
Open...	F4
Retrieve...	
Close	Ctrl+F4
Save	Shift+F3
Save As...	F3
Password...	
File Manager...	
Preferences	▶
Print...	F5
Print Preview...	Shift+F5
Select Printer...	
Exit	Alt+F4

THE QUICK LIST OPTION

WordPerfect allows you to group similar files into what are called *Quick Lists*. This feature provides an easier way of accessing and changing directories. The *Quick List* option can be found in the *Open File, Retrieve File, Retrieve Figure,* and *Save As* dialog boxes. The same *Quick List* is used in all these dialog boxes.

Figure 16. This example shows the *Quick List* option at the bottom of the *Open File* dialog box. It is currently not selected.

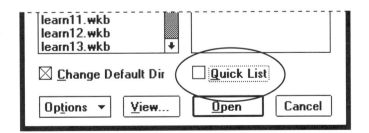

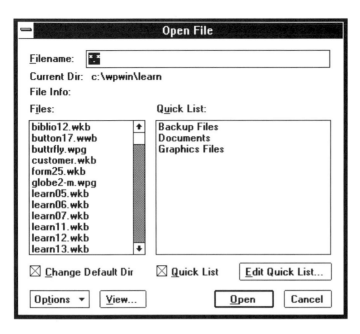

Figure 17. If you click on the *Quick List* option in the *Open File* dialog box, for example, the *Directories* list box will disappear and in its place will be the *Quick List* box. The *Edit Quick List* button will also appear. The list of names that appear in the *Quick List* will vary according to which files you have assigned default directories in the *Location of Files* dialog box (see Chapter 5 — Setting Preferences).

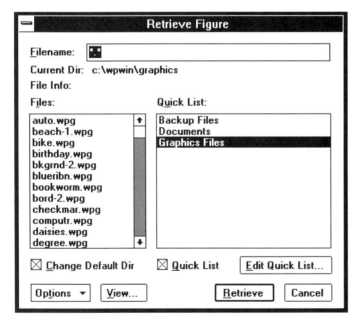

Figure 18. To access the files in a *Quick List*, double-click on the option that represents what type of file it is, and the directory that contains these files will become active. The list of files for that directory will then appear in the *Files* list. In this figure, the *Graphics Files* option was double-clicked and the files in the *graphics* directory are listed.

Figure 19. Editing a *Quick List* can be done by first clicking on the *Edit Quick List* button from Figure 18. This will activate the *Edit Quick List* dialog box as shown here. The current directory of an item selected in the *Quick List* box will appear under the *Directory/Filename* line.

To add your own option to the *Quick List,* click on the *Add* button. This will activate the *Add Quick List Item* dialog box of Figure 20.

Figure 20. In the *Descriptive Name* text box of the *Add Quick List Item* dialog box, key in the name that you would like to appear in the *Quick List* frame. For this example we used the title "Personal Documents."

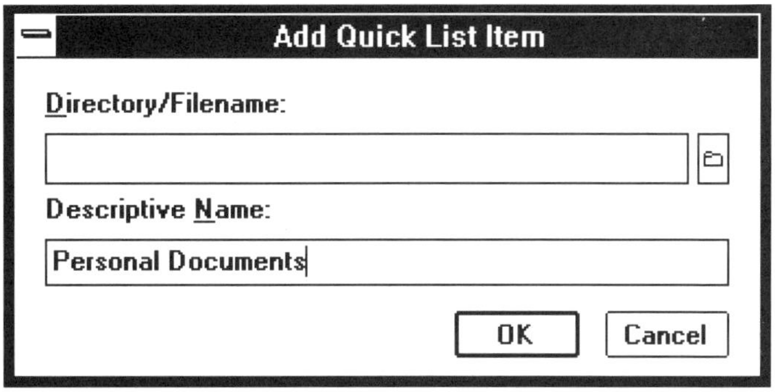

Figure 21. The next step is to locate the directory which contains the files you want to include. To do this, click on the ⌂ symbol to the right of the *Directory/Filename* text box in Figure 20. This will activate the *Select Directory* dialog box. Open the directory, in the *Select Directory* dialog box, that contains your personal documents and click on the *OK* button.

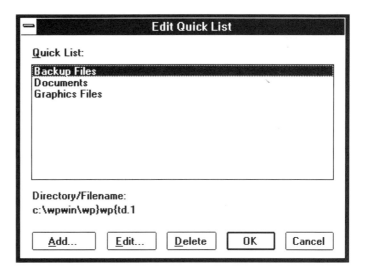

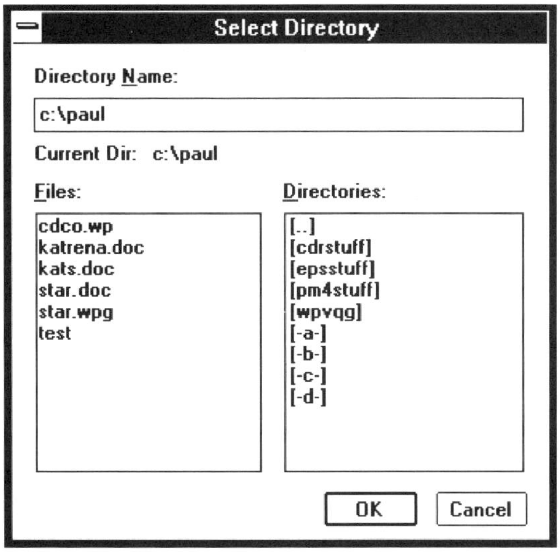

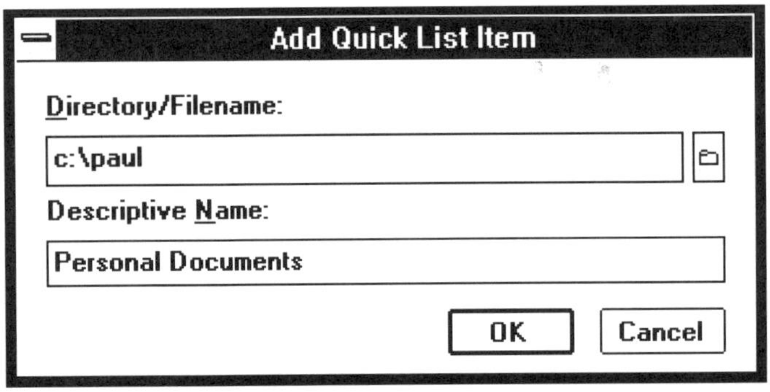

Figure 22. After clicking on *OK* in the dialog box shown in Figure 21, you will be returned to the *Add Quick List Item* dialog box, where the directory you selected in the previous dialog box will appear in the *Directory/Filename* text box.   If this is correct, click on *OK* to get back to the *Edit Quick List* dialog box.

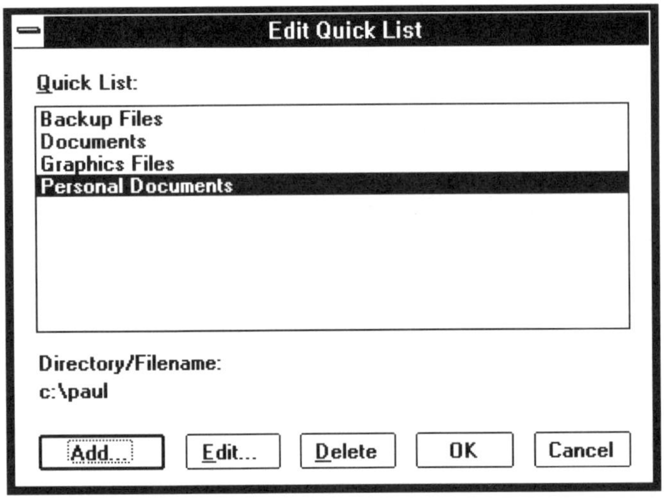

Figure 23. The "Personal Documents" option now appears in the *Quick List* box of the *Edit Quick List* dialog box.

The *Edit* button in the *Edit Quick List* dialog box activates the *Edit Quick List Item* dialog box. In this dialog box, it is possible to change the descriptive name and current directory of the *Quick List* item selected in the *Edit Quick List* dialog box. The *Delete* button will remove a selected *Quick List* item from the list.

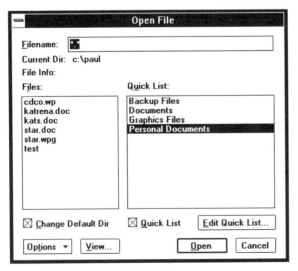

Figure 24. After clicking on *OK* in the *Edit Quick List* dialog box, you will see your *Personal Documents Quick List* item in the *Quick List* frame of the file selection dialog box where you began. In this case it was the *Open File* dialog box. Double-clicking on the *Personal Documents* item in the *Quick List* frame will activate the directory that you previously selected (see Figure 21).

To turn the *Quick List* feature off, simply deselect the *Quick List* option in one of the file selection dialog boxes.

THE FILE MANAGER

Figure 25. The *File Manager* command from the **File** menu activates the *File Manager* utility that comes with WordPerfect. With this utility, you can view, delete, print, find, get information on, and open WordPerfect files, among other things. The *File Manager* can also be accessed directly through Windows without first activating WordPerfect.

For more information on the *File Manager,* consult the **WordPerfect for Windows Reference Manual**.

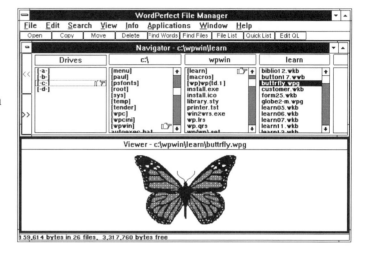

SETTING PREFERENCES 5

THE PREFERENCES SUB-MENU

The *Preferences* sub-menu lets you customize certain settings
that will determine the way WordPerfect runs. The changes
made in the dialog boxes associated with this menu will affect
all future documents, until the settings are modified again.

Figure 1. The *Preferences* sub-menu,
from the **File** menu, contains a
variety of commands. Each
command activates a dialog box
where you can select a wide range
of default settings. This chapter
looks at the twelve different default
options available from the
Preferences sub-menu.

File	
New	Shift+F4
Open...	F4
Retrieve...	
Close	Ctrl+F4
Save	Shift+F3
Save As...	F3
Password...	
File Manager...	
Preferences	
Print...	F5
Print Preview...	Shift+F5
Select Printer...	
Exit	Alt+F4

Preferences sub-menu
Location of Files...
Backup...
Environment...
Display...
Print...
Keyboard...
Initial Codes...
Document Summary...
Date Format...
Merge...
Table of Authorities...
Equations...

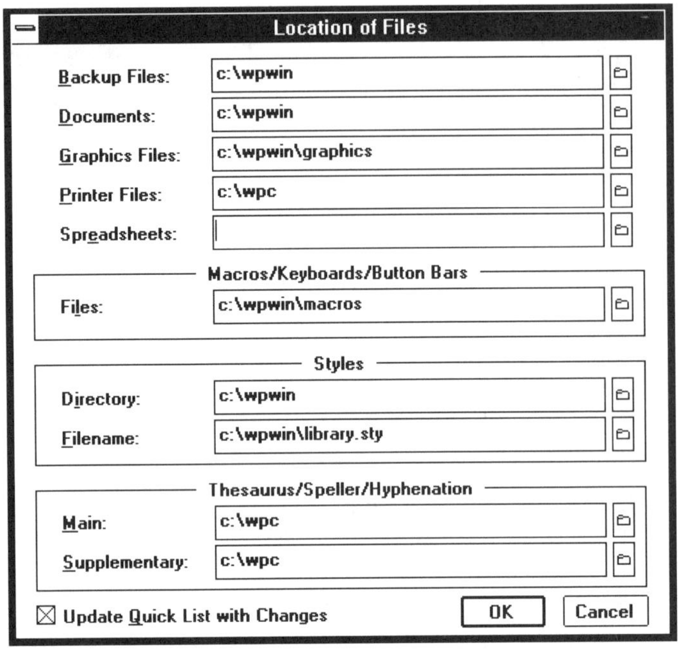

LOCATION OF FILES

Figure 2. The *Location of Files* command will activate the *Location of Files* dialog box. In this dialog box, it is possible to nominate the drive and directory into which certain files will automatically be saved.

You may edit the directory name in any of these text boxes using the mouse and keyboard. Alternatively, click on the symbol to the right of the file type for which you wish to change the default directory. This will activate the *Select Directory* dialog box. Select the directory you wish to use and click on *OK*. It will then appear in the relevant box.

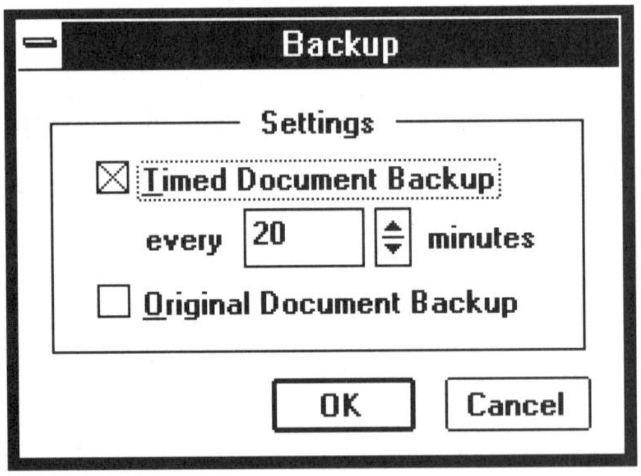

BACKUP

Figure 3. The *Backup* option in the *Preferences* sub-menu of Figure 1 activates the *Backup* dialog box. The *Timed Document Backup* option (on by default) will make a backup copy of any currently open documents, at regular intervals as specified. These files will be saved in the directory specified in the *Location of Files* dialog box (Figure 2). These backup documents are named *wp{wp}.bk* followed by the number of the document window. When you exit from WordPerfect, the files are deleted.

If you have a power failure, you can open the document as it existed at the last timed backup. When you open WordPerfect again, a *Timed Backup* dialog box appears letting you *Rename, Open* or *Delete* the backup file(s).

If you select the *Original Document Backup* option, each file you save will have a backup file saved with it in the same directory. The backup file will have the same name but an extension of *.bk!* These files can be opened using the *Retrieve* command from the **File** menu.

ENVIRONMENT SETTINGS

Figure 4. The *Environment Settings* dialog box is activated by selecting the *Environment* command from the *Preferences* sub-menu of Figure 1.

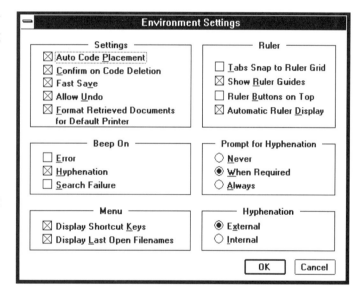

The first section of the *Environment Settings* dialog box is the *Settings* section. The first option in this section is the *Auto Code Placement* option. This option, on by default, ensures that most codes placed in your document are inserted at the correct place, often at the beginning of the paragraph or page. For more information on codes, see Chapter 2 — **Editing Text**.

Figure 5. The *Confirm on Code Deletion* option in the *Settings* section of the *Environment Settings* dialog box warns you if you are about to delete a code from your document.

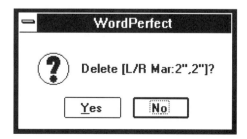

The *Fast Save* option in the *Settings* section of the *Environment Settings* dialog box of Figure 4 saves a document without the information necessary for the printer. This results in a faster save, but a longer print time, as all printer information is sent to the printer at the time of printing.

While the *Allow Undo* option is selected, the *Undo* command in the **Edit** menu can be accessed. This command allows you to reverse the last formatting or editing change you made to your document.

As a document is retrieved or opened, the *Format Retrieved Documents for Default Printer* option will format the document for the currently selected printer, even if this was not the original printer for which the document was formatted. If this option is off, WordPerfect will attempt to select the printer for which the document was last saved. If it cannot find this printer, it warns you, and then formats the document for the current printer.

```
┌─────────── Beep On ───────────┐
│  ☐ Error                      │
│  ☒ Hyphenation                │
│  ☐ Search Failure             │
└───────────────────────────────┘
```

Figure 6. The next section in the *Environment Settings* dialog box is the *Beep On* section.

If you have the *Error* option selected, you will hear a beep whenever an error dialog box appears.

The *Hyphenation* option will force a beep when the *Position Hyphen* dialog box appears. The appearance of this dialog box is determined by the option selected in the *Prompt for Hyphenation* section of the *Environment Settings* dialog box (Figure 13).

The *Search Failure* option in the *Beep On* section, if selected, will beep when the *String Not Found* message appears in the *Status Bar* after a search.

```
┌─────────── Menu ───────────┐
│  ☒ Display Shortcut Keys    │
│  ☒ Display Last Open Filenames │
└────────────────────────────┘
```

Figure 7. The next section of the *Environment Settings* dialog box is the *Menu* section.

Figure 8. With the *Display Shortcut Keys* option active, the keyboard shortcut keys that apply to a certain command will appear next to the command in the menus. The two menus in this figure show the **File** menu with, and without, the shortcut keys.

File	
New	
Open...	
Retrieve...	
Close	
Save	
Save As...	
Password...	
File Manager...	
Preferences	▶
Print...	
Print Preview...	
Select Printer...	
Exit	

File	
New	Shift+F4
Open...	F4
Retrieve...	
Close	Ctrl+F4
Save	Shift+F3
Save As...	F3
Password...	
File Manager...	
Preferences	▶
Print...	F5
Print Preview...	Shift+F5
Select Printer...	
Exit	Alt+F4

Figure 9. When you have the *Display Last Open Filenames* option selected, the four files that were most recently opened will be listed in the **File** menu. Any of these files can be re-opened by simply selecting them from the **File** menu.

File	
New	Shift+F4
Open...	F4
Retrieve...	
Close	Ctrl+F4
Save	Shift+F3
Save As...	F3
Password...	
File Manager...	
Preferences	▶
Print...	F5
Print Preview...	Shift+F5
Select Printer...	
Exit	Alt+F4
1 learn18.wkb	
2 learn17.wkb	
3 learn13.wkb	
4 learn07.wkb	

Figure 10. The next section of the *Environment Settings* dialog box is the *Ruler* section.

The *Tabs Snap to Ruler Grid* option causes all tabs to snap to every 1/16 th of an inch. If the option is on, then holding down the Shift key overrides it when setting tabs. If the option is off, then depressing the Shift key will make it act as though it is on.

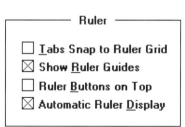

┌─ **Ruler** ─────────────┐

☐ **T**abs Snap to Ruler Grid

☒ Show **R**uler Guides

☐ Ruler **B**uttons on Top

☒ Automatic Ruler **D**isplay

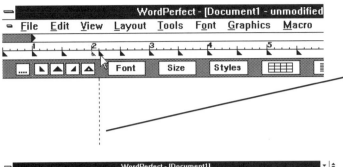

Figure 11. The *Show Ruler Guides* option in the *Ruler* section of the *Environment Settings* dialog box ensures that these guides appear when you move a tab or margin marker with the mouse.

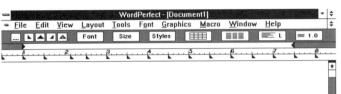

Figure 12. If you have the *Ruler Buttons on Top* option checked, the buttons, such as *Font* and *Size*, that normally run across the bottom of the *Ruler* will now be positioned above the *Ruler*.

The *Automatic Ruler Display* option, in Figure 10, ensures that the *Ruler* appears each time you start WordPerfect. If you do not wish the *Ruler* to appear on start-up, do not select this option.

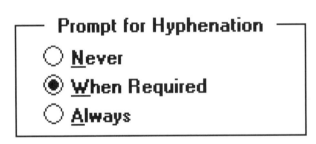

Figure 13. The *Prompt for Hyphenation* section of the *Environment Settings* dialog box contains three options. These options will only come into effect if you have selected *Hyphenation On* from the *Line/Hyphenation* command in the **Layout** menu.

The *Never* option will hyphenate a word according to the dictionary you have loaded. If the word is not in the dictionary, it will move to the next line without being hyphenated.

The *When Required* option asks you how a certain word should be hyphenated, if it does not appear in the dictionary. The *Always* option asks you to determine where a word will be hyphenated, each time a word needs hyphenation. The latter two options work in conjunction with the *Position Hyphen* dialog box.

Figure 14. The two options in the *Hyphenation* section of the *Environment Settings* dialog box determine the type of dictionary used when hyphenating.

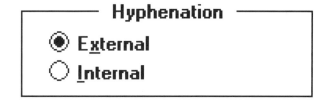

The *External* option loads the larger of the two dictionaries. It contains more words, allowing more hyphenating options but, conversely, takes up more disk space.

The dictionary files are installed with the *Speller.* If you choose not to install the *Speller,* you cannot use the *Hyphenation* option. For more information on *Hyphenation,* see Chapter 3 — **Page Formatting.**

DISPLAY

Figure 15. The *Display* command in the *Preferences* sub-menu activates the *Display Settings* dialog box.

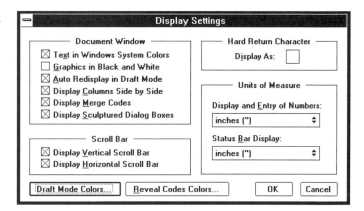

The first section of this dialog box is the *Document Window* section. The first option in this section is the *Text in Windows System Colors.* This means that the text color in WordPerfect is controlled by Windows.

The *Graphics in Black and White* option, when selected, will display all graphics in your document in black and white.

With the *Auto Redisplay in Draft Mode* option on, any changes you to make to your document in *Draft Mode* are updated automatically.

The *Display Columns Side by Side* option ensures that multiple columns in your document will display side by side as they would print. Deselecting this option, however, will display multiple columns as one long column, speeding up on-screen display time. The columns will still print side by side, irrespective of whether this feature is on or off.

The *Display Merge Codes* option will display *Merge Codes* on the screen. *Merge Codes* are displayed in conjunction with the *Merge* feature available from the **Tools** menu.

Sculptured dialog boxes have a more three-dimensional appearance, with chiseled lines on a gray background. They appear more slowly than normal Windows dialog boxes but will be activated if you have the *Display Sculptured Dialog Boxes* option selected.

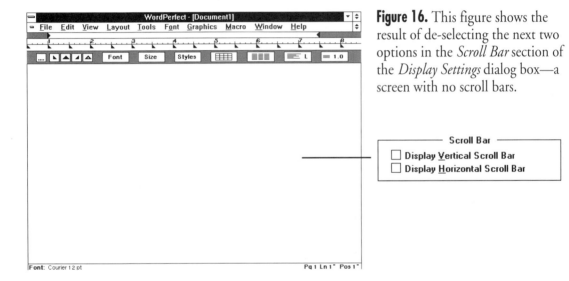

Figure 16. This figure shows the result of de-selecting the next two options in the *Scroll Bar* section of the *Display Settings* dialog box—a screen with no scroll bars.

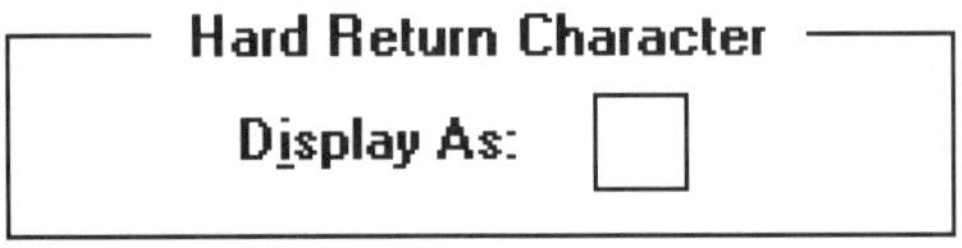

Figure 17. The *Hard Return Character* section appears at the top right of the *Display Settings* dialog box of Figure 15. If you enter a character in this section of the dialog box, it will appear in the document window each time you create a hard return. It will not print or appear in *Reveal Codes.*

Figure 18. The *Units of Measure* section of the *Display Settings* dialog box lets you determine the type of measurement used in all dialog boxes (*Display and Entry of Numbers*) and in the *Status Bar* and *Ruler* (*Status Bar Display*). Whatever style of measurement you choose from the pop-up list option shown here will be the style used.

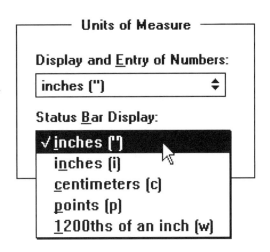

Figure 19. At the bottom left of the *Display Settings* dialog box of Figure 15 is a *Draft Mode Colors* button. If you click on this button, you will activate the *Draft Mode Colors* dialog box.

The changes you make in this dialog box affect the appearance of *Draft Mode* operation only.

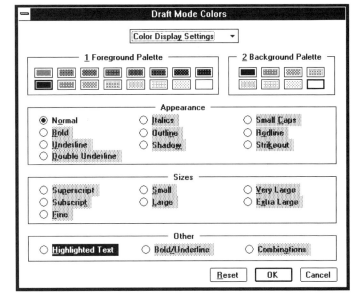

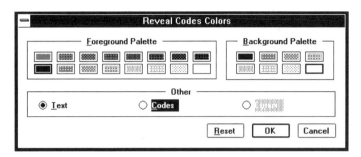

Figure 20. The *Reveal Codes Colors* dialog box is activated by clicking on the *Reveal Codes Colors* button in the *Display Settings* dialog box of Figure 15. The changes you make to the color scheme in this dialog box will change the colors used in the *Reveal Codes* window.

PRINT

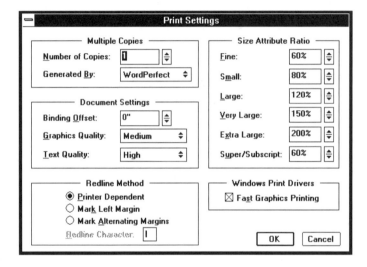

Figure 21. The *Print* command in the *Preferences* sub-menu of Figure 1 will activate the *Print Settings* dialog box.

The *Number of Copies* option determines how many copies you would like printed and the *Generated By* option decides whether WordPerfect or the printer generates the multiple copies. If you select *WordPerfect*, the multiple copies will be collated. If multiple copies are generated by the printer they will probably print faster because they are uncollated.

The *Binding Offset* option in the *Document Settings* section moves the text position if the document is to be bound. The *Graphics Quality* and *Text Quality* options let you decide the printing quality of text and graphics.

The *Redline Method* options determine how any text marked with the *Redline* feature (**Font** menu) will print.

The *Size Attribute Ratio* selections determine the size of certain text options in relation to normal text. If you have any of these options applied to any text (see *Font* dialog box in Chapter 2 — **Editing Text**), you can adjust the default size at this point.

The *Fast Graphics Printing* option in the *Print Settings* dialog box can be selected to print graphics faster with no loss of quality.

KEYBOARD

Figure 22. The *Keyboard* command in the *Preferences* fly-out menu will activate the *Keyboard* dialog box. The options in this dialog box decide what keyboard is currently in use and, therefore, which keyboard shortcuts are assigned to which commands.

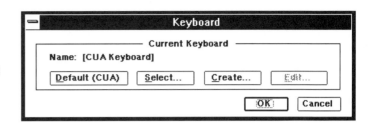

The *Default* button loads the default CUA keyboard that comes with WordPerfect. Most of these keyboard shortcuts are common to all Windows programs.

Figure 23. The *Select* button in Figure 22 activates the *Select Keyboard File* dialog box. In this figure, you can search for other keyboard files you would like to load. The DOS WordPerfect keyboard file (*wpdos51.wwk*) is shown here.

Figure 24. If you click on the *Create* button in the *Keyboard* dialog box of Figure 22, you will get the *Keyboard Editor* dialog box. With this feature, you can create your own keyboard file with personalized keyboard shortcuts.

The *Item Types* pop-up list currently contains the *Commands* option. The other options available in this list are *Menus, Text,* and *Macros.*

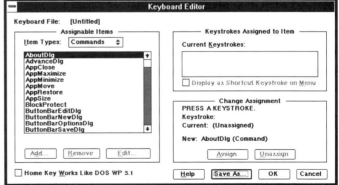

With *Commands* selected as the *Item Types* in Figure 24, all commands in WordPerfect are listed in the list box below *Item Types*. If you select a command from this list, then you are able to assign a keyboard sequence to it, or if it already has one, you can change the assignment. The keyboard sequence you select will appear in the *Change Assignment* section of the dialog box after the word *Keystroke* (Figure 25).

```
┌──────── Change Assignment ────────┐
│ Press a Keystroke.                │
│                                   │
│ Keystroke:  Ctrl+S                │
│ Current:    Font Size Menu (Submenu) │
│ New:        AboutDlg (Command)    │
│                                   │
│      ┌─────────┐  ┌──────────┐    │
│      │ Assign  │  │ Unassign │    │
│      └─────────┘  └──────────┘    │
└───────────────────────────────────┘
```

Figure 25. If the key sequence you selected already applies to a command, then it will appear after the word *Current*. In this figure, we selected the Ctrl+S key sequence for the *About* command and are shown that it already applies to the *Size* sub-menu command in the **Font** menu. You have the option here of unassigning this key sequence from the original command and applying it to a new command, or selecting another key sequence from the keyboard.

```
┌─────── Keystrokes Assigned to Item ───────┐
│                                           │
│ Current Keystrokes:                       │
│ ┌───────────────────────────────────────┐ │
│ │ Ctrl+S                                │ │
│ │                                       │ │
│ └───────────────────────────────────────┘ │
│                                           │
│ ☒ Display as Shortcut Keystroke on Menu   │
└───────────────────────────────────────────┘
```

Figure 26. If you decide that the key sequence you have selected is the right one, click on the *Assign* button from Figure 25 and this sequence will appear in the *Current Keystrokes* box shown here. More than one key sequence can be applied to a command.

The *Display as Shortcut Keystroke on Menu* option will display the newly assigned key sequence on the menu next to the command, if the keystroke assignment refers to a menu command.

Figure 27. The *Add* and *Remove* buttons in the *Assignable Items* frame of Figure 24 become available when you have the *Text* or *Macro Item Types* selected. The *Text* option in the *Item Types* pop-up list allows you to apply a key sequence to text. Every time you use the key sequence, the appropriate text will appear in the document. The *Edit Text* button allows you to edit this text at any time.

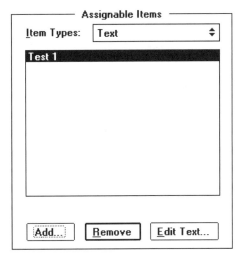

You can also assign keystrokes to macros by choosing *Macros* from the *Item Types* sub-menu.

Figure 28. The *Save Keyboard File* dialog box is activated by clicking on the *Save As* button in the *Keyboard Editor* dialog box of Figure 24. If you try to exit from the *Keyboard Editor* box without saving a new keyboard file you have created, the *Save Keyboard File* dialog box will appear, prompting you to save the file.

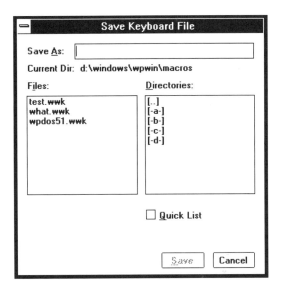

Figure 29. The *Edit* button in the *Keyboard* dialog box (Figure 22) lets you edit any keyboard files you have created.

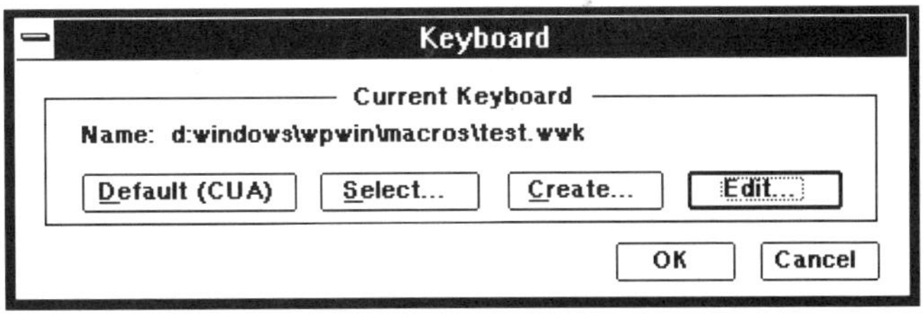

INITIAL CODES

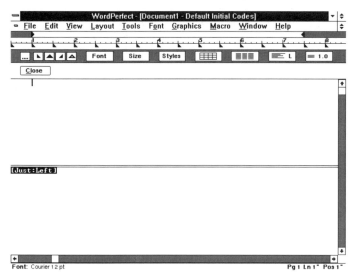

Figure 30. The *Initial Codes* command in the *Preferences* sub-menu of the Figure 1 **File** menu activates the *Initial Codes* screen. In this screen, it is possible to set up default options for all future documents. By selecting certain menu commands, codes are inserted that will format all future documents that are created. These options can be changed at any time and will be overridden by the codes inserted in the *Document Initial Codes* screen (see Chapter 3 — **Page Formatting**).

DOCUMENT SUMMARY

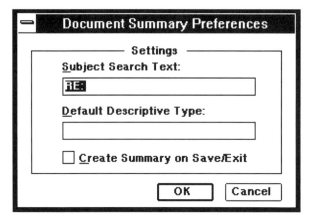

Figure 31. The *Document Summary* command in the *Preferences* sub-menu of Figure 1 activates the *Document Summary Preferences* dialog box. The *Document Summary* feature allows you to create document summaries or overviews.

The *Subject Search Text* option assumes that the standard subject entry in your document is **RE**. This, of course, can be changed to meet your needs. Clicking on the *Extract* button in the *Document Summary* dialog box of Figure 32 will display, in the *Subject* text box of the same figure, the text that follows the *Subject Search Text* option in a document. It will only copy the first 160 characters or until the next hard return code is reached.

The *Default Descriptive Type* text box allows you to insert the default type of document style. It is useful for categorizing your documents into such items as memos, letters, faxes, and so on.

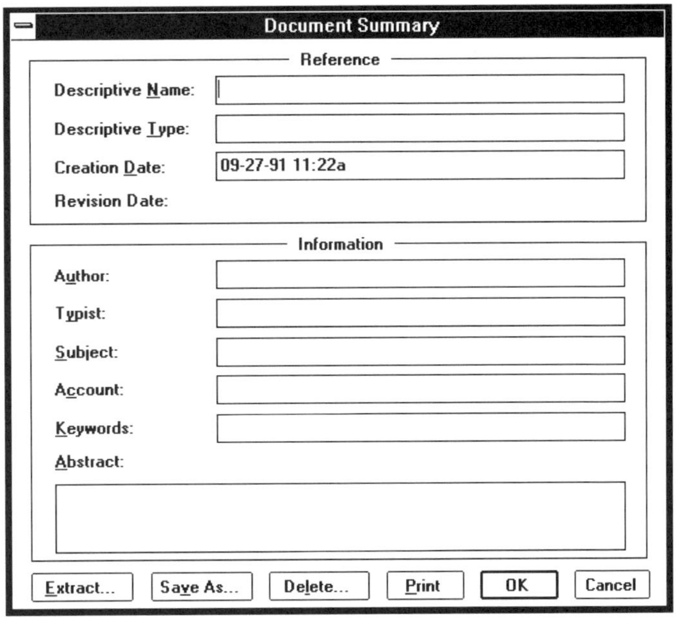

Figure 32. If you have the *Create Summary on Save/Exit* option selected in the dialog box shown in Figure 31, when you *Save* or exit your document, the *Document Summary* dialog box appears. This dialog box can also be activated by selecting the *Summary* command from the *Document* sub-menu in the **Layout** menu.

This *Document Summary* dialog box is used to create the actual overview or summary of the document. Most of the options in this dialog box are straightforward. They let you key in relevant information about the document to help you recognize it.

The *Abstract* text box can have a brief summary of the document keyed in. Alternatively, the *Extract* button will copy the first 400 characters of the document into the *Abstract* box, as well as copying the first 160 characters after the *Subject Search Text* option (Figure 31) into the *Subject* text box.

The *Save As* button lets you save the document summary as a file. The *Delete* button will remove all information from the *Document Summary* dialog box. The *Print* button allows you to print the document summary.

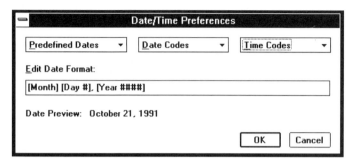

DATE FORMAT

Figure 33. The *Date Format* command from the *Preferences* sub-menu of Figure 1 activates the *Date/Time Preferences* dialog box. In this box, it is possible to change the way the date appears when you use the *Date* options, located in the **Tools** menu. You can choose a different option from the *Predefined Dates* pop-up list or create a special date format of your own.

The *Date Preview* section, at the bottom of the dialog box, displays how your selection will look.

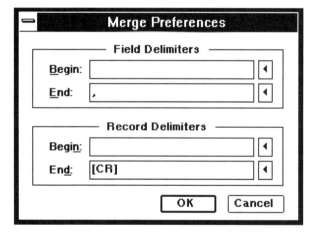

MERGE

Figure 34. The *Merge* command in the *Preferences* fly-out menu of Figure 1 activates the *Merge Preferences* dialog box.

This dialog box is used when you are merging documents with DOS files or documents from WordPerfect 4.0 (or earlier versions). The *Field Delimiters* and *Record Delimiters* must match the other program's merge settings for the merge to be successful.

TABLE OF AUTHORITIES

Figure 35. The *Table of Authorities* command in the *Preferences* menu activates the *ToA Preferences* dialog box. The *Table of Authorities* feature of WordPerfect is used mainly by the legal profession to create citation lists for legal briefs, which is similar to a contents. The options in this dialog box are set up before the table is created.

These options are self-explanatory and determine how the table is set out.

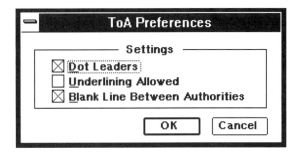

Figure 36. Once you have selected the required options from the Figure 35 dialog box, you then create the table by selecting the *Table of Authorities* command from the *Define* sub-menu in the **Tools** menu; this activates the *Define Table of Authorities* dialog box.

For more information on using the *Table of Authorities* feature, consult the **WordPerfect for Windows Reference Manual**.

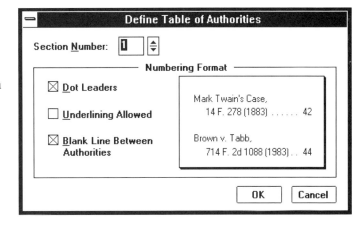

EQUATIONS

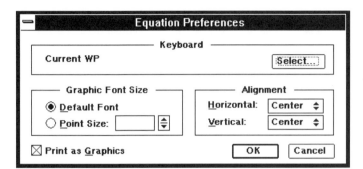

Figure 37. The *Equations* command in the *Preferences* sub-menu activates the *Equation Preferences* dialog box. This dialog box determines how equations, created through the **Graphics** menu, will appear on screen.

The *Select* button in the *Keyboard* section of this dialog box gives you access to the *Equation Keyboard* dialog box. This dialog box is similar to the Figure 22 *Keyboard dialog* box and is used in the same way.

If you have the *Default Font* option selected in the *Graphic Font Size* section of the *Equation Preferences* dialog box, the size of the equation is in relation to the size of the text in which it will appear. The *Point Size* option, when selected, allows you to set your own equation point size. The *Alignment* options determine whcrc the equation sits on the line.

Print as Graphics is normally selected, allowing WordPerfect to send all equation symbols to the printer as graphics. If this option is not selected, WordPerfect substitutes fonts for the particular symbols. If no symbols are found, it is printed as a graphics character.

For more information on the creation of graphics see Chapter 10 — **Using Graphics.**

SPELL CHECKING & THESAURUS   6

THE SPELLER

The spell checking feature of WordPerfect is common to
most word processing programs. In WordPerfect,
however, it is actually a separate program that can run on
its own. It scans your documents for any misspelled
words, giving you the choice of correcting these words or
leaving them as is.

USING THE SPELLER

Figure 1. To spell check an open
document, select the *Speller*
command from the **Tools** menu.
This will activate the *Speller*
window of Figure 2.

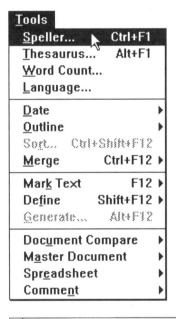

Figure 2. The options within the
Speller window are explained in the
following figures. To start the spell
checking process, simply click on
the *Start* button. When the spell
checking procedure begins, the
spell checker starts looking for
words that may be spelled
incorrectly.

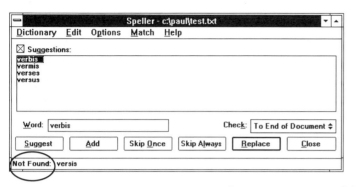

Figure 3. Once an incorrectly spelled word is found, it appears in the bottom left of the *Speller* window. The words *Not Found* refer to the fact that the spell checker has not found a match for this word in its dictionaries.

In the *Suggestions* area of the *Speller* window, the spell checker automatically makes some suggestions as to how it feels the selected word should be spelled. It is from here that you make selections with which to replace the misspelled word.

To the right of the *Speller* window is the *Check* pop-up list. Before commencing spell checking, this list will say *Document* (see Figure 2); during spell checking it will change to *To End of Document* (Figure 3). Figure 9 explains the other options.

If the selected word is spelled incorrectly, you can either correct it yourself, or make a selection from those listed under *Suggestions*. You may correct it yourself if none of the suggested words is the correct one.

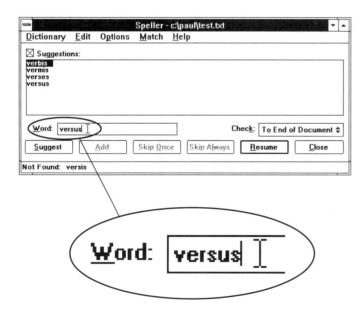

Figure 4. To correct a misspelled word yourself, key in the new word or correction in the *Word* text box.

Figure 5. Alternatively, select the appropriate word from the *Suggestions* rectangle. You will see that as the word is highlighted in the *Suggestions* rectangle, it also appears in the *Word* text box, allowing you to confirm your selection. To replace the incorrectly spelled word with the new word in the *Word* text box (regardless of whether you typed it or highlighted it from the *Suggestions* rectangle), you must click on the *Replace* button. The word is replaced in the text, and the *Speller* moves on to find other incorrectly spelled words.

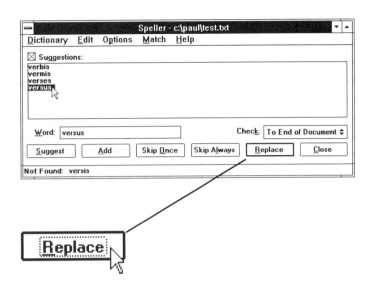

Figure 6. To the *Speller*, a misspelled word is one that is not found in its dictionaries. Of course, the best spell checker in the world cannot contain every word. You may decide that the word highlighted by the *Speller* is in fact correctly spelled. It may be the name of a person or company, or a word or acronym which is used in your particularly industry.

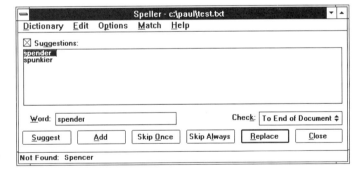

You could select one of the Skip buttons (*Skip Once* to ignore this word and move on, or *Skip Always* to ignore this word for the rest of the document), or you can add this word to the WordPerfect dictionary. This latter option is performed by clicking on the *Add* button. The word is now added to a supplementary dictionary so that it will be recognized next time it appears in a document.

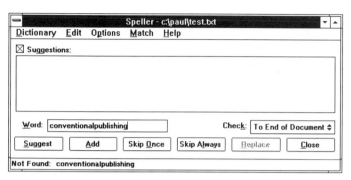

Figure 7. The WordPerfect *Speller* also highlights words that may not have a space between them. If this happens, place the cursor in the *Word* text box and add the space yourself between the words. Remember to then click on the *Replace* button so your correction replaces the mistake.

Figure 8. When the *Speller* finds two occurrences of a word in a row, such as "the the," the second word is highlighted and the *Duplicate Words Found* dialog box appears. This offers the choices of deleting the second word, disabling double-word checking, or continuing without deleting the word. (See Figure 16 for details on how to set up this option.)

Once spell checking is complete, a message box will appear. Click on *OK* to return to the *Speller* window. Then select *Close* from the *Speller* to return to your document.

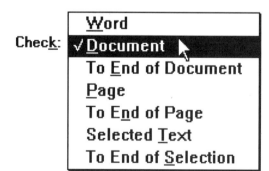

Figure 9. The options available in the *Check* pop-up list of the *Speller* window refer to which part of the current document you want spell-checked. The *Word* option only checks the current word. The *Document* option spell-checks the whole document. Once it has started, the *To End of Document* option becomes active.

If the *Page* option is selected, only the current page is checked. Once it has begun spell-checking, the *To End of Page* option becomes active. If the *Selected Text* option is active, only text that is highlighted is spell-checked. Once spell checking has begun, the *To End of Selection* option is selected.

USING THE SPELLER IN STAND-ALONE MODE

Figure 10. It is also possible to use the *Speller* outside WordPerfect. You can activate stand-alone operation by double-clicking on the *Speller* icon in the *Windows Program Manager.*

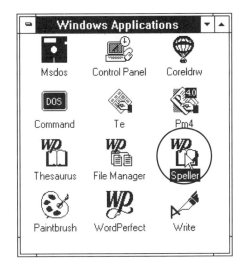

Figure 11. You can now enter individual words into the *Word* text box, and spell check them one at a time. Enter the word in this text box via the keyboard.

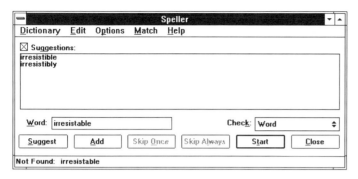

Figure 12. Once you have entered the desired word, click on the *Start* button, and a list of possible alternate spellings for this word will appear in the *Suggestions* text box, if the word is spelled incorrectly. If the word is spelled correctly, it will inform you in the bottom left corner that the word has been found in the dictionary. This indicates that the word is correctly spelled.

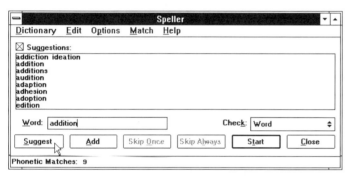

Figure 13. If you click on the *Suggest* button after entering a word, whether it is spelt incorrectly or not, you will get a list of what are called *Phonetic Matches.*

Note: If you key a word into the Speller Word *text box while in WordPerfect, the* Start *button will not have the same effect. The* Suggest *button, however, will still display a list of* Phonetic Matches *for this word. To spell-check an individual word in WordPerfect, select the word in the document before activating the* Speller. *Once the* Speller *is activated, the* Selected Text *option will appear automatically in the* Check *pop-up list; just click on the* Start *button.*

THE DICTIONARY MENU

(a)

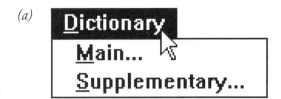

Figure 14. The options available in the *Speller* **Dictionary** menu (a) let you choose a different dictionary from the one currently loaded. The *Main* dictionary is the dictionary to which WordPerfect first refers, while the *Supplementary* dictionary is the dictionary that contains any words added to the *Speller* by you.

(b)

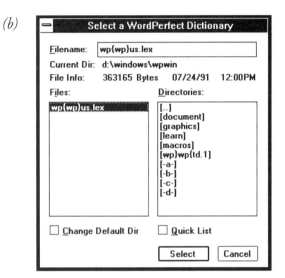

Selecting one of these options from the **Dictionary** menu will take you to a dialog box (b), where it is possible to select another dictionary you intend to load.

THE EDIT MENU

Figure 15. The most important command in the *Speller* **Edit** menu is *Undo*. This command will undo the last change made in the *Word* text box. The *Cut* command deletes whatever is in the *Word* text box and places it in the Windows *Clipboard*, whereas the *Copy* command leaves the word(s) behind as well as putting a copy in the *Clipboard*.

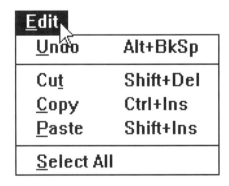

You must select one or more words before the *Cut* or *Copy* commands can be used. The *Paste* command places back, in the *Word* text box, whatever you have just previously cut or copied to the *Clipboard*. The *Select All* command highlights everything in the *Word* text box so it will display in reverse video ready to be cut and/or copied.

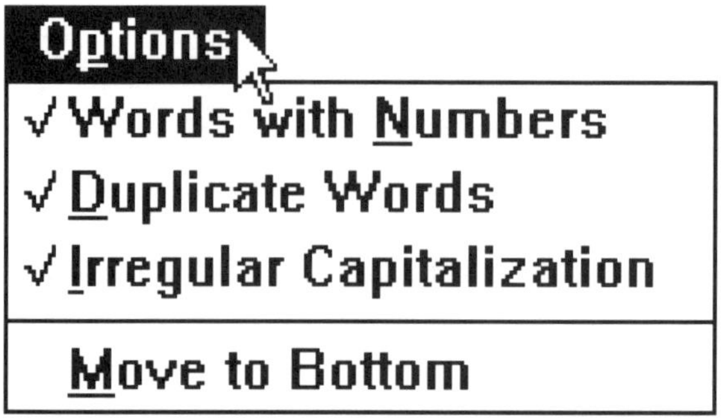

THE OPTIONS MENU

Figure 16. By default, the first three commands in the **Options** menu are checked (or active). To turn them off, select them from the menu and the check mark will disappear. If the *Words with Numbers* option is active, the *Speller* will highlight words that include numbers. If you do not want this to happen, deselect this option.

The same applies for the next two options. If you do not want the *Speller* to highlight two instances of the same word that appear in succession, deselect the *Duplicate Words* option. If you have any words in your document that may have irregular capitalization within the first three characters, and you do not want the spell checker to highlight them, turn off the *Irregular Capitalization* command.

The *Move to Bottom* command in the **Options** menu moves the *Speller* window to the bottom of the screen. This allows you to see the words that the spell checker picks up as mistakes and decide whether they are mistakes or not, based on the context.

THE MATCH MENU

Figure 17. The options in the **Match** menu let you search for words with a similar pattern. On selecting the *1 Character* option, a ? (question mark) will appear in the *Word* text box.

Figure 18. By placing the *1 Character* symbol between the letters s and y (s?y), for example, and clicking on the *Suggest* button, similar words including *say, shy, sky, sly* and *soy* appear in the *Suggestions* frame. The first word in the list replaces what was in the *Word* text box.

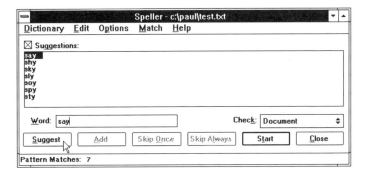

Figure 19. On selecting the *Multiple Characters* option from the **Match** menu of Figure 17 an * (asterisk) symbol will appear in the *Word* text box. This command gives you the option of displaying words that have more than one character the same.

For example, by placing the *Multiple Characters* symbol before the letters *port* (*port), and clicking on the *Suggest* button, all words in the dictionary that end in port will be listed. The bottom left-hand corner of the *Speller* tells us that there are 29 *Pattern Matches*. Again, the first word in the list replaces what was in the *Word* text box.

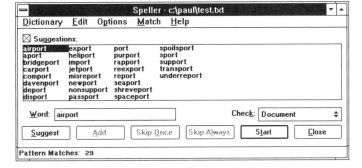

THESAURUS

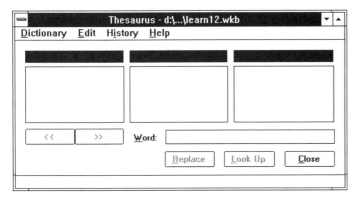

Figure 20. The *Thesaurus* feature of WordPerfect is designed to help you write your document. Like a thesaurus book, the *Thesaurus* program lists synonyms and antonyms for selected words. The WordPerfect *Thesaurus,* however, lets you view synonym listings for up to three words at a time and can update your document directly. The *Thesaurus,* like the *Speller,* is a separate program and can also run in stand-alone mode.

USING THE THESAURUS

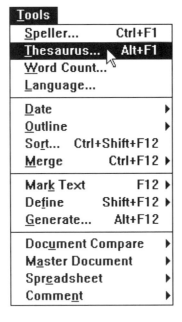

Figure 21. To see a list of synonyms for a word, place the cursor within that word, and select the *Thesaurus* command from the **Tools** menu.

Figure 22. The word with the cursor inserted appears above the first column and is known as the headword. The letter in parentheses tells us what kind of word it is (i.e., noun, adjective, etc.). A list of synonyms and antonyms appears in the first column below the word. If necessary, scroll bars will appear (see Figure 26) if the list is larger than the list window.

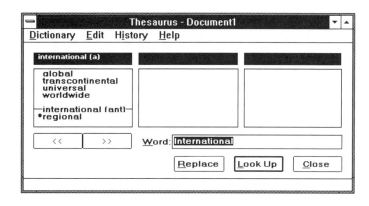

Figure 23. If you highlight a word in the synonym list, it will be placed in the *Word* text box. You can type words directly into the *Word* text box, if the word you want is not available from the list of synonyms. Clicking on the *Replace* button replaces the word in the document with whatever is in the *Word* text box.

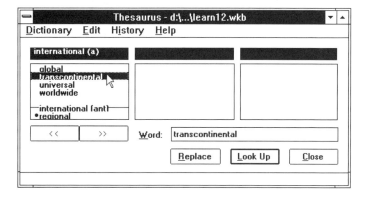

Figure 24. Once the *Replace* button is selected, the *Thesaurus* disappears, and you are returned to the document with the new word replacing the original. If the original word was capitalized, the new one is also capitalized. If you wish to return to the text without making any changes, select the *Close* button in the Thesaurus. The *Thesaurus* is reactivated by selecting the *Thesaurus* command from the **Tools** menu.

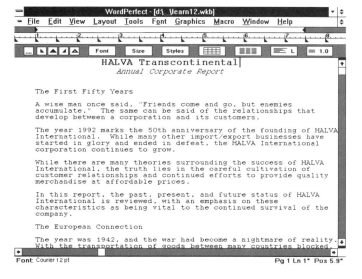

(a)

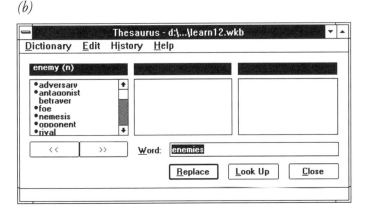

Figure 25. Before activating the *Thesaurus* again, we placed the cursor in the word "enemies" on the fourth line down (a). Notice that, even though the selected word is "enemies," the *Thesaurus* in (b) is showing synonyms for the word "enemy." This is because the word "enemies" is not in the *Thesaurus* dictionary but it has identified the word "enemy" as a related word.

(b)

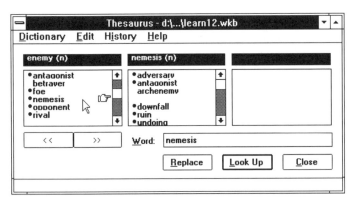

Figure 26. It is possible to click also on some of the listed synonym words in the column list to view additional synonyms and antonyms. To do this, double-click on the relevant word from the first column. In this example, the word "nemesis" was double-clicked on. The word "nemesis" is now the headword in the second column and a series of synonyms for this word appears in the list below.

Figure 27. This option, called *Reference Chaining*, may continue on for additional columns. For example, as shown here, synonyms and antonyms for a word double-clicked in the second column now appear in the third column.

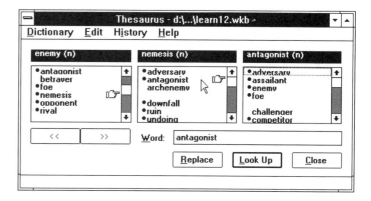

Figure 28. If you have double-clicked on more than three words, the scrolling buttons below the first column give you access to previous words in earlier or later columns.

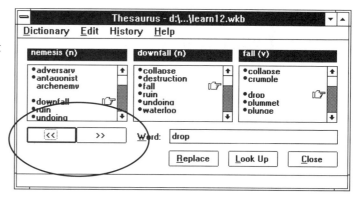

Figure 29. If you type a new word into the *Word* rectangle, you must click on the *Look Up* button to reveal a new list of words. This word appears as the headword for the first column and any words previously listed will disappear.

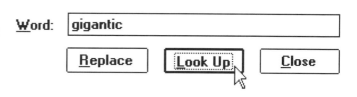

Figure 30. If the word you have typed in the *Word* text box is not in the *Thesaurus* dictionary, this is indicated in the bottom left of the *Thesaurus* window.

THE DICTIONARY MENU

(a)

Dictionary
Change Dictionary...

(b)

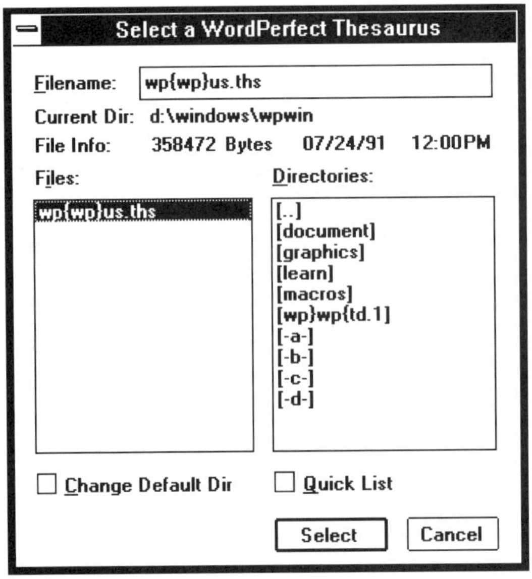

Select a WordPerfect Thesaurus

Filename: wp{wp}us.ths
Current Dir: d:\windows\wpwin
File Info: 358472 Bytes 07/24/91 12:00PM
Files:

wp{wp}us.ths

Directories:

[..]
[document]
[graphics]
[learn]
[macros]
[wp}wp{td.1]
[-a-]
[-b-]
[-c-]
[-d-]

☐ Change Default Dir   ☐ Quick List

Select   Cancel

Figure 31. The *Thesaurus Dictionary* menu (a) loads a new language dictionary as the current dictionary. This is done through the *Select a WordPerfect Thesaurus* dialog box (b) activated by selecting the *Change Dictionary* command.

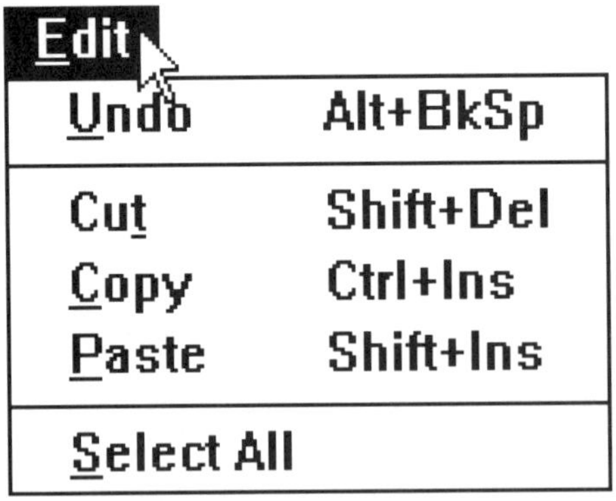

THE EDIT MENU

Edit

Undo   Alt+BkSp

Cut   Shift+Del
Copy   Ctrl+Ins
Paste   Shift+Ins

Select All

Figure 32. The most important command in the *Thesaurus* **Edit** menu is the *Undo* command. On selecting this command, any changes you have just made in the *Word* text box are reversed. The *Cut* command cuts whatever is in the *Word* text box and places it in the Windows *Clipboard*. The *Copy* command makes a copy of whatever is in the *Word* text box for the *Clipboard,* as well as leaving the original behind.

The text in the *Word* text box
must be selected before the *Cut* or
Copy commands are used. The
Paste command places a copy of
whatever is in the *Clipboard* into
the *Word* text box. The *Select All*
command highlights whatever is
in the *Word* text box, in reverse
video, so that the *Cut* and/or *Copy*
commands can be used.

THE HISTORY MENU

Figure 33. The History menu
contains all the words that have
been looked up since activating the
Thesaurus. If you select a word
from this menu, it appears as the
headword for column one with its
synonyms below it, replacing the
previous contents of this column.

History
drop
fall
downfall
annulment
waterloo
undoing
foe
antagonist
nemesis
enemies

PRINTING FROM WORDPERFECT 7

THE PRINT COMMAND

Printing your document in WordPerfect is achieved through the *Print* command located in the **File** menu. The options connected with printing from WordPerfect are extremely varied, allowing you to customize the way your document is printed.

Figure 1. Selecting the *Print* command from the **File** menu activates the *Print* dialog box of Figure 2.

File	
<u>N</u>ew	Shift+F4
<u>O</u>pen...	F4
<u>R</u>etrieve...	
<u>C</u>lose	Ctrl+F4
<u>S</u>ave	Shift+F3
Save <u>A</u>s...	F3
Pass<u>w</u>ord...	
<u>F</u>ile Manager...	
Pr<u>e</u>ferences	▶
<u>P</u>rint...	F5
Print Pre<u>v</u>iew...	Shift+F5
Se<u>l</u>ect Printer...	
E<u>x</u>it	Alt+F4

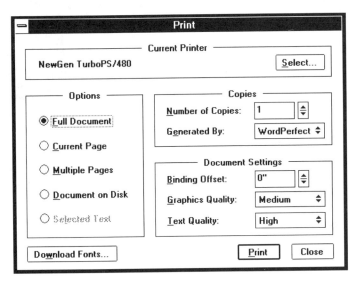

Figure 2. In the *Print* dialog box there are a number of options from which to choose. Any changes you make in this dialog box override the selections in the *Print Settings* dialog box from the *Preferences* sub-menu in the **File** menu. The top section of this dialog box lists the currently selected printer.

Number of Copies: Specify the number of copies you wish to print. *Generated By:* For multiple copies choose either *WordPerfect* or *Printer.* The printing time is faster if you select *Printer* for multiple copies.

Options: Most of these options are self explanatory. The *Multiple Pages* option invokes a dialog box where you specify the page number range. *Document on Disk* also invokes a dialog box where you name the file on disk to be printed. The *Selected Text* option is available only if you have highlighted text within your document.

Document Settings: The *Binding Offset* option allows you to specify the amount of space to move the text, to the right on odd numbered pages and to the left on even numbered pages, if the document is to be bound. The *Graphics* and *Text Quality* options determine the quality of text and graphics for printing.

SELECTING PRINTERS

Figure 3. Clicking on the *Select* button at the top right of the *Print* dialog box of Figure 2 invokes the *Select Printer* dialog box. This is the same dialog box activated by the *Select Printer* command from the **File** menu.

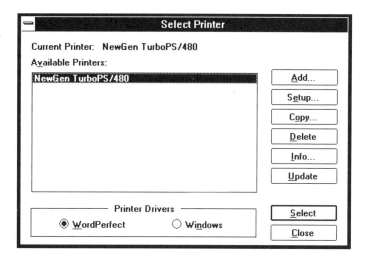

In this box you can modify the printer settings. To change the printer, first select either *WordPerfect* or *Windows* to specify the type of printer driver you are using. Then select a different printer name listed in the window (if available), or select the *Add* button to activate the dialog box of Figure 4. This lets you add printer names to the list.

Once you have modified this dialog box to your requirements, click on the *Select* button to return to the WordPerfect screen. If you have the *Windows Printer Drivers* option selected, the *Add* button is not available. In this case, click on the *Setup* button to activate the Windows print dialog box.

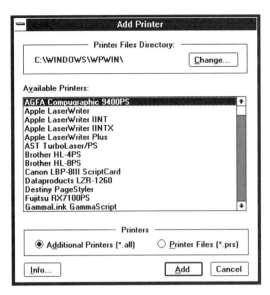

Figure 4. In the *Add Printer* dialog box (for *WordPerfect Printer Drivers*), select the printer you require and click on the *Add* button. A dialog box appears telling you the filename of the printer just selected. Click on *OK* and you will be returned to the *Select Printer* dialog box of Figure 3, with the name of your selected printer shown in the *Available Printers* list.

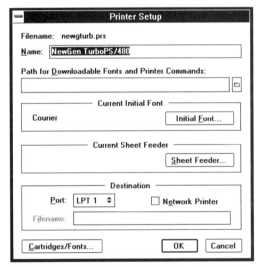

Figure 5. This *Printer Setup* dialog box is activated by clicking on the *Setup* button in the *Select Printer* dialog box of Figure 3. This assumes that you have the *WordPerfect* option selected in the *Printer Drivers* section of the *Select Printer* dialog box. Before clicking on the *Setup* button, select the relevant printer from the *Available Printers* list.

The name of the printer appears in the *Name* text frame with the *Filename* above it.

The *Path for Downloadable Fonts and Printer Commands* text frame should contain the directory where WordPerfect searches for font files and printer command files. To adjust this location, click on the 🗁 button to activate the *Select Directory* dialog box. In this latter dialog box, you can locate the directory that contains the relevant files for the printer. Click on *OK* to return to Figure 5.

The *Current Initial Font* option in the *Printer Setup* dialog box of Figure 5 lets you determine the default font for the printer.

The *Current Sheet Feeder* option in the Figure 5 *Printer Setup* dialog box lets you decide on the sheet feeder, if your printer is capable of handling one.

The *Port* option in the *Destination* section of the *Printer Setup* dialog box lets you choose your printer port from a variety of serial and parallel connections. The *File* option is selected from the *Port* pop-up list if you are printing to disk. A filename and path must be inserted in this case.

The *Cartridges/Fonts* button activates a dialog box where it is possible to select any cartridges or fonts you wish to use for printing.

Figure 6. The *Copy* button in the Figure 3 *Select Printer* dialog box is available only if you have the *WordPerfect* option selected in the *Printer Drivers* section of the dialog box. It activates the *Copy Printer* dialog box, as shown here. In this dialog box a slightly different filename appears for the printer selected in the *Select Printer* dialog box. Click on *OK* to add this printer to your list.

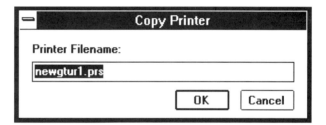

You will now have two variations of the same printer in the *Available Printers* list of Figure 3. Because they have different filenames, you can now choose two different setup configurations for the same printer.

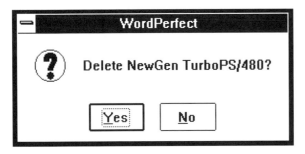

Figure 7. The *Delete* button in the *Select Printer* dialog box of Figure 3 removes the current printer that is selected in the *Available Printers* list. You must first confirm that you want to delete this printer before it is removed.

Figure 8. The *Info* button of the *Select Printer* dialog box of Figure 3 activates the *Printer Information* dialog box. If your printer has any special characteristics when working with WordPerfect, it will tell you in this dialog box.

The *Update* button in the *Select Printer* dialog box shown in Figure 3 updates your printer resource files (.prs) if you have installed a new file containing printer information (.all).

For more information on printing, see the *Print* command in Chapter 5 — **Setting Preferences**.

PRINT PREVIEW

Figure 9. Select the *Print Preview* command from the **File** menu to activate the *Print Preview* window.

File	
New	Shift+F4
Open...	F4
Retrieve...	
Close	Ctrl+F4
Save	Shift+F3
Save As...	F3
Password...	
File Manager...	
Preferences	▶
Print...	F5
Print Preview... Shift+F5	
Select Printer...	
Exit	Alt+F4

Figure 10. The *Print Preview* window allows you to view your document exactly as it will print. This will include things such as headers, footers, and page numbers that do not appear in the normal document window. Menu commands and/or *Button Bar* items are selected in the *Print Preview* window to alter the way the document is viewed while in *Print Preview* mode.

For example, you can view different pages or zoom in and out at different magnifications.

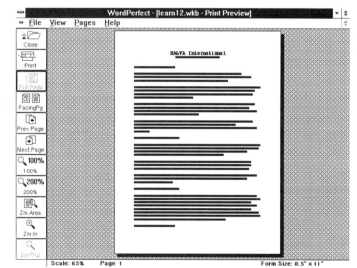

CREATING TABLES

8

WORDPERFECT TABLES

The Table feature of WordPerfect lets you create professional looking tables, schedules, worksheets, calendars, and more. It lets you arrange information into multiple rows and columns that you set up to suit your specific needs. This information can be manipulated in various ways using the range of commands available through the *Tables* sub-menu from the **Layout** menu.

THE TABLES SUB-MENU

Figure 1. Creating tables in WordPerfect is achieved through either the *Ruler* (see Chapter 1) or the *Create Table* dialog box. To activate this dialog box, select the *Create* command in the *Tables* sub-menu from the **Layout** menu.

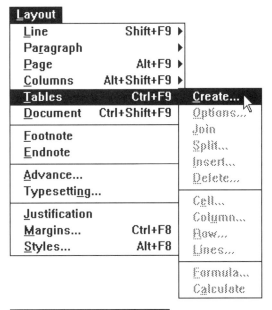

Figure 2. Once the *Create Table* dialog box appears, key in the required number for columns and rows in the appropriate boxes and click on *OK*. For this example, we chose 3 *Columns* and 3 *Rows*.

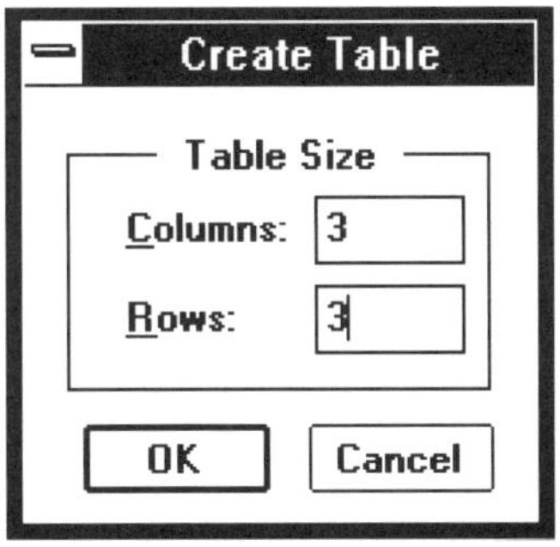

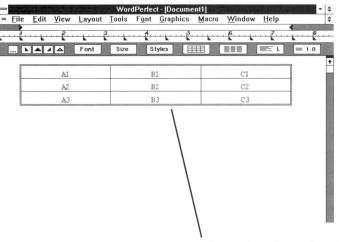

Figure 3. The table created in the previous dialog box is now displayed on screen. To key text into a cell, insert the cursor inside the required cell and start typing. The *Tab* key moves you to the next cell, while the *Shift+Tab* keys return you to the previous cell. This allows you to move around the table without using the mouse. Alternatively, the arrow keys on your keyboard will move you between cells in the table.

The text keyed into this table shows how WordPerfect actually references individual cells within a table. Columns are referenced by letters and rows by numbers. When the cursor is inside a table, the cell reference is shown in the *Status Bar.*

When working with tables, you can gain faster access to the *Tables* sub-menu by loading the default tables *Button Bar* from the *Button Bar Setup/Select* command from the **View** menu.

TABLE OPTIONS

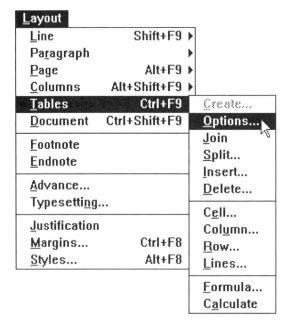

Figure 4. Once the table has been created, you will notice that the remaining options in the *Tables* sub-menu can now be selected. The next option after *Create* in this sub-menu is *Options.* Selecting this command will activate the *Table Options* dialog box of Figure 5. The cursor must be located inside the table before this command can be activated.

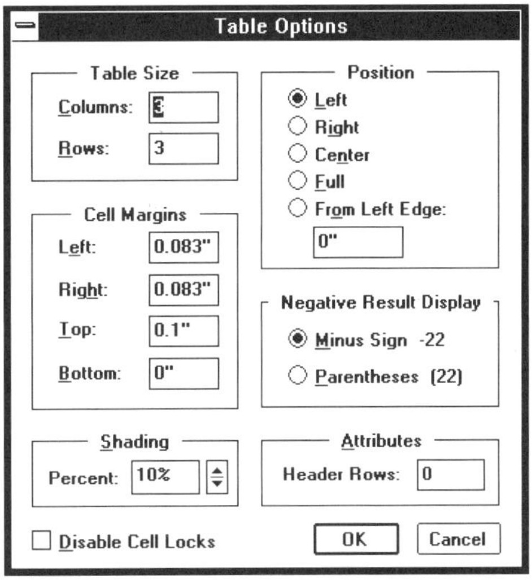

Figure 5. The first section of the *Table Options* dialog box is the *Table Size* section. This lets you alter the number of columns or rows in an existing table by changing the figures in the *Columns* and *Rows* boxes. Columns are added/deleted to the right of the table and rows are added/deleted at the bottom.

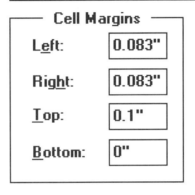

Figure 6. The *Cell Margins* section of the Figure 5 dialog box determines the space between the text and borders of each cell. Whatever changes you make here will affect all cells in the table.

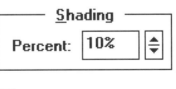

Figure 7. Any changes you make to the *Shading* feature of the *Table Options* dialog box only affects a cell that has had the *Shading* option applied to it in the *Format Cell* dialog box (see Figure 22). In altering the shading of this square, keep in mind that 100% is black.

The *Disable Cell Locks* option (below *Shading*) overrides the *Lock* feature that can be selected in the *Format Cell* dialog box, available from the *Cell* command in the *Tables* sub-menu. See Figure 22 for more details.

Position

- ● **L**eft
- ○ **R**ight
- ○ **C**enter
- ○ **F**ull
- ○ **Fr**om Left Edge:

```
0"
```

Figure 8. The *Position* group of the *Table Options* dialog box lets you alter the position of the table on the page. The *Left, Right,* and *Center* choices are self explanatory, while the *Full* option spreads the table across the page from the left to the right margin. The *From Left Edge* option allows you to key in a measurement in the box below, which determines how far the table sits from the left edge of the page.

When a table is created, it stretches from margin to margin by default. Once the table is displayed, you can then change the size of cells so that the *Left, Right,* and *Center* choices in this dialog box can be used, if required.

Negative Result Display

- ● **M**inus Sign -22
- ○ **P**arentheses (22)

Figure 9. The *Negative Result Display* section of the *Table Options* dialog box gives you the choice of displaying negative calculated results with a minus sign or parentheses. For more information see the *Formula* command, from Figure 31 onwards.

Attributes

Header Rows: `0`

Figure 10. The last section of the *Table Options* dialog box is the *Attributes* section. If your table is interrupted by a page break, you can create *Header Rows* that appear at the top of the following page making the table easier to understand. The number you key into the *Header Rows* box is the number of header rows that will appear.

SELECTING CELLS

Figure 11. To select individual cells, move the mouse to the left hand wall of a cell, until you see a left facing arrow (a), and click the mouse. Double-clicking will select the full row. The same result can be achieved by moving the mouse to the ceiling of a cell, until an upward facing arrow appears (b) and then click the mouse. Double-clicking, in this case, will select the full column.

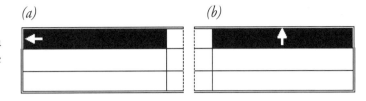

Figure 12. To select the whole table, hold the mouse down in the top left cell and drag it down and to the right. As you move down and across the table, all cells you pass will become selected. Keep dragging to the bottom right cell and release the mouse when this cell becomes highlighted. Using this approach you can select as many or as few adjoining cells as you like.

Alternatively, the full table can be selected by triple-clicking over any section of the table when either the vertical or horizontal mouse pointer arrows of Figure 11 (a) or (b) appear.

SELECTING TEXT IN CELLS

Figure 13. Text inside individual cells is selected as text is normally selected in WordPerfect. That is, either swiping text with the mouse or double-clicking over it. Text is also edited as you would edit text outside of a table.

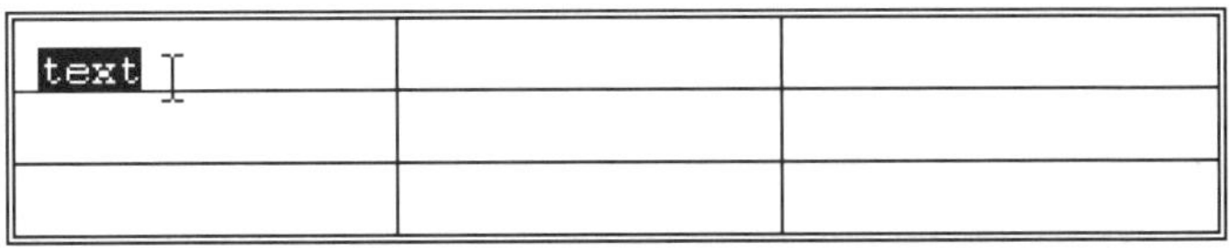

text	text	text
text	text	text
text	text	text

I

Figure 14. To select all text in a table, hold the mouse down in the top left cell and drag it down and to the right. As you move down, all cells you pass will become highlighted as in Figure 12. Keep dragging the mouse past the table so that the highlighting of the cells switches to the text. The text can now have its attributes changed or deleted.

THE JOIN COMMAND

Figure 15. The next option in the *Tables* sub-menu of Figure 1 is the *Join* option. This option will join any cells you have selected, at the time of choosing this command, so that they become one larger cell. Here the first and second cells of row 1 were selected and the *Join* option was chosen. They are now one cell.

THE SPLIT COMMAND

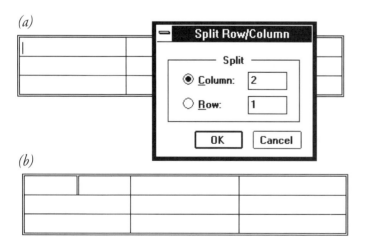

(a)

(b)

Figure 16. The *Split* command, after the *Join* command in the *Tables* sub-menu of Figure 1, can split any existing cell or cells into a number of smaller cells. In this example we placed the flashing cursor in the top left cell of the table and selected the *Split* command (a). In the *Split Row/ Column* dialog box, we placed a 2 in the *Column* frame. After selecting *OK*, the top left cell has been split into two columns (b).

THE INSERT COMMAND

Figure 17. The option after the *Split* command in the *Tables* sub-menu of Figure 1 is the *Insert* command. New columns and rows are inserted to the left and above, respectively, of the cell in which the cursor is located. In the *Insert Rows/Columns* dialog box, key in the figure for the amount of columns or rows you want to insert and click on *OK*. In this example (a), we placed the cursor in the third cell in the top row of the table, and placed a 2 in the *Columns* frame of the *Insert Rows/Columns* dialog box and selected *OK*. Figure (b) shows the result.

(a)

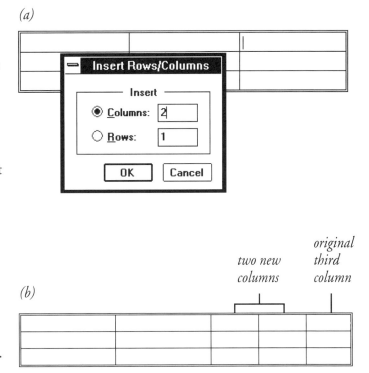

Note that in (b) two columns have been added to the table in front of the original third column.

(b)

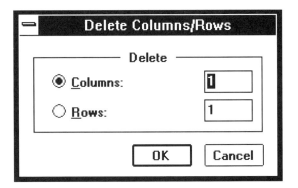

THE DELETE COMMAND

Figure 18. The next option that appears in the *Tables* sub-menu of Figure 1 is the *Delete* option. Insert the cursor in the column or row you wish to remove and select *Delete* to activate the *Delete Columns/Rows* dialog box. Choose *Columns* or *Rows* (you can't delete both at once) and how many (if you wish to delete more than one) and click on *OK*. If you actually select multiple columns or rows, you do not need to key in a number.

You can also delete the contents of a row or column without deleting the actual structure. Select either the row(s) or column(s) and press Backspace or Delete. Make your choice from the dialog box that appears and click on *OK*.

CAR WASH	Saturday	Sunday
Sharon	25 cars	37 cars
James	45 cars	15 cars

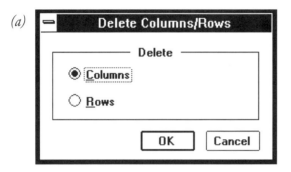

Figure 19. For example, if you wish to delete the middle column of this table, you would insert the cursor somewhere in this column, or select the whole column, or select the first cell (as we have done here).

(a)

(b)

CAR WASH	Sunday
Sharon	37 cars
James	15 cars

Figure 20. In the *Delete Columns/Row* dialog box (a), select either the *Columns* or *Rows* option and then *OK.* In this case we selected the *Columns* option. The middle column has now been deleted as in (b).

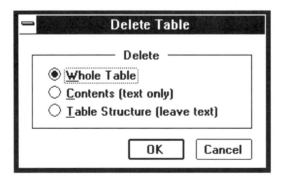

Figure 21. If you press the Delete key on the keyboard, with the whole table selected, you will get the *Delete Table* dialog box. In this case, you are given the option of deleting the whole table, just the text, or the table structure without deleting the text.

FORMATTING CELLS

Figure 22. The *Cell* command of the Figure 1 *Tables* sub-menu activates the *Format Cell* dialog box. Any changes made in this dialog box will affect the text in one or more selected cells. The *Appearance* and *Size* options in this dialog box are the same options found in the *Font* dialog box from the **Font** menu (see Chapter 2 — **Editing Text**).

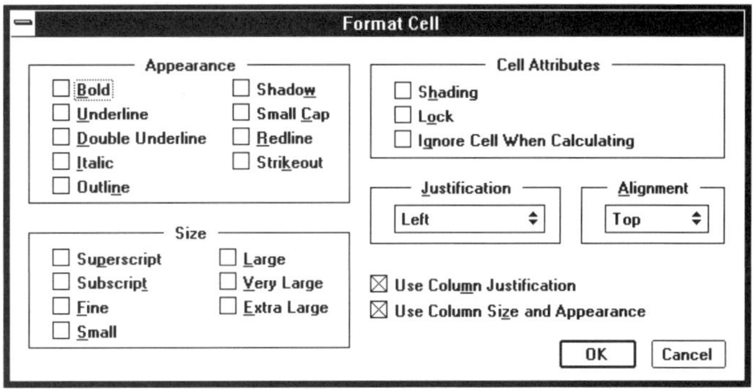

Figure 23. The first option available in the *Cell Attributes* section of the dialog box shown in Figure 22 is *Shading*. This allows you to apply a shade to the selected cell(s). The darkness of the shading is set in the *Table Options* dialog box (see Figure 7).

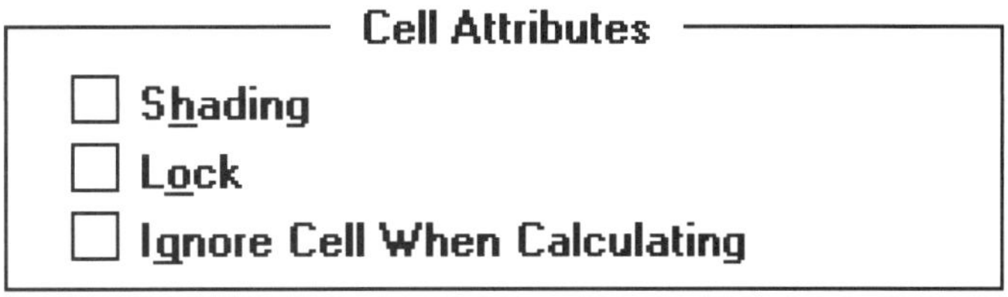

The *Lock* option below *Shading* protects the contents of the selected cell(s) so that the information cannot be changed until this option is deselected.

If the *Ignore Cell When Calculating* option is applied to a selected cell, WordPerfect will ignore this cell (or cells) when calculating a formula. (See Figure 31 onwards for using formulas within tables.)

 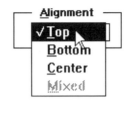

Figure 24. The *Justification* and *Alignment* options in the *Format Cell* dialog box of Figure 22 determine how the text will flow in each selected cell or cells. The options available in the *Justification* list, which apply to the horizontal positioning within cells, are *Left, Full, Center, Right, Decimal Align,* and *Mixed*.

The options available in the *Alignment* list are *Top, Bottom, Center,* and *Mixed*. These options determine the vertical alignment of text. The changes you make to the *Alignment* of text will not appear in the document but will display in the *Print Preview* window.

☐ **Use Column Justification**

☒ **Use Column Size and Appearance**

In this example, the selected cell(s) will use Justification from the Format Cell dialog box and Size and Appearance will be defined through the Format Column dialog box.

Figure 25. The *Use Column Justification* option, at the bottom right of the *Format Cell* dialog box, will allow (when deselected) the *Justification* settings of the *Format Cell* dialog box to override the column's justification for the selected cells. Column *Justification* (See Figure 26) normally applies to all cells in that column.

The *Use Column Size and Appearance* option works in the same way and applies to the choices available in the *Appearance* and *Size* sections of the dialog box.

FORMATTING COLUMNS

Figure 26. The next option available in the *Tables* sub-menu of Figure 1 is the *Column* command, which activates the *Format Column* dialog box. The options available in this dialog box affect the whole Column in which the cursor is situated. The *Appearance, Size,* and *Justification* options in this dialog box are the same options available in the *Format Cell* dialog box.

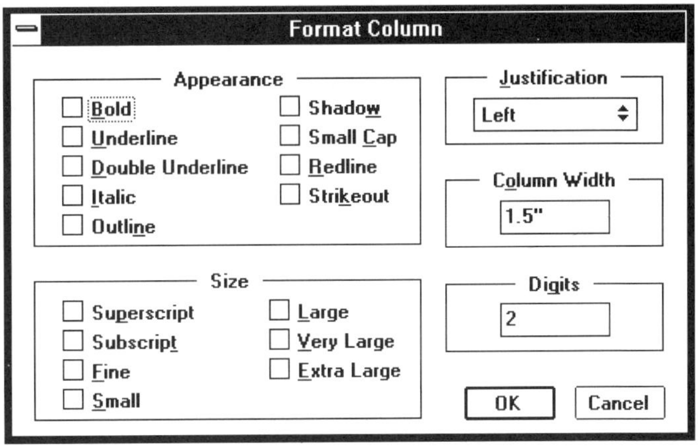

The *Column Width* option allows you to change the width of the selected column(s) by keying in a new size. The *Digits* option determines the number of digits appearing after a decimal point, for all numbers within the column.

Figure 27. The width of a column can also be adjusted through the *Ruler.* If the cursor is inserted in the table, the white section of the *Ruler,* above the tabs, contains markers that represent the columns of the table. By holding the mouse down on one of these markers, you can adjust the width of a column.

If you hold the Control key down while you are repositioning one of these markers, the right margin of the document also moves.

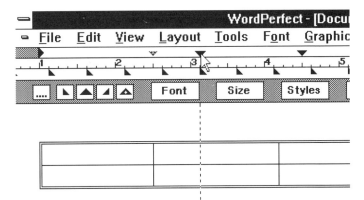

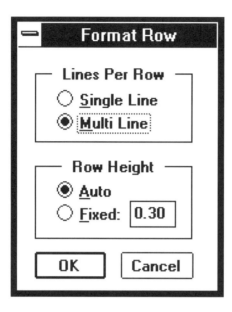

FORMATTING ROWS

Figure 28. The *Row* command, within the *Tables* sub-menu of Figure 1, activates the *Format Row* dialog box. The *Single Line* option in the *Lines Per Row* section ensures that only one line of text appears in a cell. The *Multi Line* option allows more than one line of text to appear that will wrap within the cell.

If the *Auto* option is selected in the *Row Height* section, WordPerfect automatically determines the height of the row according to the height of the current font. If you have the *Fixed* option selected, you can key in your own size which will de-activate the *Auto* option.

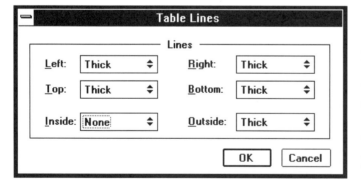

THE LINES COMMAND

Figure 29. The *Lines* command of the *Tables* sub-menu gives you access to the *Table Lines* dialog box. Making any changes in this dialog box will affect the border around a cell, or selected cells. For this example, the top middle cell of a 3 x 2 table was selected and all the options were set to *Thick*. The result is shown in Figure 30.

Figure 30. The result of the adjustments of Figure 29; the originally selected cell now includes a thick border on all sides.

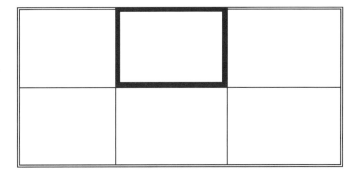

THE FORMULA COMMAND

Figure 31. The *Formula* command activates the *Tables Formula* dialog box. This gives you the option of performing calculations in cells based upon simple formula rules. You have the ability to add, subtract, multiply, and divide. See Figures 32 through 35 for examples of the *Formula* option.

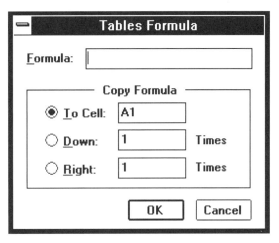

Figure 32. The *Formula* command is made up using the following symbols:

+ for addition

- for subtraction

* for multiplication

/ for division.

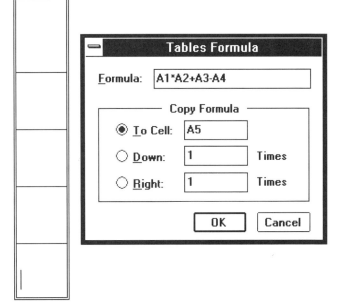

In the example in Figure 32, the cursor was placed in the bottom cell (A5) and the *Formula* command from the *Tables* sub-menu was selected. In the *Formula* text box, a path is established for the calculation to follow. For this example, the path A1*A2+A3-A4 is keyed in as the formula. The letters and numbers refer to the position of each cell in the table with A1 being the first cell in column 1, row 1.

(See Figure 3 for the labeling convention for individual cells.)

The Formula result will appear in the cell location contained in the *To Cell* text box. This can be changed in the *Tables Formula* dialog box if required.

Figure 33. After clicking on *OK* in the Figure 32 dialog box, you are returned to the screen and the table. The cell in which we inserted the formula will initially have 0.00 in it. After keying in the figures in the first four cells as shown here, select the *Calculate* command from the *Tables* sub-menu.

```
10.00
1.00
25.00
15.00
0.00
```

Figure 34. The formula path set for the first four cells has now been calculated and the answer is placed in the fifth cell.

Note: Setting up a path like this in the Tables Formula dialog box can be done in any random order, from any cell to any other. Adding, multiplying, subtracting, and dividing can all be used in one formula.

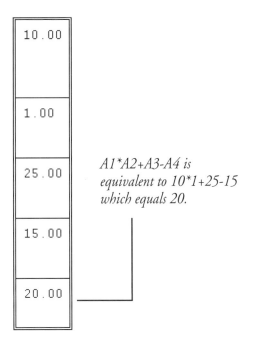

A1*A2+A3-A4 is equivalent to 10*1+25-15 which equals 20.

Figure 35. The *Copy Formula* section of the *Tables Formula* dialog box allows you to copy a formula from one cell to another. This is done by placing the cursor in the cell containing the formula you wish to copy and then selecting the *Formula* command from the *Tables* sub-menu. In the *To Cell* frame, type the new cell location for the formula, and click on *OK*.

The *Down* and *Right* options can also be used to copy the formula down or to the right of a cell, as many times as the number you key into the corresponding box.

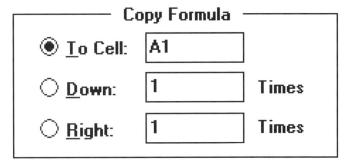

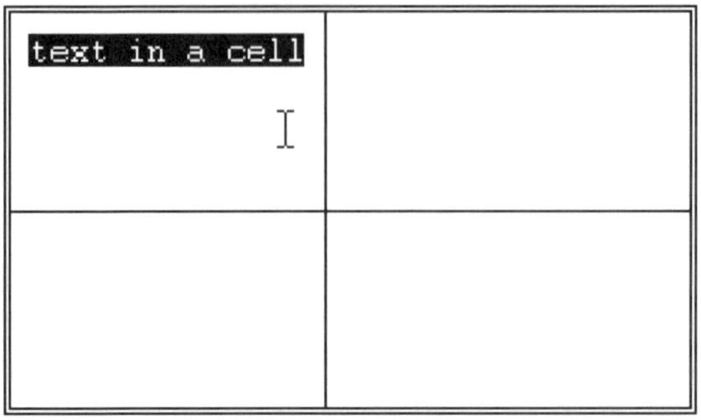

CUTTING, COPYING, AND PASTING

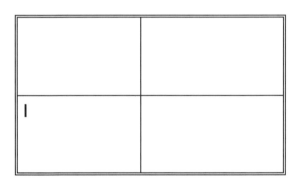

Figure 36. Text in cells can be cut or copied, and then pasted from cell to cell, or even to other sections of your document outside the table. To do this, you must first select the text inside the cell.

Once the text is selected, choose either the *Cut* or *Copy* command from the **Edit** menu. A copy of the text will now be in the Windows *Clipboard.*

Figure 37. Insert the cursor where you would like the text from the *Clipboard* to appear and select the *Paste* command.

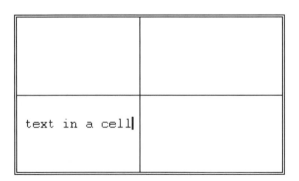

Figure 38. The text is now pasted back into the document.

Figure 39. It is also possible to *Copy* and *Paste* certain sections of the table to form another table. Selecting the *Copy* command from the **Edit** menu, with a cell or cells of a table selected, activates the *Table Cut/Copy* dialog box. Here we have selected the top row of a table.

Figure 40. In the *Table Cut/Copy* dialog box, you have the option of cutting or copying the *Selection of* cells from Figure 39, or the *Row(s)* or *Column(s)* of which the selected cell or cells are a part.

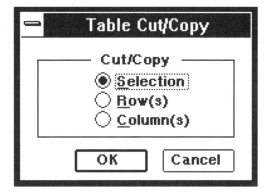

Figure 41. If you choose the *Selection* option, move the cursor below the table and select the *Paste* command. The new smaller table we copied from Figure 39 will now appear at this point.

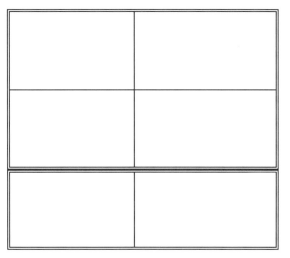

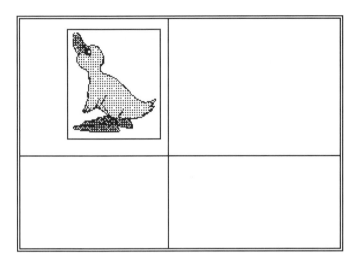

PUTTING GRAPHICS IN TABLES

Figure 42. To place a graphic inside a table, insert the cursor in the cell in which you would like the graphic to appear, and retrieve the graphic in the normal way (see Chapter 10 — **Using Graphics**).

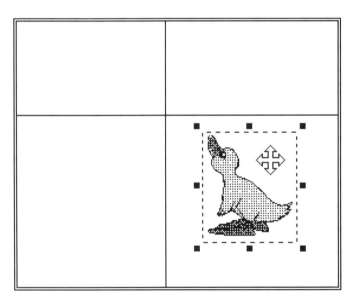

Figure 43. Once the graphic is inside the table, it can be enlarged, reduced or moved to another cell.

A graphic that has been retrieved outside a table can also be dragged into the table with the mouse.

CREATING TABLES FROM EXISTING TEXT

Figure 44. Text that is already on the page can be converted to a table. Select the text you want included in the table and then select the *Tables/Create* command from the **Layout** menu.

Figure 45. The *Convert Table* dialog box gives you two choices, depending on the sort of text you have selected. If the sections of the text are separated with tabs, select the *Tabular Column* option. If the text is arranged in parallel columns, select the *Parallel Column* option.

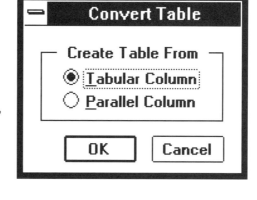

Figure 46. This figure is the result of applying the *Tabular Columns* option in Figure 45 to the text of Figure 44. This text is now contained in its own table.

	lunedi	martedi	mercoledi	giovedi	venerdi
9					
10					
11					
12					

STYLES & OUTLINES 9

STYLES

Styles can be set up in WordPerfect to make formatting a
document or section of text quicker and easier. Each style
can be made up from a variety of formatting instructions
which can be applied to all or part of a document in one
operation.

CREATING STYLES

Figure 1. Selecting the *Styles*
command from the **Layout** menu
is the first step to take in the
creation of styles. This activates the
Styles dialog box of Figure 2.

Layout	
Line	Shift+F9 ▶
Paragraph	▶
Page	Alt+F9 ▶
Columns	Alt+Shift+F9 ▶
Tables	Ctrl+F9 ▶
Document	Ctrl+Shift+F9 ▶
Footnote	▶
Endnote	▶
Advance...	
Typesetting...	
Justification	▶
Margins...	Ctrl+F8
Styles...	Alt+F8

Figure 2. The *Styles* dialog box lists
any styles that come with
WordPerfect, or any styles you
may have created and saved
previously. Click on the *Create*
button to create a new style. This
activates the *Style Properties* dialog
box of Figure 3.

Styles

Name	Type	Description	
Bibliogrphy	Paired	Bibliography	Create...
Bullet List	Paired	Indented Bullet List	Edit...
Doc Init	Paired	Initialize Document Sty	Delete...
Heading 1	Paired	Centered Heading	
Heading 2	Paired	Underlined Heading Flu	Retrieve...
Pleading	Open	Header for Numbered F	Save As...
Tech Init	Open	Initialize Technical Styl	

On | Off | Close

145

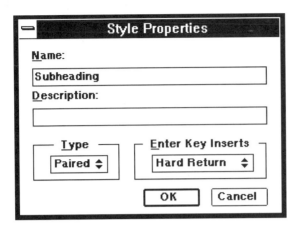

Figure 3. In the *Style Properties* dialog box, the *Name* text box contains the name of the style that you are going to create. In this example we keyed in the *Name* Subheading. In the *Description* text box, key in any details you wish displayed in the *Styles* dialog box of Figure 2 under the *Description* column.

(a)

[Style On:style 1]this is a paired style[Style Off:style 1]

(b)

[Open Style:style 2]this is an open style[HRt]

Note: Open styles are generally used for page formatting and options that will affect the whole document. Paired styles are used for smaller sections of text.

Figure 4. The *Type* section of the *Style Properties* dialog box gives you two options relating to styles:

(a) The default option is *Paired.* With this option selected, a *Style On* and a *Style Off* code is inserted before and after the group of codes that make up your style. This ensures that once a *Paired* style is turned off, its attributes will not affect any following text.

(b) The *Open* option will effect all text following the cursor, until modified by other codes.

The *Enter Key Inserts* options of the *Style Properties* dialog box of Figure 3 are available only with *Paired* styles. These choices control what function the *Enter* key plays in connection with this style. The default option is *Hard Return.* With this selected, the *Enter* key works as it would normally. The *Style Off* option turns the style off when the *Enter* key is pressed, and the *Style Off/On* option turns the style off, then on again, when you press the *Enter* key. Once you have set up the *Style Properties* dialog box, click on the *OK* button.

Figure 5. Clicking on *OK* in the *Style Properties* dialog box of Figure 3 activates the *Style Editor* window. The *Title Bar* of this window tells you the name of the style you are currently creating. In the top half of the screen is a message telling you that anything inserted before the message will be included in the style, and anything inserted after it will come into effect after the style is turned off. This message appears as a Comment code in the *Reveal Codes* section of the screen.

In this screen you begin selecting the attributes that you want included in this style.

*Note: The Auto Code Placement option, in the Settings section of the Environment Settings dialog box, will place codes that are supposed to be at the beginning of a paragraph or page, in the correct place. This option is on by default, but it cannot be selected while the Style Editor window is active. For more information on Reveal Codes see Chapter 2 — **Editing Text.***

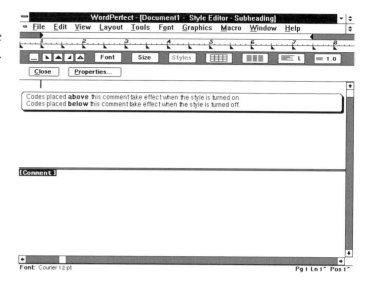

(a)

(b)

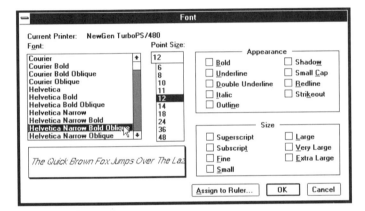

Figure 6. Codes are selected in the same manner as you select commands and options in the normal layout screen. In this example, the first code being applied to the style is a font attribute. A new font can either be selected from the *Font* menu on the *Ruler* (a) or through the *Font* dialog box accessed through the **Font** menu (b).

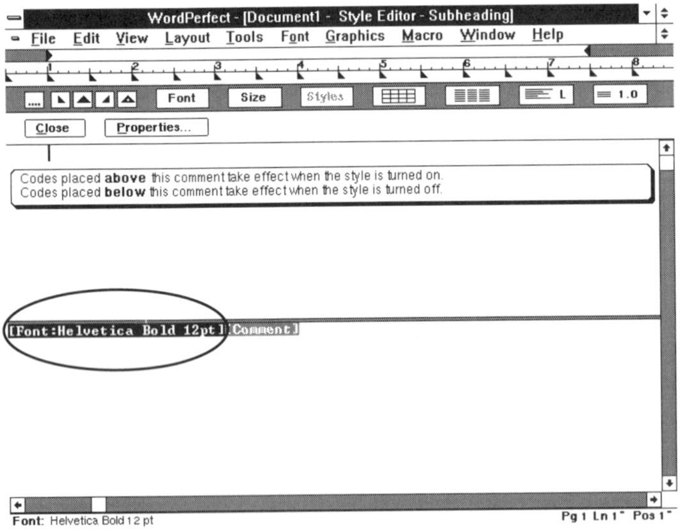

Figure 7. Once you select a new *Font,* you see the code appear in the *Reveal Codes* section of the screen.

Figure 8. You can also add a *Justification* code to the style. Do this either through the *Justification* button on the *Ruler* (a), or through the **Layout** menu (b).

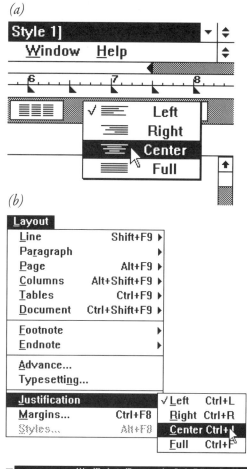

Figure 9. After selecting a *Justification* option, you immediately see the relevant code in the *Reveal Codes* section of the screen.

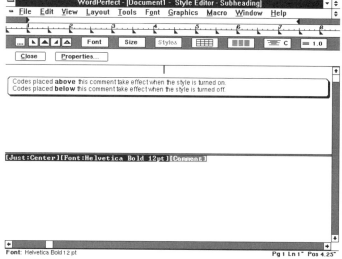

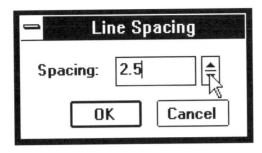

Figure 10. We are now adding a *Line Spacing* code to the style in this dialog box. The *Line Spacing* dialog box is activated from the *Line* sub-menu in the **Layout** menu. You can also activate the *Line Spacing* dialog box by double-clicking on the *Line Spacing* button on the *Ruler*. Alternatively, for common options, the *Line Spacing* button on the *Ruler* can be used.

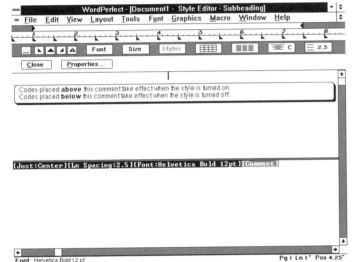

Figure 11. All the codes for this style have now been inserted. Click on the *Close* button to return to the *Styles* dialog box.

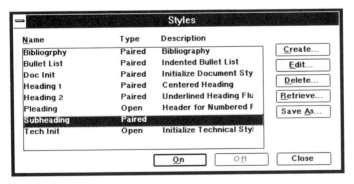

Figure 12. The Subheading style you just created appears in the *Styles* dialog box. You can now either click on the *On* button to return to the document with this style turned on, or click on *Close* to remove the dialog box.

Note: There is no entry under the Description column. This is because we did not enter any comment into the Description text box in the Figure 3 Style Properties dialog box.

Figure 13. If you clicked on the *Close* button to remove the *Styles* dialog box of Figure 12, the style you created is not active, but appears in the list of styles that is activated when the mouse is held down on the *Styles* button in the *Ruler*. Styles are turned on by selecting them from the *Styles* menu in the *Ruler*.

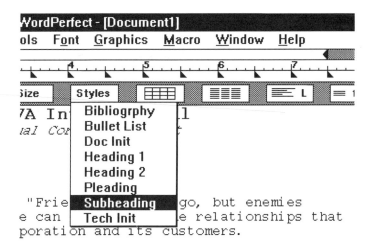

APPLYING STYLES

Figure 14. To apply a paired style to text, highlight the text, then select the required style from the list of styles in the *Ruler*.

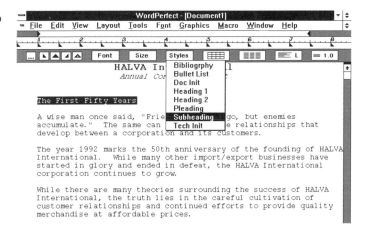

Figure 15. The text selected in Figure 14 now takes on the attributes of that style.

Note: If you Retrieve some text into a section of a document where a paired style is active, all text will take on the attributes of that style.

EDITING STYLES

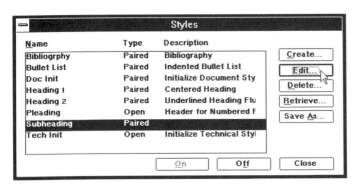

Figure 16. From the list of styles in the *Styles* dialog box, select the style you wish to edit and click on the *Edit* button. Again, you will return to the *Style Editor* window as though you are creating a new style.

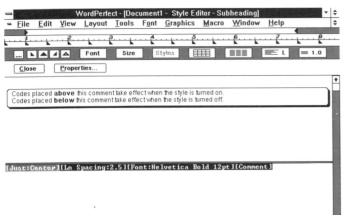

Figure 17. The *Style Editor* window appears, showing all the codes that belong to the style. It is now possible to add or remove any features of this style. If you want to change a code that is already there, the first one must be deleted in the *Reveal Codes* section at the bottom of the screen. The new one can then be added in the fashion previously described.

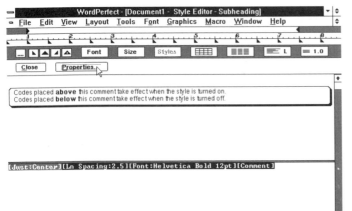

Figure 18. If you click on the *Properties* button in the *Style Editor* window, you activate the *Style Properties* dialog box of Figure 19.

Figure 19. With this *Style Properties* dialog box activated, it is possible to change the *Name, Description, Type,* and *Enter Key Inserts* options for the style. After clicking on *OK,* you are returned to the *Style Editor* window.

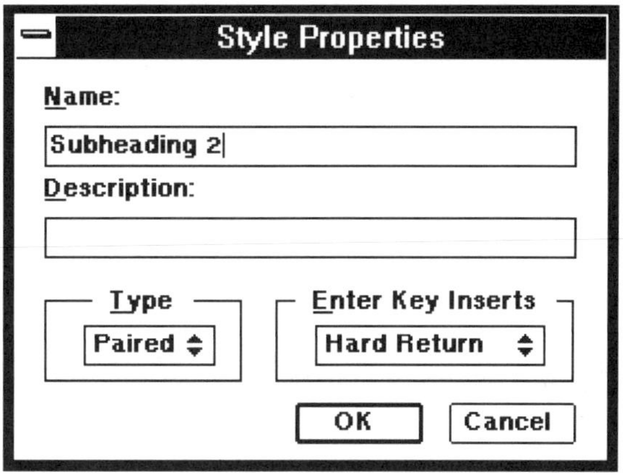

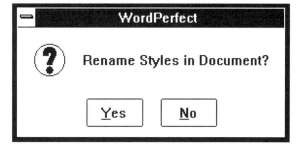

Figure 20. If you have renamed a style, the *Rename Styles in Document?* screen prompt appears after clicking on the *Close* button in the *Style Editor* window. If you click on *Yes,* the style name in both the *Styles* dialog box and the document changes. If you click on *No,* a new style is created with the new name.

When WordPerfect comes across text with the original style applied to it, the original style name is placed back in the list of styles. This allows you to base a new style on one already existing. This can save time if a new style you intend to create is very similar to one you have created already.

SAVING STYLES

Unless styles are saved as a file on your hard disk, they are only available to the document in which they were created. Saving these styles as a file allows you to use them in other documents.

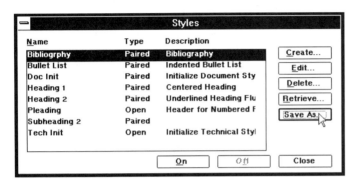

Figure 21. To save the styles of a current document, click on the *Save As* button in the *Styles* dialog box. This will activate the *Save Styles* dialog box of Figure 22.

Figure 22. The *Save Styles* dialog box lets you save styles anywhere on your hard disk. It is recommended that you create a directory for your styles and give them a *.sty* extension to avoid confusion with other *WordPerfect* files. Click on the *Save* button after naming the style file. All styles in the current document will be saved in this file.

RETRIEVING STYLES

Figure 23. Click on the *Retrieve* button in the dialog box shown in Figure 21 to activate the *Retrieve Styles* dialog box. Search for the required style file and double-click on it to retrieve it, or select it from the list of files and click on the *Retrieve* button. You are then returned to the *Styles* dialog box. Any changes made to a style that has been retrieved will only affect the current document.

Figure 24. If any of the styles in the document have the same name as any of the styles you are retrieving, you are asked if you want to replace them.

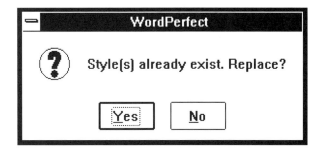

DELETING STYLES

Figure 25. To delete a style, select it from the list of styles in the *Styles* dialog box and click on the *Delete* button. This activates the *Delete Style* dialog box, where there are three options. The first is the *Leave Format Codes* option. If you select this option, the style is deleted from the document but all codes connected with the style are replaced by normal codes.

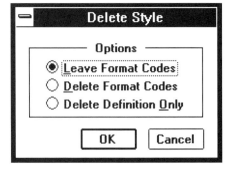

The *Delete Format Codes* option deletes the style from the document and the relevant codes are not replaced. The *Delete Definition Only* option deletes the style from the document but the style codes that have been applied to sections of text remain intact.

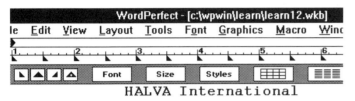

Figure 26. If a style needs to be removed from text, the style codes must be selected and then deleted in *Reveal Codes*. In this example, the *Style On: Heading 1* code is selected currently. Pressing the *Delete* key now will remove this style from the text.

GRAPHICS, TABLES, AND TEXT IN STYLES

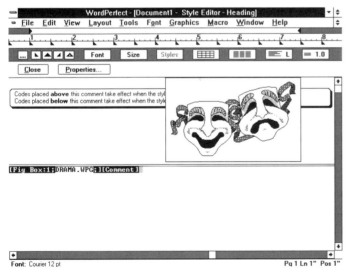

Figure 27. It is possible to include graphics, tables, and text in styles. This is done by adding them in the *Style Editor* window when you are creating the style. In this figure, we have added a graphic to this style. Every time you use this style the graphic will appear. If you create a table, retrieve a graphic, or add some text to a style it cannot be edited in the document. You must return to the *Style Editor* window to do this.

When adding a graphic to a style, you must use the *Graphic on Disk* option (see Chapter 10 — **Using Graphics**, for more information).

FURTHER NOTES ON STYLES

Some page format codes, including *Center Page, Force Odd/ Even Page, Headers, Footers, Top/Bottom Margins, Page Numbering, Paper Size/Type*, and *Suppress Page Format* included in a style remain active once you have turned the style off.

Normally, codes placed after the *Comment* code in the *Style Editor* window will come into effect once the style has been turned off. There are two exceptions, however. *Left/right margins* and *tabs* is one and conflicting codes, such as a *font* code before and after the comment code, is the other. This is because text reverts to its original state once the style is turned off.

USING OUTLINES

The *Outline* feature of WordPerfect allows you to create outlines with different levels and numbered paragraphs. These outlines will update automatically if you add or remove any entries.

Figure 28. Select the *Outline On* command from the *Outline* sub-menu of the **Tools** menu to turn the *Outline* feature on. The word "Outline" then appears on the left side of the *Status Bar*.

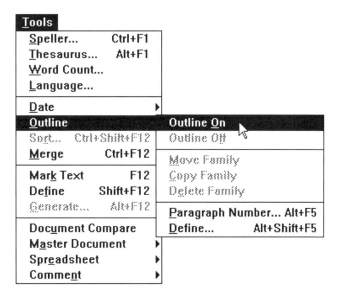

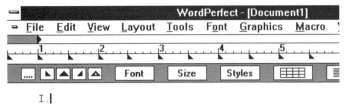

Figure 29. Press the Enter key to get a first-level number to appear. If you have not changed any options in the *Define Paragraph Numbering* dialog box (explained later), this first level entry will appear as an I.

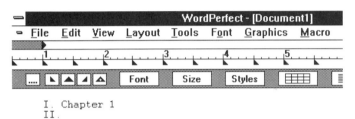

Figure 30. Each time you press the Enter key, after adding some text, another first-level entry will appear. It will increase in number each time.

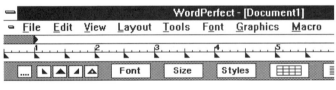

Figure 31. To get a second-level entry, press the Enter key and then the Tab key. The second-level entry in this figure is represented by the A. Some text has also been added to the second-level entry. To move levels back and forth, the cursor must be situated to the immediate right of the number or letter.

Figure 32. Pressing the Tab key continues to move you across to the next level. Eight levels are possible, and each level has a different numbering style.

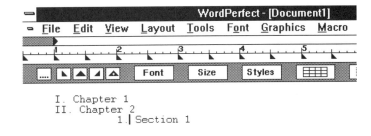

```
I. Chapter 1
II. Chapter 2
        1. Section 1
```

Figure 33. The Shift+Tab keys move you to the previous level. In this figure, level 8 has been returned to level 7 by using the Shift+Tab keys.

```
I. level 1
    A. level 2
        1. level 3
            a. level 4
                (1) level 5
                    (a) level 6
                        i) level 7
                        ii) level 8
```

Figure 34. The *Outline Off* command in the *Outline* sub-menu of the **Tools** menu turns the *Outline* feature off.

Note: The Alt and arrow keys can be used in an outline to move the cursor around.

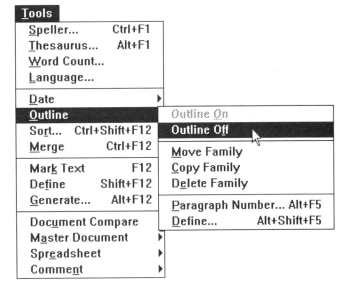

MOVING/COPYING AND DELETING FAMILIES

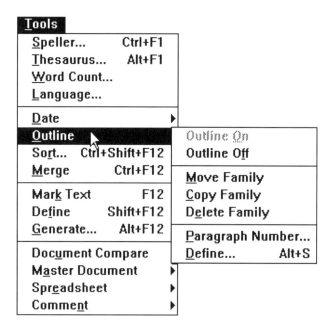

Figure 35. After the *Outline Off* command, the next three commands in the *Outline* sub-menu concern sections of an outline referred to as a family. They are the *Move Family, Copy Family,* and *Delete Family* commands.

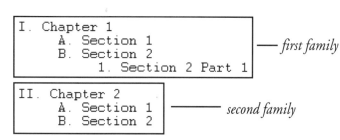

— *first family*

— *second family*

Figure 36. A family consists of the paragraph number and text where the cursor is located, plus any subordinate levels. The cursor must be inserted in the family you want to move, copy, or delete.

If you choose the *Move Family* command from the *Outline* sub-menu of Figure 35, then the family with the cursor located inside it will become selected. The arrow keys on the keyboard can now be used to alter the position of the selected family.

The up and down arrow keys will move the family up or down a section. The outline numbering system will update automatically when a family changes position.

The *Home + up arrow* keys move the family to the top of the outline while the *Home + down arrow* keys move the family to the bottom of the outline. The left and right arrow keys move the family across or back a level (with a maximum two levels to the left or right). When you are happy with the new position of the selected family, press the Enter key and the family will be situated in its new position.

The *Copy Family* command works the same way as the *Move Family* command, only it leaves the original family behind and moves a copy. Again, the Enter key is used to plant the family in the new position.

If you select the *Delete Family* command, you will be confronted with the *Delete Outline Family* screen prompt where you must confirm your deletion choice by clicking on either the *Yes* or *No* buttons. When you delete a family from an outline, it remains on disk as a temporary file. If you want to retrieve it, select the *Undelete* command from the **Edit** menu and then click on the *Restore* button in the *Undelete* screen prompt. The family returns at the location of the cursor.

PARAGRAPH NUMBERING

Figure 37. The next option in the *Outline* sub-menu is the *Paragraph Number* command. Paragraph numbering is used to create an outline, or to number paragraphs individually. An outline can be created without having to use the *Outline* command. As with outlines, paragraph numbers are updated automatically if numbers are added or removed.

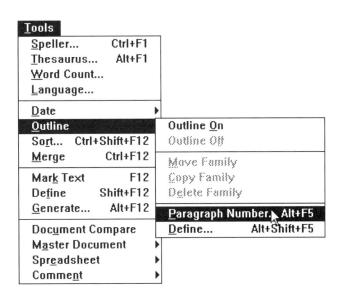

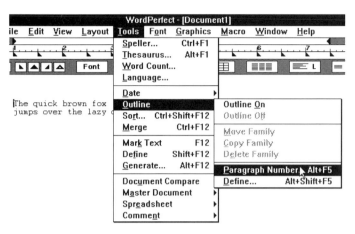

Figure 38. To insert a paragraph number, move the cursor to where you want the number to be located, and select the *Paragraph Number* command from the *Outline* sub-menu in the **Tools** menu.

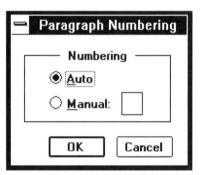

Figure 39. In the *Paragraph Number* dialog box that appears, select *Auto*, if it is not already selected, and click on the *OK* button.

```
I.The quick brown fox
jumps over the lazy dog
```

Figure 40. Once you confirm the auto paragraph numbering in the dialog box of Figure 39, a number will be placed in your document. Once this number is on the page, its level can be moved up and down in the same way that outlines are moved.

Figure 41. If you choose the *Manual* option in the *Paragraph Number* dialog box, you must specify a level in the relevant frame and then click on *OK*.

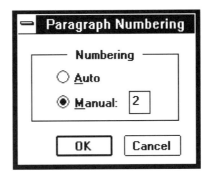

Figure 42. The number that appears in your document relates to the level you inserted in the *Paragraph Number* dialog box, regardless of its position. In this figure there is a second-level entry number at the first-level entry position.

```
I.The quick brown fox
jumps over the lazy dog
A.|
```

The number will now be fixed there. The level of this paragraph number cannot be changed using the Tab and Shift+Tab keys.

A paragraph number can be inserted in an outline by selecting the *Paragraph Number* command while in an outline.

An automatic paragraph number inserted in an outline is moved the same way a normal outline level is moved. A paragraph number inserted in an outline with the *Manual* option selected (see Figure 41) can have its level changed by using the Tab or Shift+Tab keys. This will not alter its position.

THE DEFINE PARAGRAPH NUMBERING DIALOG BOX

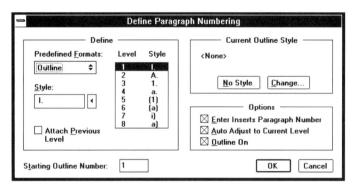

Figure 43. Selecting the *Define* command from the *Outline* sub-menu of Figure 37 presents you with the *Define Paragraph Numbering* dialog box. The first section of this dialog box is the *Predefined Formats* options. The options available provide different ways of identifying levels in both outlines and paragraph numbering.

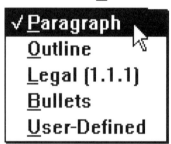

Figure 44. On selecting a different option from the *Predefined Formats* pop-up list, you will see the options in the *Level/Style* frame change.

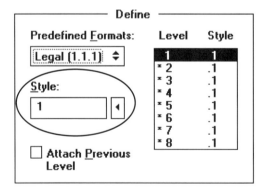

Figure 45. The *Style* section of the *Define Paragraph Numbering* dialog box lets you define your own style. Select a style from the *Level/Style* frame (Level 1 is selected when you open this dialog box), and either key in a new number or letter in the *Style* text box, or select a new numbering style from the *Style* pop-up list. The *Style* pop-up list is activated by holding the mouse down on the left-facing arrow to the right of the *Style* text box.

Figure 46. Click again on the *Level* option in the *Level/Style* frame that you selected to change. The new character you keyed into the *Style* text box will then become the new level style. Each level, in turn, can be changed in this way.

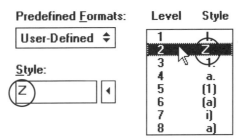

Figure 47. The next option available in the *Define Paragraph Numbering* dialog box is the *Attach Previous Level* option. Checking this option (a) places an asterisk next to the selected level. This option connects the next level of an outline with the previous level as in (b). For example, Level 2 will read I.A. if level 1 is I.

(a)

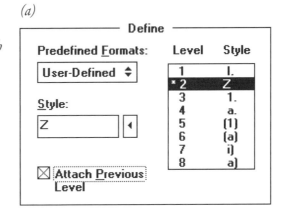

(b)

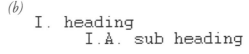

CREATING OUTLINE STYLES

Figure 48. The *Current Outline Style* section of the *Define Paragraph Numbering* dialog box lets you create and apply a style to an outline. Click on the *Change* button to create, change, or edit a style. These styles are created in the same way that normal text formatting styles are created.

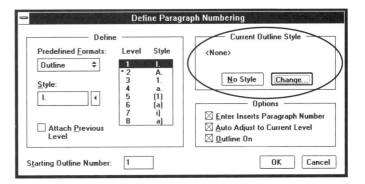

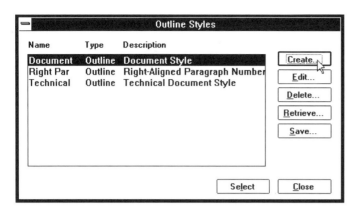

Figure 49. Clicking on the *Change* button activates the *Outline Styles* dialog box. Some styles may already listed; these are provided by WordPerfect. To create a style, click on the *Create* button.

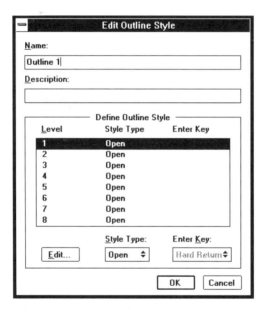

Figure 50. Clicking on the *Create* button in the *Outline Styles* dialog box activates the *Edit Outline Style* dialog box. In this dialog box, you enter a name in the *Name* box and, if you wish, a description of the style to help you identify it. It is possible to include codes for each of the eight different levels in the one style. After selecting the level for which you wish to create the style, click on the *Edit* button.

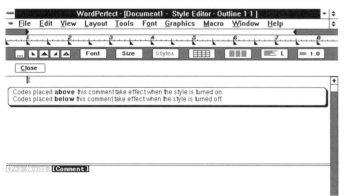

Figure 51. Clicking on the *Edit* button in Figure 50 activates the *Style Editor* window. A level number (or letter) will appear after the cursor. You can now set up your outline style.

Figure 52. Click on the *Close* button in the *Style Editor* window of Figure 51 once you have created your style. This returns you to the *Edit Outline Style* dialog box. Click on *OK* in this dialog box, to return to the Figure 53 dialog box.

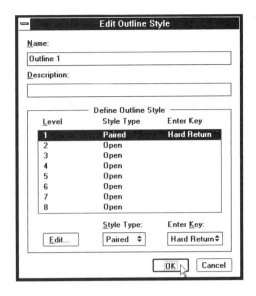

Figure 53. In the *Outline Styles* dialog box, click on either the *Close* or *Select* button. The *Close* button exits from the dialog box with the just-created style saved, but not active. If you click on the *Select* button, the style that is selected in the list of styles in this dialog box will be active.

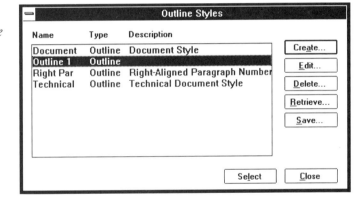

Figure 54. Whichever way you exited from the previous dialog box, you are returned to the *Define Paragraph Numbering* dialog box. If you clicked on *Select* in the previous dialog box, the style name that was selected appears in the *Current Outline Style* section of the dialog box. Click on *OK* to return to your document.

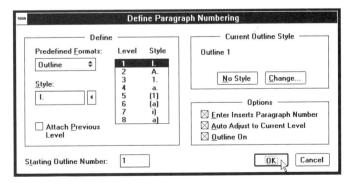

When you click on *OK* in the *Define Paragraph Number* dialog box with a style active, the outline from the cursor onward will be affected.

If you wanted to change this style, insert the cursor at the position where you want to make the changes, and then select the *Define* command from the *Outline* sub-menu in the **Tools** menu. In the associated dialog box, click on the *Change* button. In the *Outline Styles* dialog box, click on the style you want and then click on the *Select* button. This will return you to the *Define Paragraph Numbering* dialog box where you would click on *OK*. The sections of the outline concerned with this style will change.

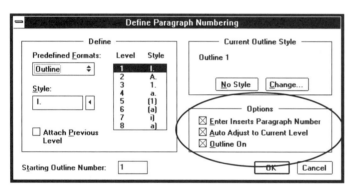

Figure 55. When the *Enter Inserts Paragraph Number* option is on, a new paragraph number is inserted when you press the Enter key. If it is deselected, pressing the Enter key ends the current line of text without inserting a new paragraph number.

When the *Enter Inserts Paragraph Number* option is on, the Shift+Enter keys will insert a new line without adding a new number. The *Page Break* option from the *Page* sub-menu in the **Layout** menu will insert a page break for you. The Ctrl+Enter keys will insert a paragraph number and a page break.

The *Auto Adjust to Current Level* option inserts the next level entry at the same level as the previous one. If this option is disabled, the next paragraph number will be inserted as a first level entry.

The *Outline On* option turns the *Outline* command on as soon as you click on *OK* to exit from the dialog box.

Figure 56. The *Starting Outline Number* option determines the first number of an outline. This is useful further on in a document if you turn on a second outline that you wish to run in numeric order with any previous outlines.

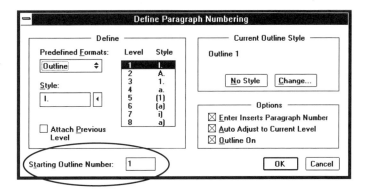

USING GRAPHICS 10

GRAPHICS

WordPerfect is compatible with most graphics file formats. Any graphic files that have been created with programs that can produce compatible formats with WordPerfect can be imported into your document. WordPerfect also has the ability to alter the way an imported graphic looks. Basic graphics, such as rectangles and lines, can also be created in WordPerfect.

You can create various types of graphics boxes, such as *figure, text, table,* and *user* boxes. (The table graphics box is not to be confused with the normal table feature.)

You can put graphics images, tabulated tables, or text into any type of box. The type of box does not refer to its contents, but rather to its defaults and the list to which it belongs (if you need lists of graphics in your document). For example, a figure box has a single line border by default, whereas a user-defined box has no border. The defaults of all types of boxes may be changed, so anything said about one type of box applies to other types as well.

RETRIEVING GRAPHICS

Figure 1. To import a graphic file into your document, select the *Retrieve* command from the *Figure* sub-menu of the **Graphics** menu. This activates the *Retrieve Figure* dialog box of Figure 2.

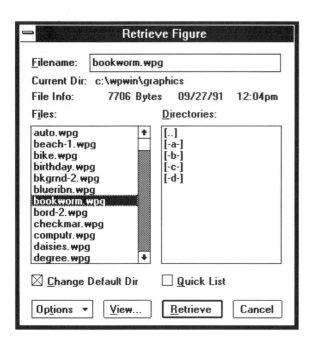

Figure 2. The *Retrieve Figure* dialog box gives you access to your computer's drives and directories. The current directory is indicated on the *Current Dir* line at the top of the dialog box. The *Filename* and certain information about the file selected in the *Files* list will also appear at the top of this dialog box.

The *Options* pop-up list at the bottom of the *Retrieve Figure* dialog box lets you delete a selected file, copy a selected file to a different drive or directory, move or rename a file, or find a file.

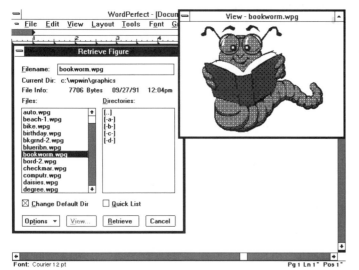

Figure 3. The *View* button at the bottom of the *Retrieve Figure* dialog box lets you see what a selected file looks like before it is imported into your WordPerfect document.

Figure 4. Once you have selected the graphic you wish to place in your document, click on the *Retrieve* button, and the file will be inserted into your document at the cursor location.

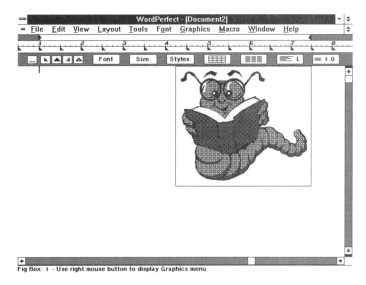

Figure 5. If there was any text in the document, by default, it will be wrapped around the graphic.

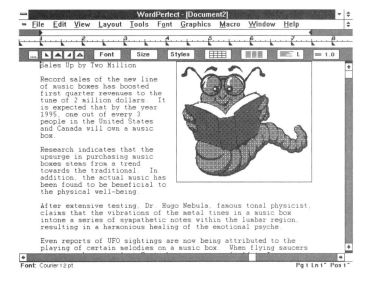

MOVING/RESIZING GRAPHICS

A graphic is selected by clicking on it once with the mouse. When a graphic is selected, eight small black handles and a dotted line will appear around its border.

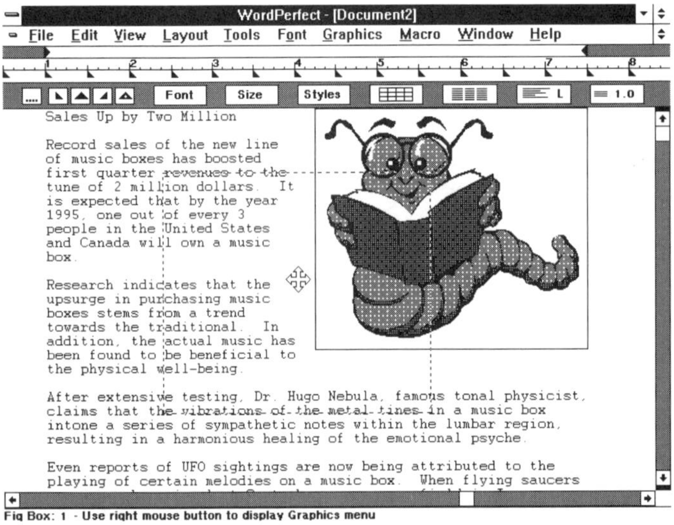

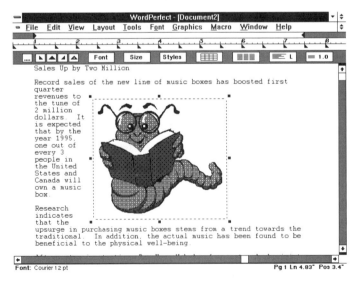

Figure 6. When you move the mouse over a selected graphic, the mouse pointer will change to a four headed arrow.

To move the graphic, hold the mouse down, drag the graphic to a new position, and release the mouse. A dotted outline will follow the mouse as you drag it around.

Figure 7. Once you release the mouse, any text in the document, by default, will reformat around the newly positioned graphic.

Figure 8. If you position the mouse exactly on top of a black handle of a selected graphic, the cursor changes to a two-headed arrow. Holding the mouse down on a handle and dragging it alters the size of the graphic. Once you release the mouse, the graphic redraws at the new size.

Figure 9. The *Position* command in the *Figure* sub-menu of the **Graphics** menu can be selected to activate the *Box Position and Size* dialog box. This dialog box provides an alternative to moving and resizing graphics. Choose this command once the graphic is selected.

Graphics	
Figure	Retrieve... F11
Text **B**ox	Create...
Equation	**E**dit... Shift+F11
Table Box	**P**osition...
User Box	**C**aption...
Line	New Number...
	Options...

Figure 10. An alternative way to activate the *Box Position and Size* dialog box is to move the mouse over the graphic and press the right mouse button. This activates a sub-menu where you select the *Box Position* command to activate the *Box Position and Size* dialog box of Figure 11.

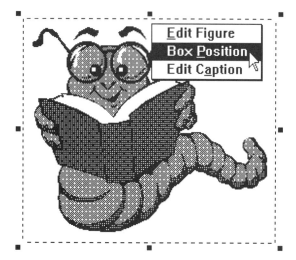

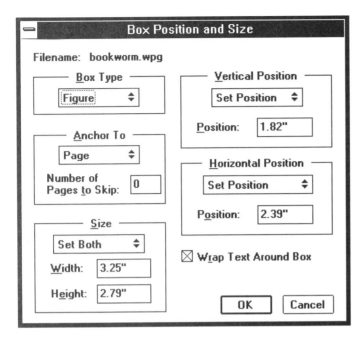

Figure 11. The *Filename* of the selected graphic appears at the top of the *Box Position and Size* dialog box.

The *Box Type* section of the dialog box provides a pop-up list allowing you to change the type of box containing the graphic. It is currently a *Figure* box because we used the *Retrieve* command in the *Figure* sub-menu of the **Graphics** menu (see Figures 1 through 5) to import the graphic.

In this dialog box it is also possible to anchor the graphic to a specific page, paragraph or character in the *Anchor To* section. The *Page* option in the *Anchor To* pop-up list ensures the graphic remains on the current page.

The *Paragraph* option in the *Anchor To* pop-up list keeps the graphic with its paragraph, even if this paragraph is later moved. The *Character* option in the *Anchor To* pop-up list treats the graphic as part of the text. The *Number of Pages to Skip* option in the *Anchor To* section ensures a graphic anchored to a page will not necessarily appear on the page in which it is inserted, but on the page to which it is skipped.

The *Size* options in the *Box Position and Size* dialog box let you specify an exact width and height for the graphic. This is done by keying in the required figures in the *Width* and *Height* frames. If you prefer to use centimeters for the resizing of the graphic and inches is the current unit of measurement, place a "c" after the keyed-in figure.

The *Vertical Position* and *Horizontal Position* options let you determine the position of the graphic on the page. If you have one of the *Anchor To* options active, other than the *Page* option, this will affect your selections in the *Position* options.

The *Wrap Text Around Box* option is on by default and ensures that the text does not run through the graphic—rather it runs around it. Deselect this option if you want to overlay a graphic with text.

EDITING GRAPHICS

Figure 12. To edit a graphic, select the *Edit Figure* command from the sub-menu that appears when you click the right mouse button on the graphic. This activates the *Figure Editor* screen of Figure 14.

Figure 13. Alternatively, the *Figure Editor* screen can be activated by selecting the *Edit* command from the *Figure* sub-menu in the **Graphics** menu.

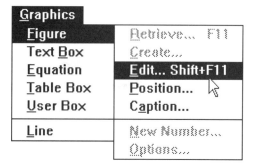

Figure 14. The *Figure Editor* screen has its own *Button Bar*, which can be modified in the same way as the normal document *Button Bar*.

Using the options in either the *Button Bar* or the menus, you can change the size, appearance and position of the graphic. These changes modify the graphic in the *Figure Editor* screen allowing you to see the changes before they are applied to the graphic in the document.

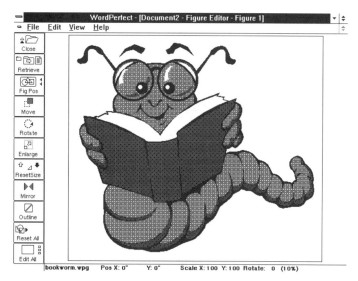

The **Edit** menu provides a range of commands allowing you to move, rotate, scale, mirror, invert, outline, and remove the colors from a graphic.

The *Graphic on Disk* option in the **File** menu of Figure 14, lets you save the graphic as a separate file, rather than as part of the document. If the graphic is changed before you complete the document, the graphic will then be updated automatically. This feature also conserves disk space if you happen to use the same graphic more than once in a document, or in a merge operation.

Click on the *Close* button in the *Figure Editor Button Bar* or select *Close* from the **File** menu to exit the *Figure Editor*, after making any required changes to the graphic.

Note that the Status Bar in the Figure Editor provides vital information on the graphic as you make changes.

DELETING GRAPHICS

To delete a graphic, select it with the mouse and press the *Delete* key on your keyboard. A graphic code can also be deleted from *Reveal Codes*. If you delete a graphic by mistake, the *Undo* or *Undelete* commands in the **Edit** menu can be used to restore it. (For more information on *Reveal Codes* and the *Undo* and *Undelete* commands, see Chapter 2 —**Editing Text**.)

CREATING A CAPTION

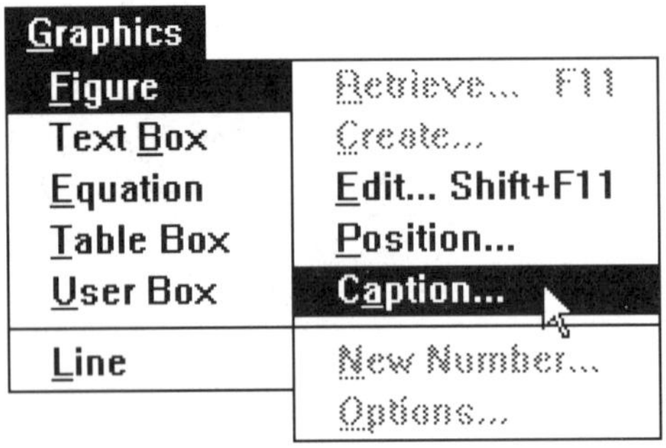

Figure 15. To create a caption for a graphic, select the graphic, and then choose the *Caption* command in the *Figure* sub-menu of the **Graphics** menu. Alternatively, click on the right mouse button, with the mouse over the graphic, to activate the graphic sub-menu (see Figure 12) and select the *Edit Caption* option.

Figure 16. The action of Figure 15 activates the *Caption Editor* screen as shown here. Since this is the first graphic in the document, the words "Figure 1" automatically appear. These words can be backspaced over and changed if you wish. You then key in the caption text and apply formatting commands as you would with normal text in your document. The *Box Number* option inserts the Figure "x" text back into the *Caption Editor* if you have previously deleted it.

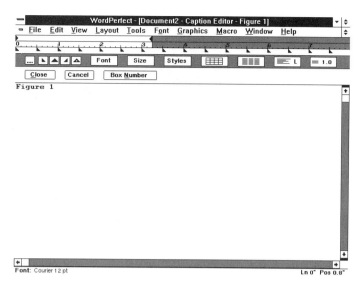

Click on the *Close* button when you have finished this operation. WordPerfect keeps track of figure numbers, so that the following figure numbers will automatically be set to 2, 3, 4, and so on.

Figure 17. The caption now appears, by default, below the graphic. For this example we also keyed in some text. This caption moves with the graphic.

Figure 1 This is a bookworm

THE CREATE COMMAND

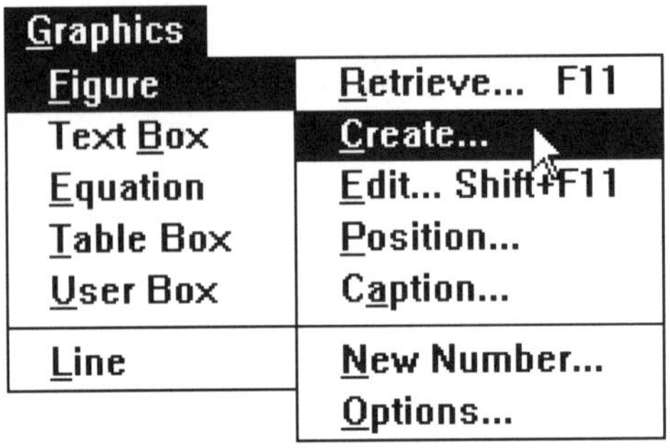

Figure 18. The *Create* command in the *Figure* sub-menu of the **Graphics** menu also activates the *Figure Editor* shown again in Figure 19 (see also Figures 12 through 14).

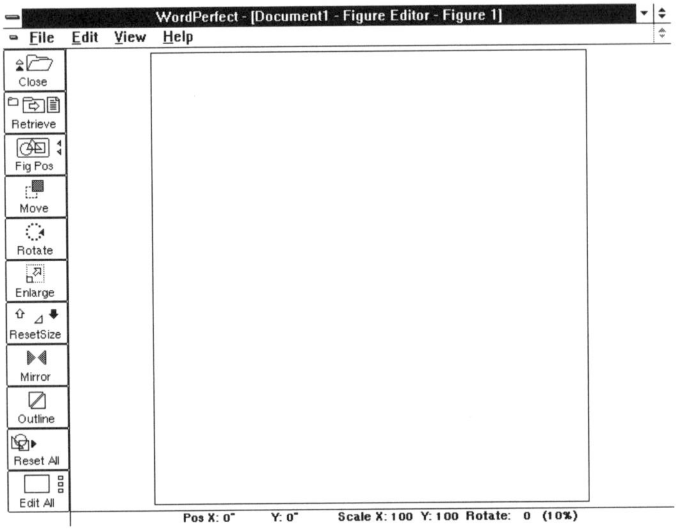

Figure 19. Because the *Create* command from the *Figure* sub-menu can only be chosen when there is no graphic selected in your document, the *Figure Editor* is initially blank. It is possible to retrieve a graphic into this *Figure Editor* and edit it using the menu and/or *Button Bar* commands. Alternatively, if you click on the *Close* command in the *Button Bar*, or select *Close* from the **File** menu, an empty box will appear on the page that you can resize and move around as you wish.

THE NEW NUMBER COMMAND

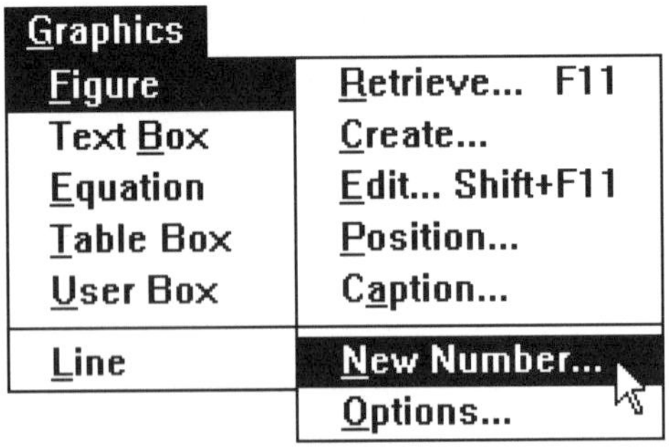

Figure 20. The *New Number* option from the *Figure* sub-menu in the **Graphics** menu activates the *Figure Number* dialog box of Figure 21.

Figure 21. The *Figure Number* dialog box lets you determine the next number when you add a caption to a figure.

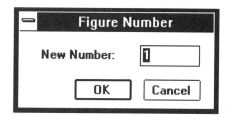

THE OPTIONS COMMAND

Figure 22. The *Options* command in the *Figure* sub-menu of the **Graphics** menu activates the *Figure Options* dialog box of Figure 23. In this dialog box you can adjust the many options affecting the appearance of all future figure boxes.

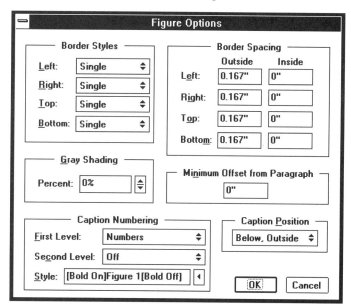

Figure 23. The *Border Styles* section of the *Figure Options* dialog box contains four pop-up lists that determine the thickness of the lines of the figure box. There are seven options from which to choose, ranging from *None* to *Extra Thick*.

The *Gray Shading* option, underneath *Border Styles*, lets you select a percentage fill of black.

The *Caption Numbering* options adjusts the various caption parameters. The *First Level* pop-up list contains four choices concerning the type of numbering system. You can either turn it off, or choose between *Numbers, Letters,* or *Roman Numerals.* The default setting is *Numbers,* i.e. Figure 1.

Note: The changes made in this dialog box affect all future figure boxes you create . You may want to alter the options for an existing graphic box. In this case make sure your cursor is placed before the code for the box you want to change, then change the graphics options. Similarly, if you move a graphic with the mouse, you may place it in front of the options code, making the options no longer effective.

The *Second Level* pop-up list contains the same options as the *First Level* pop-up list but is for second-level captions. Normally *Second Level* caption numbering is disabled. If enabled, it provides box numbering as 1.1, 1.2, 1.3, and so on, up to a maximum second level numbering of 31.

The *Style* text box lets you change the "Figure 1" default caption that appears automatically in the *Caption Editor* of Figure 16. You may change it to say something like "Picture 1," for example.

Figure 24. The *Border Spacing* section of the *Figure Options* dialog box of Figure 23 determines the amount of space between the text surrounding the box and the actual box. You can also adjust the amount of space between the inside walls and whatever is contained in the figure box. In this example, a 1 inch setting was placed in the *Left* and *Top Inside* options. The graphic is pushed one inch away from the top and left walls of the box.

The *Minimum Offset from Paragraph* option in the *Figure Options* dialog box of Figure 23 ensures that a graphic anchored to a paragraph will stay with this paragraph. This is unless the distance between the text and the graphic becomes smaller than the measurement in this dialog box. The graphic will then be moved to the next column or page.

The *Caption Position* option in the *Figure Options* dialog box determines where a caption will appear in relation to the figure box. The default setting is *Below, Outside*, which can be seen in the caption created in Figure 17.

PUTTING TEXT IN BOXES

Text may be inserted into a graphics box. In this case you would choose a *Text Box*, but you could also select a *Table* or *User* box just as well. The differences are in the default options.

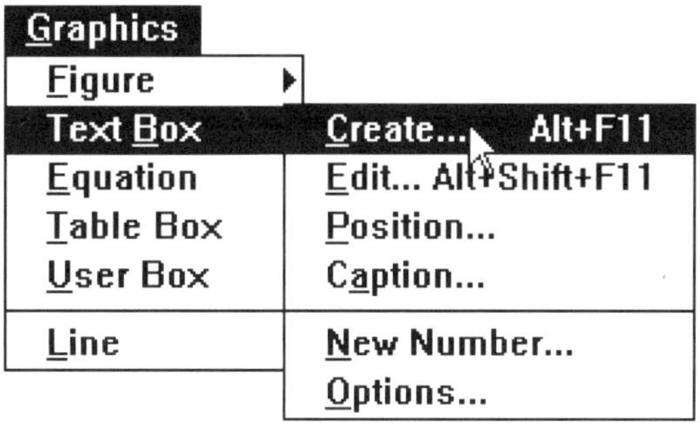

Figure 25. To create a text box, select the *Create* command from the *Text Box* sub-menu in the **Graphics** menu. This activates the *Text Box Editor* of Figure 26.

Figure 26. In the *Text Box Editor*, key in the text you would like to appear in the text box. Apply any formatting attributes as you normally would with text in a WordPerfect document. The *Box Position* button activates the *Box Position and Size* dialog box described in Figure 11.

The *Rotate* button activates the *Rotate Text* dialog box where it is possible to rotate the text, appearing in the text box, in 90 degree increments. If you do rotate the text, it can be viewed only on the *Print Preview* screen.

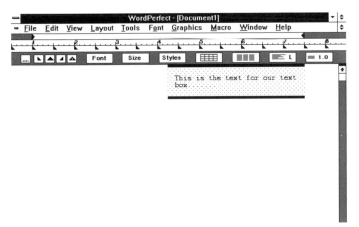

Figure 27. After clicking on the *Close* button in the Figure 26 *Text Box Editor*, the text box appears in the document at the cursor location. This box can be moved, resized, and edited in the same way as figure boxes.

Figure 28. To edit the text in the text box once it is on the page, click on the text box with the right mouse button, and select the *Edit Text Box* command from the sub-menu that appears. This activates the *Text Box Editor* with the text included, ready for editing. (The *Text Box Editor* can also be activated by choosing the *Edit* command from the *Text Box* sub-menu in the **Graphics** menu, after selecting the text box.)

As can be seen in the sub-menu in this figure, it is also possible to assign captions to text boxes (see Figure 16). The *Box Position and Size* dialog box of Figure 11 can also be activated.

The *Text Box* sub-menu of Figure 25 also has a *New Number* command and an *Options* command which are explained in Figures 21 and 23 respectively.

EQUATIONS

Equations also appear in boxes
similar to figure and text boxes,
and can be edited in a similar way
(except for content type).

Figure 29. The *Create* command
from the *Equation* sub-menu in the
Graphics menu activates the
Equation Editor dialog box of
Figure 30.

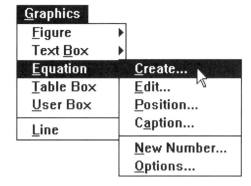

Figure 30. In the *Equation Editor*
dialog box you can create (but not
calculate), mathematical and/or
scientific equations. The list box to
the left of the *Equation Editor*
dialog box contains a variety of
symbols and commands you can
use in your equations.

The *Equation* sub-menu of Figure
29 also contains the same options
as the *Figure* and *Text Box* sub-
menus which are explained earlier
in this chapter.

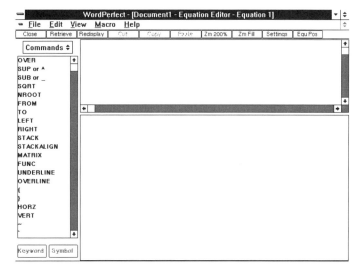

Figure 31. Once an equation box
appears in the document it can be
moved, resized, and edited like
other WordPerfect graphic boxes.

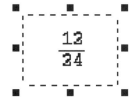

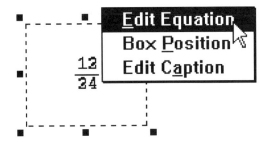

Figure 32. To edit the equation, select the *Edit Equation* command from the sub-menu that appears when you click the right mouse button on the equation box. Alternatively, choose the *Edit* command from the *Equation* sub-menu in the **Graphics** menu after selecting the equation box (see Figure 29). Equations can also have captions assigned (see Figure 16) and they have their own *Box Position and Size* dialog box (Figure 11) that can be activated through this sub-menu (or the *Position* command of Figure 29).

TABLE BOXES AND USER BOXES

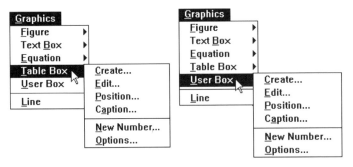

Figure 33. The *Table Box* and *User Box* commands also allow you to create graphic boxes that will not be affected by changes made to the options of other graphic boxes in a document. These boxes are created, moved, edited, and resized in exactly the same way as the figure boxes previously described.

CREATING LINES

Figure 34. The *Horizontal* command from the *Line* sub-menu in the **Graphics** menu activates the *Create Horizontal Line* dialog box of Figure 35.

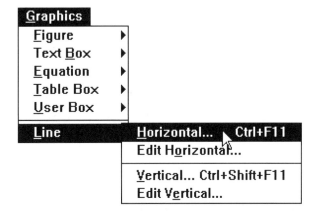

Figure 35. Through this dialog box you can create horizontal lines for your document. The *Line Size* options determine the length and thickness of a line. You may not be able to select the *Length* option initially.

The *Gray Shading* section of this dialog box lets you apply a percentage of black shading to a line. Remember that 100% is black.

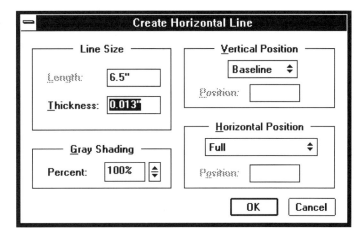

The *Vertical Position* pop-up list gives you two choices for the vertical positioning of a horizontal line. The *Baseline* option places the line on the baseline at the cursor position. If you select the *Specify* option, you key in the distance by which you want the line to appear from the top of the page. Key in the amount in the *Position* frame after selecting *Specify*.

If you select the *Left, Right,* or *Center* options from the *Horizontal Position* pop-up list, you can then alter the length of the line in the *Line Size* section of this dialog box. The *Full* option spreads the horizontal line from the left to the right margin. The *Specify* option lets you key in the distance, in the *Position* frame, that the line will appear from the left of the page.

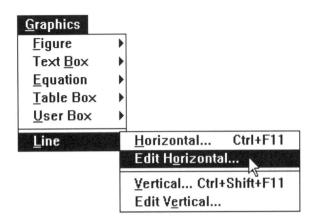

Figure 36. The *Edit Horizontal* command activates the *Edit Horizontal Line* dialog box. This dialog box contains the same options as the *Create Horizontal Line* dialog box of Figure 35. Select the line you want to edit before selecting this command.

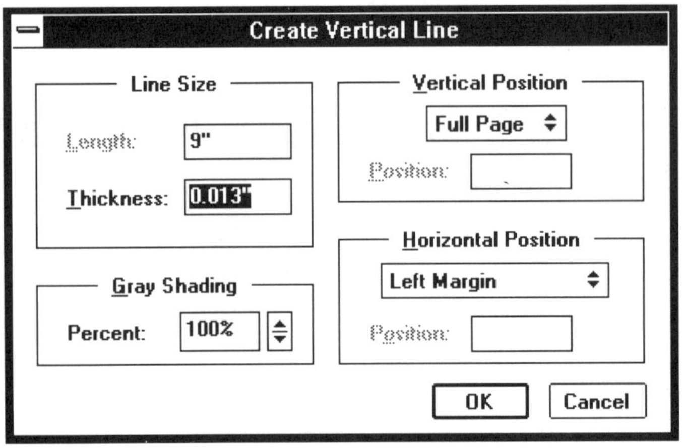

Figure 37. The *Create Vertical Line* dialog box is activated by selecting the *Vertical* command from the *Line* sub-menu of Figures 34 or 36. The options available in this dialog box are the same as in the *Create Horizontal Line* dialog box but will place vertical lines in your document.

CUT, COPY, AND PASTE

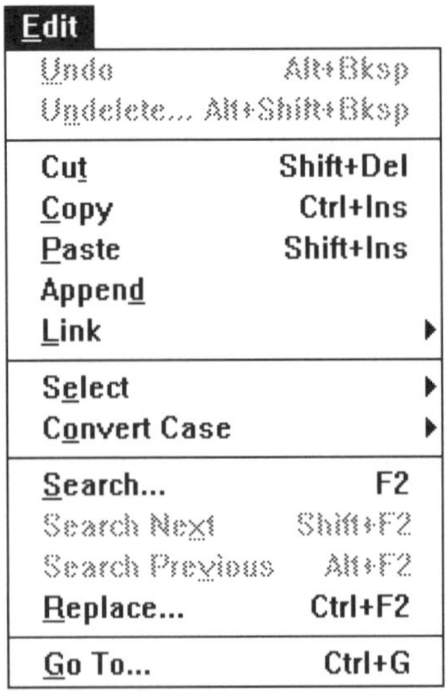

Figure 38. The *Cut* command from the **Edit** menu removes a selected graphic from your document and places it in the Windows *Clipboard*. The *Copy* command places a copy of a selected graphic in the Windows *Clipboard*, while leaving the original graphic in the document. The *Paste* command places a cut or copied graphic back into the document at the cursor location.

MERGE 11

THE MERGE COMMAND

When you use the *Merge* command in WordPerfect, you are combining information from two separate files for the creation of new, multiple documents. This type of merge is often called a mail-merge, because one file generally is a letter, while the other document contains the names and addresses to be included in the letter. In this case, the letter is known as the *Primary File*, while the list of names and addresses is the *Secondary File*.

THE SECONDARY FILE

A secondary file is made up of fields and records. It may be, for instance, a name and address list. All the particulars about a person are called a *Record*. Each separate piece of information in that record, such as a name, address or zip code is a *Field*. In the secondary file, an end field code must be inserted after each field and an end record code at the end of each record.

Figure 1. As an example of a secondary file, we will produce a name and address field, four records long, with three fields in each record. The first field in the record is the name—in this figure "Dean Fallon."

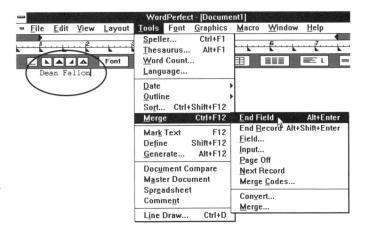

After keying in the required text for the first field, select the *End Field* command from the *Merge* sub-menu in the **Tools** menu. This inserts an end field code after the text.

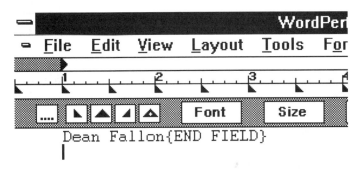

Figure 2. You will then see an *{END FIELD}* code appear after the cursor in your document. A hard return is also inserted automatically. This moves the cursor to the next line.

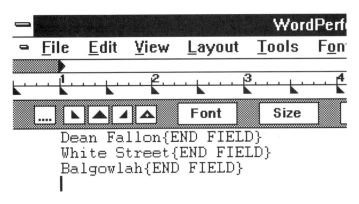

Figure 3. The street address and suburb are entered and, in the same fashion as Figures 1 and 2, an *{END FIELD}* code is inserted after each field.

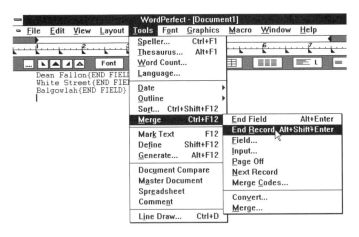

Figure 4. This finishes the first record. To let WordPerfect know this fact, select the *End Record* command from the *Merge* sub-menu in the **Tools** menu. This inserts an *{END RECORD}* code at this point—the result is shown in Figure 5.

Figure 5. The actions of Figure 4 insert an *{END RECORD}* code at the bottom of your fields as well as a hard page break after this.

You can now key in the relevant information for the second record. Figure 6 shows four records entered.

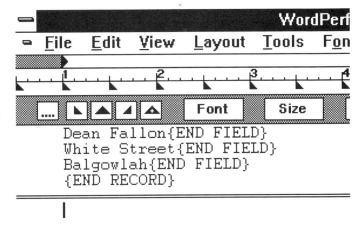

Figure 6. Each record must contain the same number of fields and each field must contain the same type of information. For example, if the first field of the first record is the name of a customer, the first field in all records in this file must be the customer name. In this example, each record has three fields, with the same type of information in each field.

Note: If you leave a field empty in one or more records, it still must have an {END FIELD} code inserted. A secondary file can contain as many records as you like with as many fields of any length as you like.

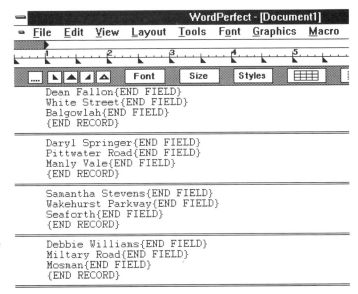

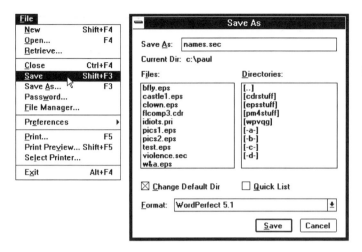

Figure 7. Save the document the way you would save any WordPerfect document. In this case, we called it *names.sec*.

THE PRIMARY FILE

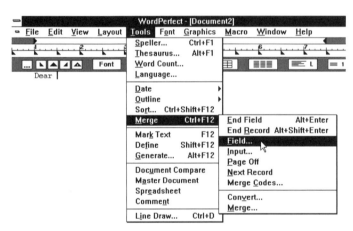

Figure 8. In this example, the primary file is a letter; start creating it the same way you would create any letter. When you reach the section of the letter which requires information from the secondary file, select the *Field* command from the *Merge* sub-menu in the **Tools** menu. Make sure you put a space after the text so the field code appears one space away from the text.

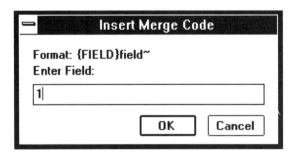

Figure 9. In the *Enter Field* text frame of the *Insert Merge Code* dialog box that now appears, key in the number of the field you want inserted in this section of the letter. If you need to insert the name here, and the name is the first field of your secondary file, key in '1' and click on *OK*. Figure 10 shows the result.

Figure 10. A *{FIELD}1*- code is inserted in the text. Continue entering the text of the letter as normal, inserting field codes in the above fashion wherever you require them.

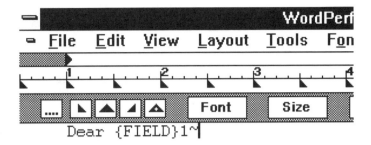

Figure 11. Once you have keyed in the letter with all field codes in the correct place, save this document. Remember, each time you enter a field number in the *Insert Merge Code* dialog box, it must relate to the correct field in the secondary file. Three field codes have been used in this example.

This file is saved as the primary file. We called it *letter1.pri.*

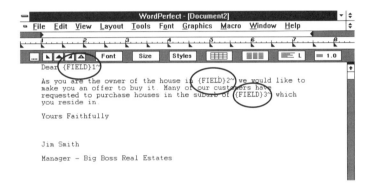

MERGING FILES

Figure 12. The primary and secondary files are now merged to produce a series of "form" letters. To do this, open a new WordPerfect document and select the *Merge* command from the *Merge* sub-menu in the **Tools** menu. This activates the *Merge* dialog box of Figure 13.

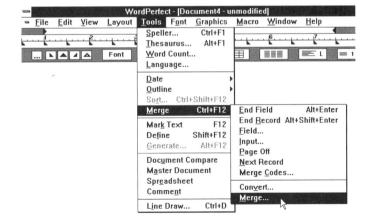

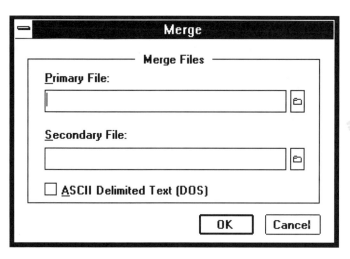

Figure 13. If you remember the name of the *Primary File*, you can key it directly into the text box at the top of this dialog box. If you need to check its name in the list of files, click on the symbol next to the *Primary File* text box to activate the *Select File* dialog box of Figure 14.

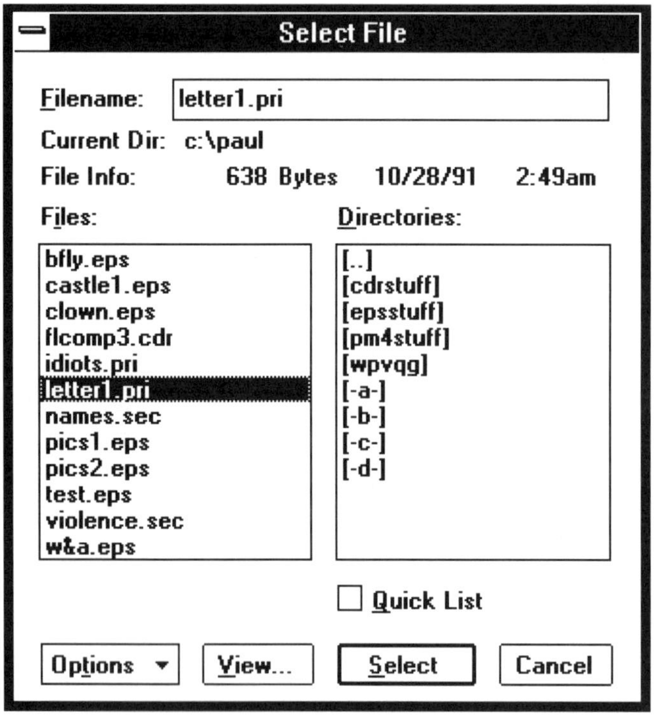

Figure 14. Select the file that you created as your primary file in the *Select File* dialog box and click on *OK*. The path and filename now appear in the *Primary File* text box of the *Merge* dialog box, shown again in Figure 15.

Figure 15. Do the same for the *Secondary File* as you did for the *Primary File*, so that its path and filename appear in the *Secondary File* text frame. Exit the *Merge* dialog box by clicking on *OK*. The merge now takes place.

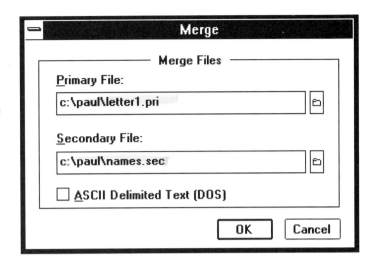

Figure 16. In a short time, depending on how large your secondary file is, a new document is created as a result of the merge between the primary and secondary files. A hard page break is inserted between each record. This newly created document is untitled, so you may wish to save it before printing. The name, address, and suburb in this example have been inserted in the correct positions. The vertical scroll bar can be used to view the other letters in the merge.

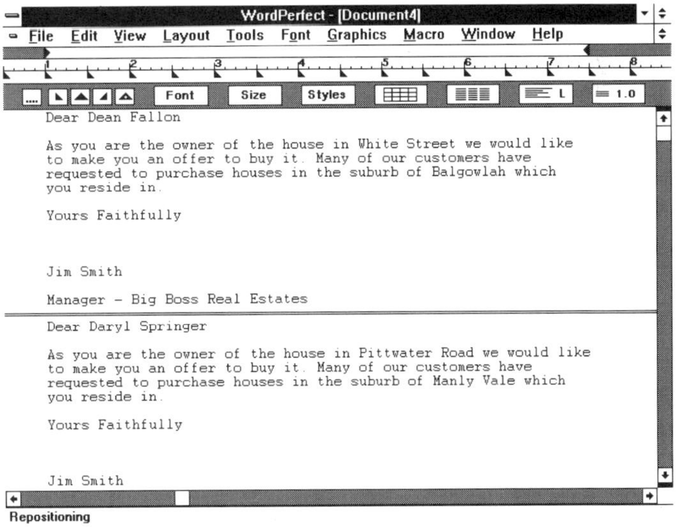

Note: To cancel a merge while it is happening, press the Esc key.

Figure 17. If you are using a graphic in a merge, make sure you have the *Graphic On Disk* option selected (see Chapter 10 — **Using Graphics**) so that a new graphic file is not used for each record. This speeds the merge operation and saves disk space.

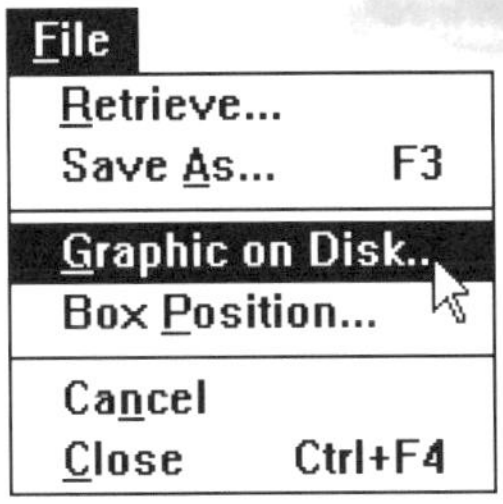

(a)

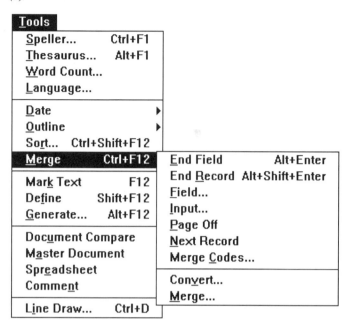

Figure 18. WordPerfect can also add merge codes, such as the date, to a primary file. To do this, select the *Merge Codes* command from the *Merge* sub-menu in the **Tools** menu (a).

In the *Insert Merge Codes* dialog box that appears (b), select a code from the list; clicking on the *Insert* button inserts the selected code into your document. For more information on what each of these codes mean, see the **WordPerfect for Windows Reference Manual**.

(b)

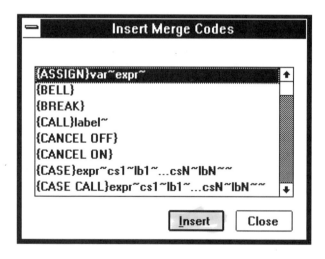

Figure 19. The *Convert* command in the *Merge* sub-menu converts any 4.2 or 5.0 WordPerfect merge codes that may be in your document, if they were created in an earlier version of WordPerfect. The *Convert Old Merge Codes* screen prompt is activated when you select this command. You must confirm whether you want WordPerfect to proceed with this conversion.

CREATING MACROS 12

USING MACROS

Macros are used in WordPerfect to record a series of commands that perform a common task. They can then be played back quickly and easily to achieve this task. Almost anything you can do in WordPerfect for Windows has a corresponding macro command. The creation and playing back of macros is all done through the **Macro** menu.

RECORDING A MACRO

Figure 1. Select the *Record* command from the **Macro** menu to begin recording a macro.

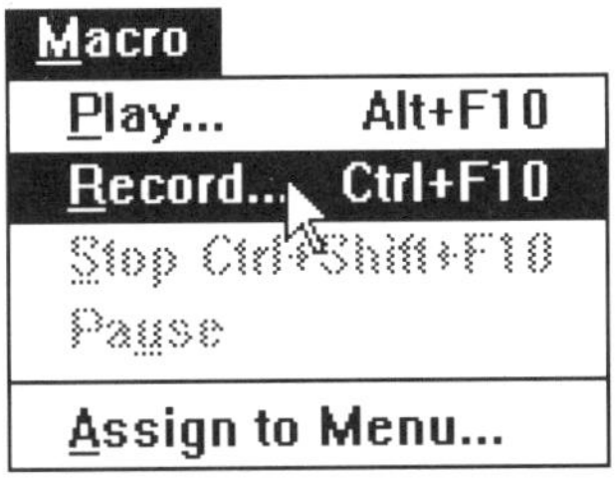

Figure 2. Selecting the *Record* command from the **Macro** menu activates the *Record Macro* dialog box. In this dialog box, type in a name for the macro you are about to record, in the *Filename* text box. If you do not give this name any extension, WordPerfect will automatically append a *.wcm* extension.

The *Descriptive Name* text box is available if you wish to give the macro a more descriptive name. If you need to key in more information about the macro, including a summary of steps, key this into the *Abstract* text box. Click on the *Record* button to begin recording the macro.

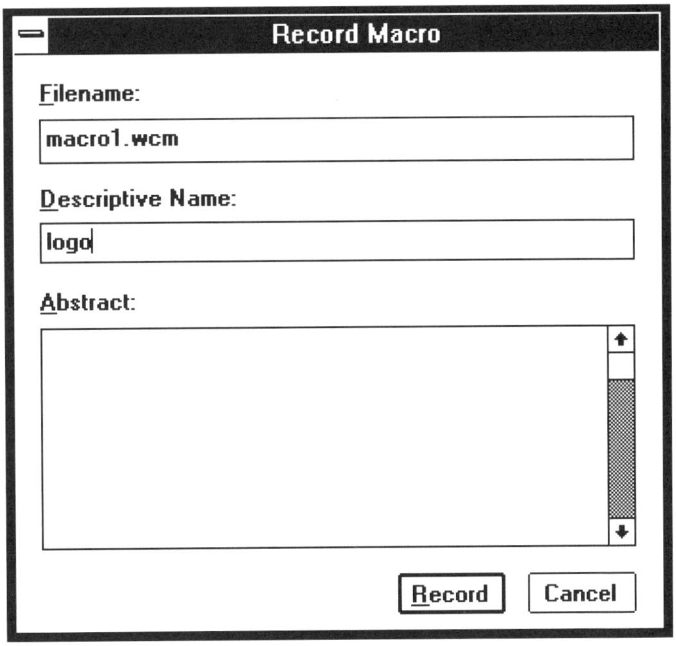

*Note: A macro file is saved into the directory that you have specified in the Location of Files dialog box. (See Chapter 5 — **Setting Preferences** for more information.)*

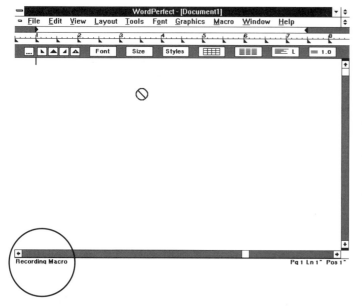

Figure 3. After clicking on the *Record* button in the dialog box of Figure 2, you are returned to the document window. The *Status Bar* indicates that you are currently recording a macro. The cursor changes shape as well, which reminds you that the position of the cursor cannot be changed with the mouse when recording a macro.

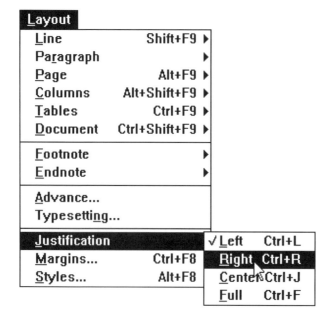

Figure 4. Any commands you select from the menus, or steps you perform, are recorded in the macro. In this case, the *Right* option from the *Justification* sub-menu in the **Layout** menu is being selected.

Figure 5. Now the *Bold* command from the **Font** menu is being selected.

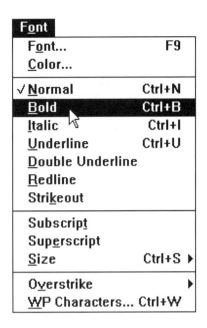

Figure 6. Next, a company name and address is keyed in.

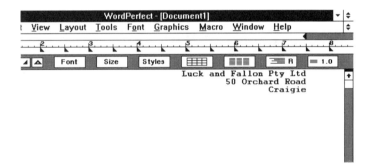

Figure 7. Select the *Stop* command from the **Macro** menu, once you have finished recording the macro.

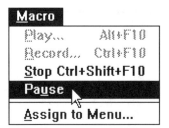

Figure 8. The *Pause* option in the **Macro** menu, lets you pause the recording of a macro. Anything you do after selecting the *Pause* option will not be part of the macro. Select the *Pause* command again to resume macro recording.

PLAYING MACROS

Figure 9. Select the *Play* command from the **Macro** menu to play back a macro in any WordPerfect document.

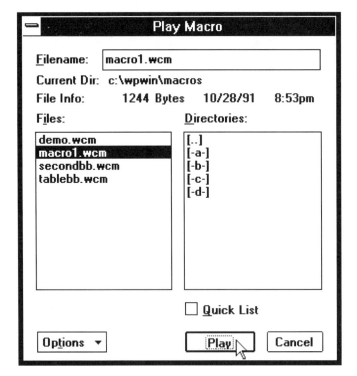

Figure 10. From the list of macro files, select the macro you just created, and click on the *Play* button.

Figure 11. After a few moments, the macro you selected in the *Play Macro* dialog box of Figure 10 appears in your document at the cursor position.

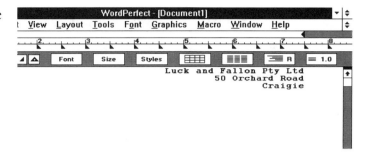

ASSIGNING MACROS TO THE MENU

Figure 12. To simplify macro use, any macro can be assigned to the **Macro** menu. Selecting the *Assign to Menu* command from the **Macro** menu activates the *Assign Macro to Menu* dialog box of Figure 13.

Figure 13. With this dialog box, it is possible to select macros so that they appear at the bottom of the **Macro** menu, making it easier to play them back. Click on the *Insert* button to activate the *Insert Macro Menu Item* dialog box of Figure 14.

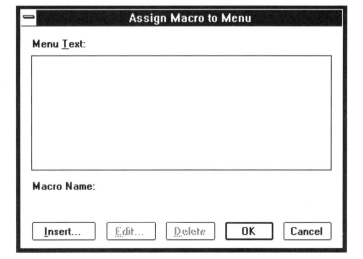

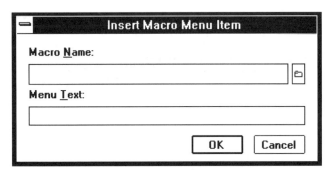

Figure 14. Click on the ▭ symbol in the *Macro Name* text box in the *Insert Macro Menu* item dialog box to activate the *Select File* dialog box.

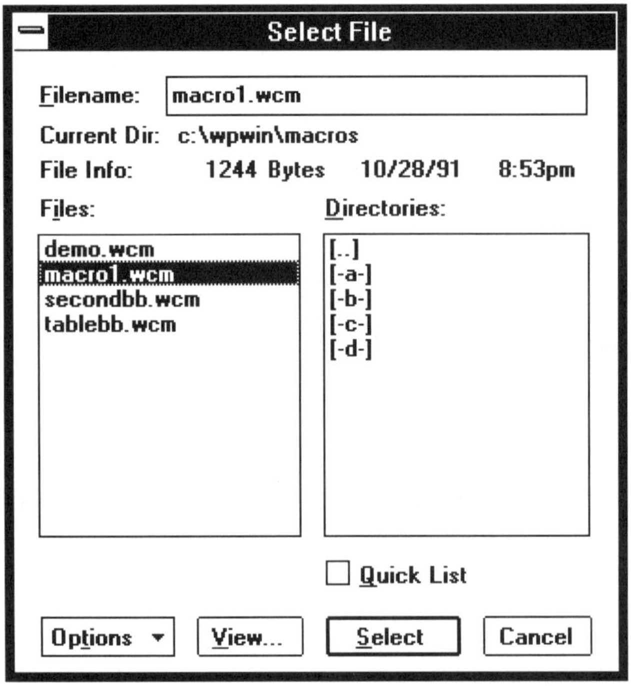

Figure 15. Locate and select the required macro file in the *Select File* dialog box, then click on *OK*.

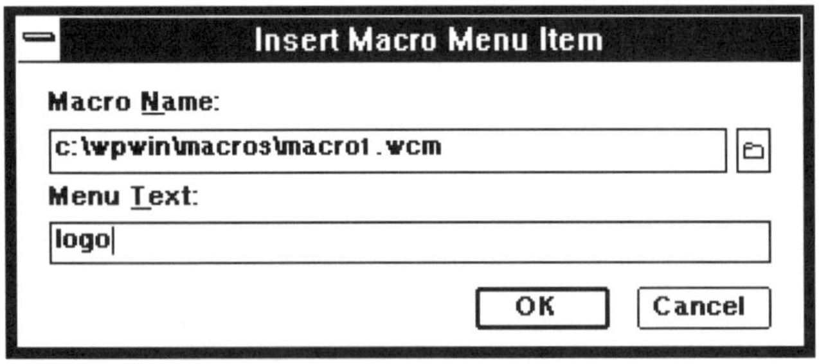

Insert Macro Menu Item

Macro **N**ame:

c:\wpwin\macros\macro1.wcm

Menu **T**ext:

logo

OK   Cancel

Figure 16. The path and filename of the macro selected in Figure 15 now appear in the *Macro Name* text frame of the *Insert Macro Menu Item* dialog box. In the *Menu Text* text box, the word "logo" is displayed automatically. This is because "logo" was chosen as the *Descriptive Name* for this macro back in Figure 2.

If you did not enter such a description, key one in now or, if you wish, leave it blank. Whatever appears in the *Menu Text* text box will appear in the **Macro** menu as the name of the macro. If it is left blank, then the macro filename will appear in the **Macro** menu. Click on *OK* in Figure 16.

Figure 17. The macro you selected now appears in the *Menu Text* list in the *Assign Macro to Menu* dialog box. Click on *OK* to exit from this dialog box and to return to the document.

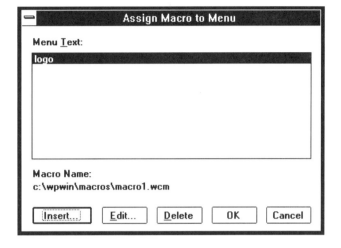

Figure 18. The macro is now available through the **Macro** menu. Selecting the *logo* option from the **Macro** menu will perform the macro just created.

Note: Macros are opened and edited in the same way WordPerfect documents are.

Figure 19. Macros can be assigned to the *Button Bar* using the *Assign Macro to Button* option in the *Edit Button Bar* dialog box. For more information on the *Button Bar,* see Chapter 1 — **WordPerfect for Windows.**

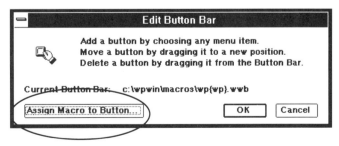

THE TOOLS MENU 13

THE TOOLS MENU COMMANDS

Some of the commands found in the **Tools** menu have been discussed in earlier chapters of this book. The remaining commands, discussed here, cover a variety of additional WordPerfect features.

Figure 1. The first two commands in the **Tools** menu, *Speller* and *Thesaurus,* are discussed in Chapter 6. The first option to look at in this chapter is the *Word Count* command.

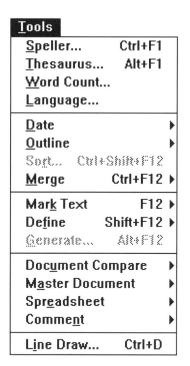

WORD COUNT

Figure 2. Selecting the *Word Count* command from the **Tools** menu of Figure 1 displays the *Word Count* dialog box. This dialog box tells you the number of words in the current document or selected text.

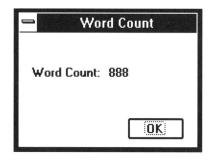

LANGUAGE

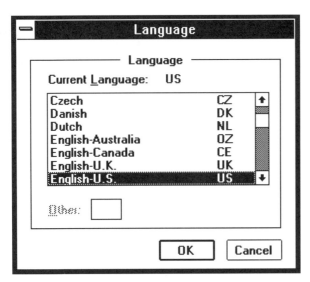

Figure 3. Selecting the *Language* command from the **Tools** menu of Figure 1 activates the *Language* dialog box. The *Language* feature lets you specify the language of text in your documents. These language codes are used for such things as date, sort, and spell checking. The correct language dictionary must first be installed. Your cursor needs to be at the beginning of the foreign language text before selecting this code.

DATE

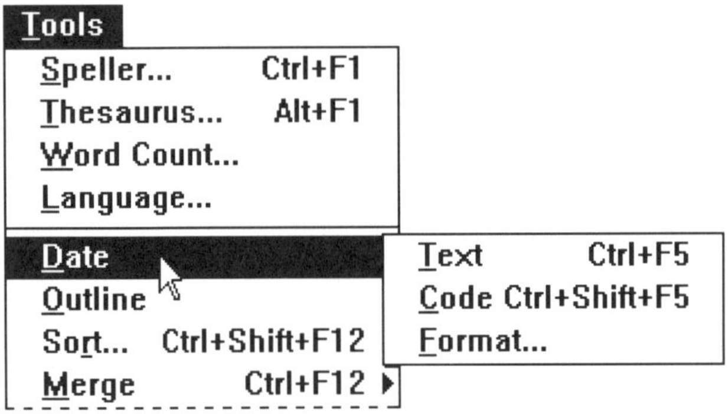

Figure 4. The next option in the **Tools** menu of Figure 1 is the *Date* command. Selecting this command activates the *Date* sub-menu.

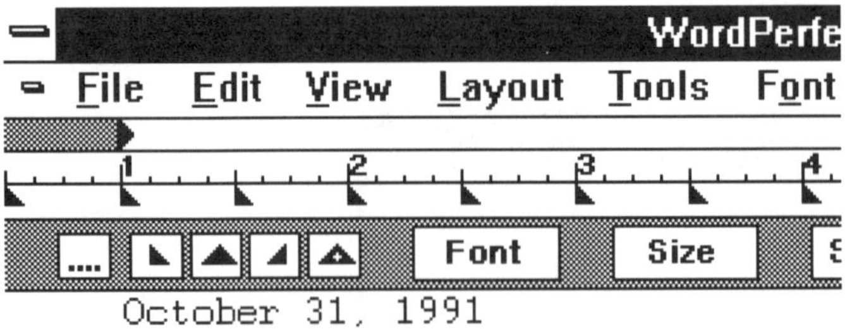

Figure 5. The first option in the *Date* sub-menu of Figure 4 is the *Text* command. Selecting this command inserts the current date in the document at the cursor position. The date is inserted as normal text, just as if you had typed it yourself.

Figure 6. The *Code* command in the *Date* sub-menu of Figure 4 inserts the date as a code. Every time you open the document in the future, the date will change to reflect the current date.

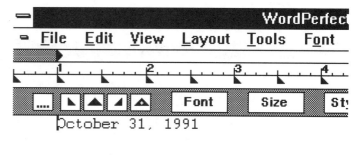

Figure 7. The *Format* command in the *Date* sub-menu of Figure 4 activates the *Document Date/Time Format* dialog box. The options in this dialog box let you change the way the date appears in your document. You can select a standard option from the *Predefined Dates* pop-up list, or combine the options in the *Date Codes* and *Time Codes* pop-up lists with your own text.

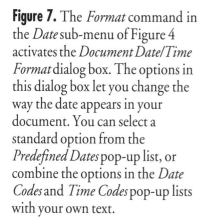

The *Edit Date Format* text frame changes to reflect any selections made in one or more of the three pop-up lists. You can also edit the information in this text frame directly. The *Date Preview* section of the dialog box shows you the actual date format as you make changes.

The next option in the **Tools** menu of Figure 1 is the *Outline* option. This is discussed in Chapter 9.

SORT

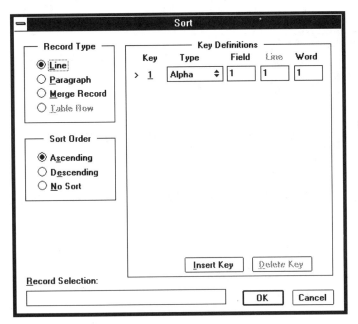

Figure 8. The *Sort* command in the **Tools** menu for Figure 1 displays the *Sort* dialog box. In this box, you can alphabetically sort text such as lines, paragraphs, rows of information in a table, or merge file records (usually names and addresses). You can sort selected text or the whole document. The default settings, as shown, will sort each line in a list, in alphabetical order, by the first word in the line.

In the *Record Type* section, you let WordPerfect know what type of information you wish to sort. This option is set to *Line*. Often you will want to sort a number of lines in which the different parts of information (fields) are separated by spaces or tabs. If the information for each record only takes up one line, then the *Line* option is what you need. Should the information for each record take up more than one line, then the *Paragraph* option must be chosen. *Merge Record* is selected if you are sorting a secondary merge file containing {End Field} and {End Record} codes. If your cursor is positioned inside a WordPerfect table, the default will be *Table Row*, which allows you to sort a WordPerfect table.

The *Sort Order* section is where you indicate whether you want items sorted from A–Z (ascending), or from Z–A (descending).

In the *Key Definitions* section, the *Type* pop-up list lets you select either *Alpha* or *Numeric*, depending on whether you are sorting words or numbers. The *Field, Line,* and *Word* options determine how the items are to be selected and sorted—these vary depending upon *Record Type* selection. (For example, if you have *Table Row* selected as the *Record Type,* then these options will change to *Cell, Line,* and *Word.*) Accepting the defaults here means that your list is sorted alphabetically by the first word in each line. For sorting purposes, a *line* ends with a Return code, a *word* is separated by a space, and a *field* is separated by a tab.

For example, you may have a list of first and last names, such as:

> Paul Smithers
>
> Roger James
>
> Fred Smith
>
> Carrie Smith

Figure 9. The list may need to be sorted first by surname and then by first name. This would require two keys. Click on the *Insert Key* button, to provide another line for you to enter the details for *Key 2.* Under *Word* in *Key 1* enter 2, for the second word. The *Key 2* default of *Word 1* is correct. Click on *OK* for the sort to start.

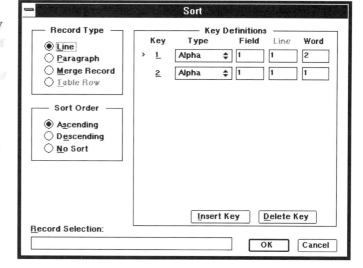

The result is as follows:

> Roger James
>
> Carrie Smith
>
> Fred Smith
>
> Paul Smithers

The *Merge* options in the **Tools** menu of Figure 1 are discussed in Chapter 11 — **Merge**.

MARK TEXT

INDEX

Figure 10. The first option in the *Mark Text* sub-menu is the *Index* command. Before choosing this command, select the text that you want to appear in the index (a).

(a)

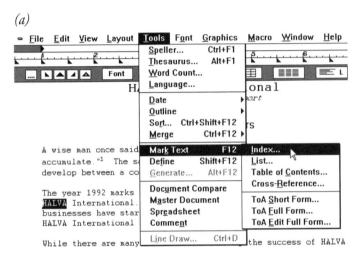

The word selected in (a) appears in the *Heading* text frame of the *Mark Index* dialog box (b).

If you want this word to be a subheading, key in a heading in the *Heading* text frame and click the mouse in the *Subheading* text frame. The word then appears in the *Subheading* frame.

(b)

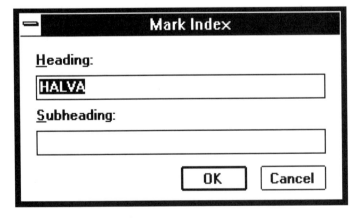

After clicking on *OK*, the text in this dialog box will be included in the index, when it is generated. To create more index entries, select the required word and re-select the *Index* command from the *Mark Text* sub-menu. In the *Mark Index* dialog box, decide whether it is to be a heading or a subheading, as discussed above.

CREATING A CONCORDANCE FILE

As an alternative to marking text manually, you may create a concordance file. A concordance file automatically creates an index without your searching through the entire document to select each word that you want indexed.

Figure 11. To create a concordance file, start a new WordPerfect document. In this new document window, list all words you want to appear in the index. Once you have keyed in your list, sort it in alphabetical order.

This list was sorted with the defaults options selected in the *Sort* dialog box.

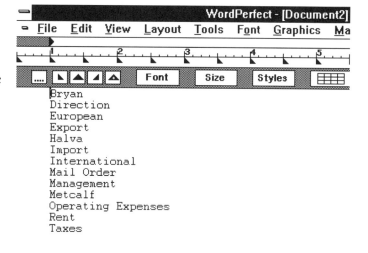

Figure 12. The next step is to save the concordance file as a WordPerfect document.

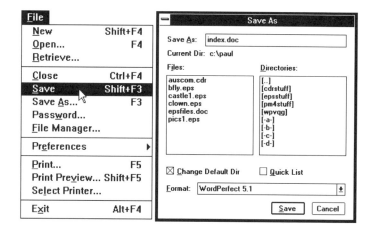

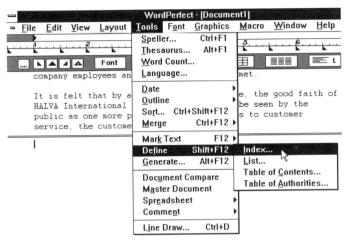

Figure 13. Open the document for which you wish to create the index and place the cursor at the beginning of a new page, at the end of the document. Select the *Index* command from the *Define* sub-menu in the **Tools** menu, to activate the *Define Index* dialog box.

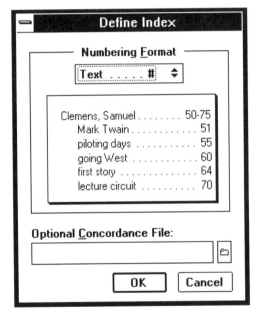

Figure 14. From the *Numbering Format* pop-up list in the *Define Index* dialog box, choose the style of numbering you want for your index. There are five different *Numbering Format* options, differing only in how the text and page numbers are positioned and formatted. The option you choose is displayed in the example below the pop-up list.

If you are using a concordance file and you remember its name, key it into the *Optional Concordance File* text box. If you need to search for it, click on the ☐ symbol to the right of the *Optional Concordance File* to activate the *Select File* dialog box.

Figure 15. In the *Select File* dialog box, locate and select the file that contained the list of words you saved in Figure 12 and click on *OK*. This returns you to the *Define Index* dialog box, with the path and filename of the file you just selected in the *Optional Concordance File* text box. Click on *OK* to return to the document.

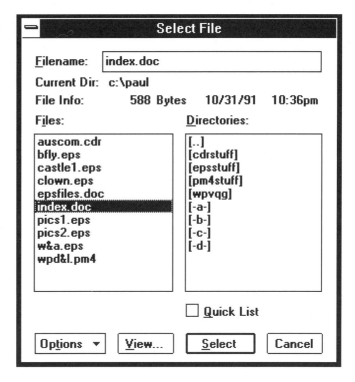

Figure 16. To compile the index, select the *Generate* command from the **Tools** menu.

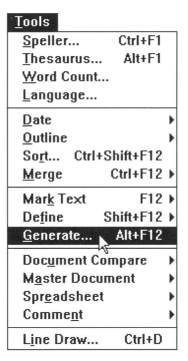

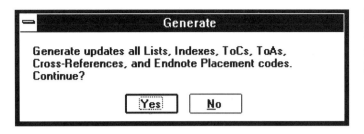

Figure 17. Selecting the *Generate* command activates the *Generate* screen prompt. Click on the *Yes* button to begin the index creation.

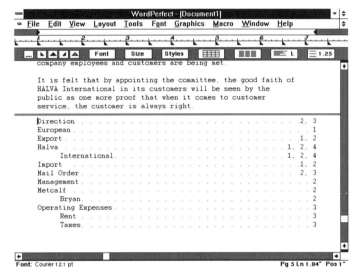

Figure 18. After a few moments, the index appears at the position of the cursor. It is a good idea to start a new page at the end of the document on which your index is to appear. This can be edited as any other text in a document.

Note: If you want any of the headings in the index to be subheadings, select them when you are creating the concordance file and follow the steps under Mark Text in Figures 9 and 10 above. In this example the indented words were assigned as subheadings of the words they appear beneath.

CREATING LISTS

A list is similar to a table of contents. It can be created for such things as figures or captions in a document. When a list is generated, the items are listed in the order in which they appear in the document.

Figure 19. You can generate up to ten lists in a document. The first step in generating a list is to select the text and choose the *List* command from the *Mark Text* sub-menu.

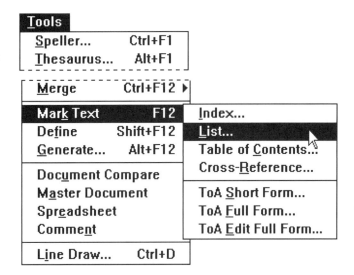

Figure 20. The *List* command activates the *Mark List* dialog box.

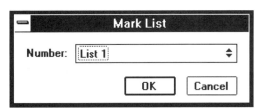

Figure 21. The *Number* pop-up list in the *Mark List* dialog box provides ten options for creating the ten different lists. The last five options in this list are for graphic captions. If you select the *Text Box Captions* option, for example, all text box captions will appear in the list without your having to mark each one individually.

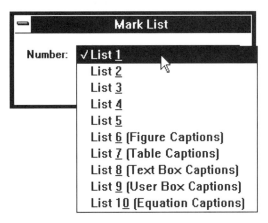

These last five graphic caption options do not have to be used specifically for graphic captions. They can be used in the same way as the first five options. For this example, we are going to select the *List 1* option.

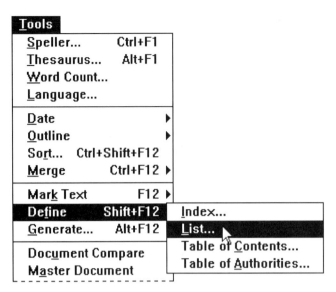

Figure 22. Once you have marked all required text in the document, and included it in your list, select the *List* command from the *Define* sub-menu in the **Tools** menu. This activates the *Define List* dialog box of Figure 23.

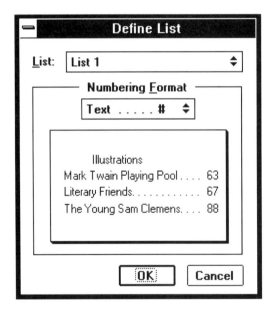

Figure 23. In the *List* pop-up list, select the list number to which you assigned the selected text. In this case we used the *List 1* option. If we had used the *List 5* option in the *Mark List* dialog box shown in Figure 21, for example, we would have chosen the *List 5* option in this dialog box. After selecting the *Numbering Format* style you want for the list (five different styles are available as for indexing), click on *OK* to return to the document.

Figure 24. After placing the cursor where you want the list to appear, select the *Generate* command from the **Tools** menu.

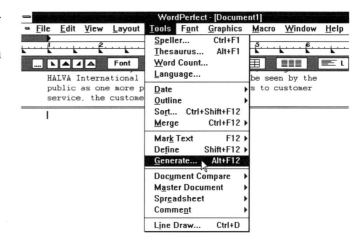

Figure 25. After clicking on the *Yes* option in the *Generate* screen prompt, the list is generated. As with the index, this can be edited like any text in your document.

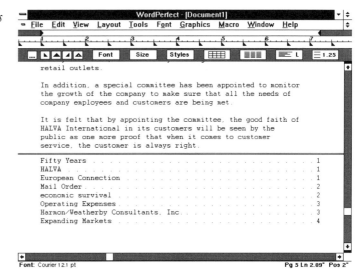

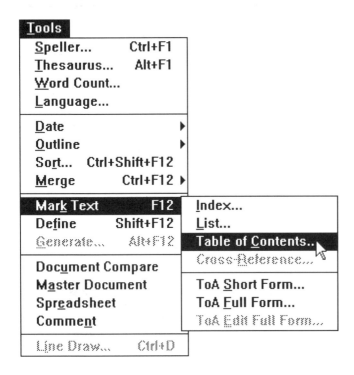

TABLE OF CONTENTS

Figure 26. WordPerfect can generate an automatic table of contents for your document. Three steps are required: mark text; define the table location and format; and generate the table.

This menu illustrates the first step—select some text and choose the *Table of Contents* command from the *Mark Text* sub-menu.

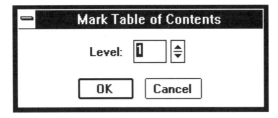

Figure 27. Selecting the *Table of Contents* command activates the *Mark Table of Contents* dialog box. In this dialog box you specify the level of the selected text in the table of contents; for example, a major heading is considered as *Level 1* and the next subheading as *Level 2*. There are five level options from which to choose.

Once you have selected the level, click on *OK* to return to the document. Follow these steps for all the headings, subheadings, and text you want to include in the table of contents.

Figure 28. Once you have marked all the intended entries for the table of contents, move to the beginning of the document and create a new page. Before defining and generating the table of contents, you may like to set a new page number from the second page onwards, otherwise the page created for the table of contents will be included in the numbering.

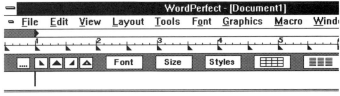

HALVA International
Annual Corporate Report

The First Fifty Years

A wise man once said, "Friends come and go, but enemie accumulate."[1] The same can be said of the relationshi develop between a company and its customers.

Figure 29. The next step is to select the *Table of Contents* command from the *Define* sub-menu in the **Tools** menu. This activates the *Define Table of Contents* dialog box of Figure 30.

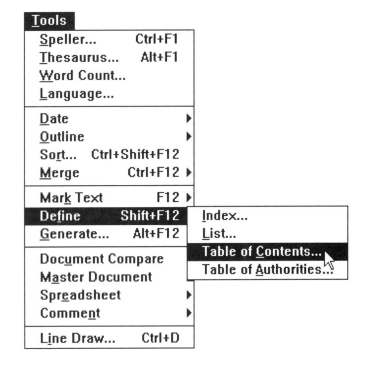

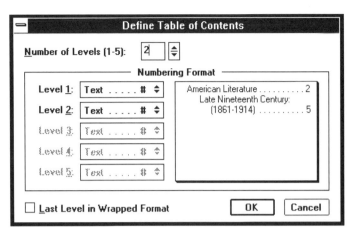

Figure 30. At the top of the *Define Table of Contents* dialog box, select the level you reached when you were marking the content entries. Then, for each level you are using, select the numbering style you want in each of the *Numbering Format* pop-up lists that correspond to each level. Click on *OK* as soon as you have set up this dialog box.

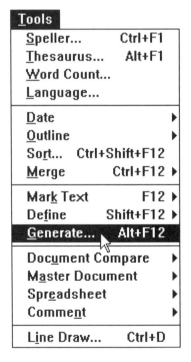

Figure 31. To create the table of contents, select the *Generate* command from the **Tools** menu making sure the cursor is in the correct position. Click on the *Yes* option in the *Generate* screen prompt.

Figure 32. After a few moments, the table of contents appears in the document. This can be edited in the same way as other text in your document.

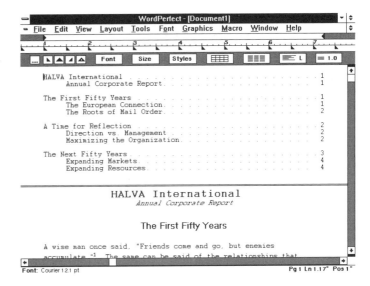

CROSS-REFERENCE

Figure 33. WordPerfect provides cross-reference capability where references to page numbers, figure numbers, and so on, can be updated automatically as these target numbers change. To generate cross-references, select the *Cross-Reference* command in the *Mark Text* sub-menu of the **Tools** menu. This activates the *Mark Cross-Reference* dialog box of Figure 34.

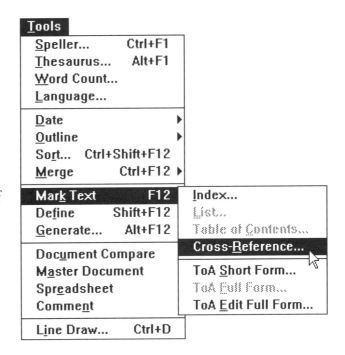

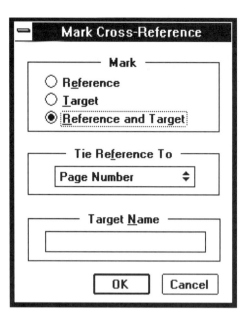

Figure 34. The options in this dialog box allow you to create cross-references throughout your document. The *Reference* option in the *Mark* section creates a reference point at the current position of the cursor. (Before activating this dialog box and selecting *Reference,* you may like to type some cross-reference text, such as *Refer to* or *See,* in the document.)

The *Target* option (the place where you are telling the reader to look) is for creating a corresponding point for any references you might have created. Again, the cursor must first be inserted at the point where you want to create the target. When creating references and corresponding targets, you must include a target name that links the words. This name is keyed into the *Target Name* text frame at the bottom of the *Mark Cross-Reference* dialog box.

It is possible to generate the *Reference* and the *Target* at separate times. The *Reference and Target* option in Figure 34 lets you mark both the reference and the target points at the same time without having to return to the dialog box. The cursor must be placed where you want the reference point to be. After typing in a *Target Name* and clicking on *OK,* you are asked to move to the target point in the document, where you insert the cursor after the target point and press Enter.

The default option of *Page Number* in the *Tie Reference To* pop-up list determines to what item the cross-reference is tied. You can also cross-reference footnote and endnote numbers, paragraphs, outlines, figures, and boxes.

Once you have marked the reference and target points in the document, select the *Generate* command from the **Tools** menu to link the cross-references together.

TABLE OF AUTHORITIES

Figure 35. The *ToA Short Form, ToA Full Form,* and *ToA Edit Full Form* options in the *Mark Text* sub-menu refer to the *Table of Authorities* option in the *Define* sub-menu. The *Table of Authorities* feature of WordPerfect is used mainly in the legal profession to list citations. For more information on *Table of Authorities,* see the WordPerfect for Windows Reference Manual.

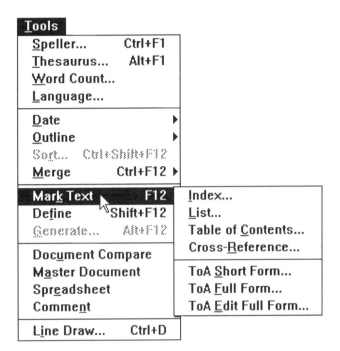

DOCUMENT COMPARE

Figure 36. The first option in the *Document Compare* sub-menu from the **Tools** menu is the *Add Markings* command. You would use this command if a document was edited elsewhere and you wanted to compare it with the original. The changes made to the document are marked with redline codes, strikeout codes, or messages indicating if any text has been moved.

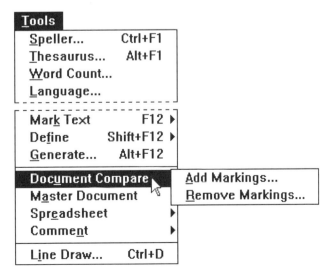

The *Remove Markings* command in the *Document Compare* sub-menu takes out the markings and restores the document to the way it was before the comparison was made.

MASTER DOCUMENT

The *Master Document* feature allows you to manage very large documents. The master document contains codes linking it to subdocuments, which, as an example, could be chapters in a book.

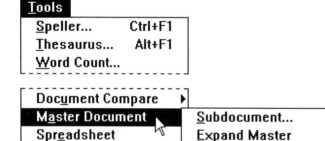

Figure 37. The options in the *Master Document* sub-menu let you include any number of *Subdocuments* into the master document. *Subdocuments* are just normal WordPerfect files except they are included as part of a larger document, the *Master Document*.

Figure 38. The first command from the *Master Document* sub-menu in the **Tools** menu is the *Subdocument* command. Selecting this command activates the *Include Subdocument* dialog box. If you select a filename from the list of files in this dialog box and click on the *Include* button, a comment bar, representing the file selected, appears in the document at the cursor location.

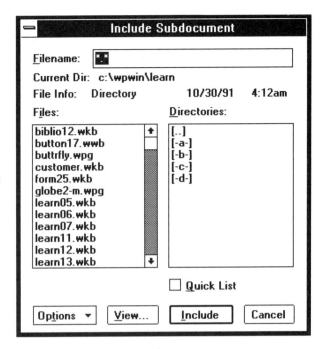

Figure 39. The order that the comment bars appear in this file determines the order in which the files appear in the master document.

The files represented by the comment bars are subdocuments linked to the master document. A subdocument can be removed from the master document by deleting the comment code in *Reveal Codes.*

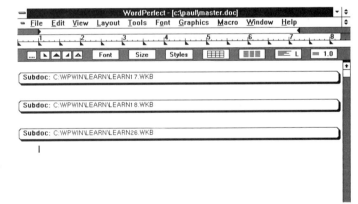

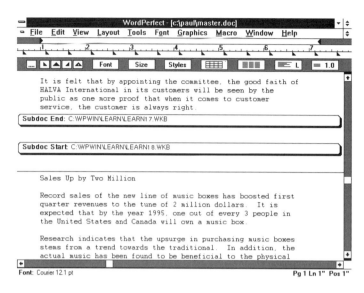

Figure 40. The *Expand Master* command in the *Master Document* sub-menu of Figure 37 retrieves all subdocuments into the master document. A comment bar will sit in front of, and after, each subdocument in the master document. In this example, you can see the bottom of the *learn17.wkb* file and the beginning of the *learn18.wkb* file.

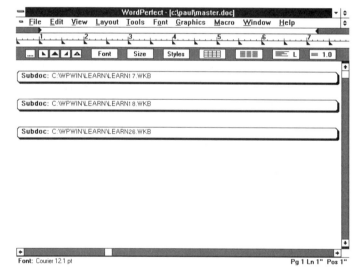

Figure 41. The *Condense Master* command in the *Master Document* sub-menu of Figure 37 removes the subdocuments from the master document, but they remain linked, and the comment bars remain in the master document. If you have made any changes to the subdocuments in their expanded form in the master document, you are prompted to save the documents when you condense them. Saving them overwrites the original document on disk.

SPREADSHEET

Figure 42. The first option in the *Spreadsheet* sub-menu allows you to import spreadsheet information from an outside program such as Lotus 1-2-3. The remaining link options allow you to establish a link between the spreadsheet program and the information imported from it into WordPerfect. This ensures that when the spreadsheet is updated, the changes are reflected in the information imported into WordPerfect.

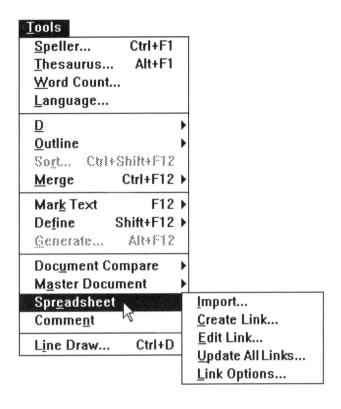

COMMENT

A *Comment* is a bar that sits in your document but does not print. It can be used as a reminder to edit a document at a later date.

Figure 43. The first command in the *Comment* sub-menu is the *Create* command. This activates the *Create Comment* dialog box of Figure 44.

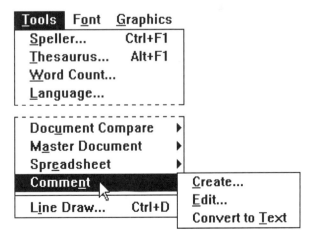

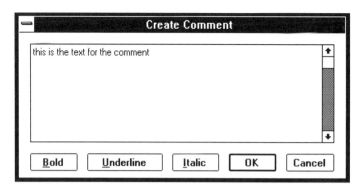

Figure 44. The *Create Comment* dialog box includes a text frame allowing you to key in your comment text. You can apply the *Bold, Underline,* and/or *Italic* commands to selected text in this dialog box.

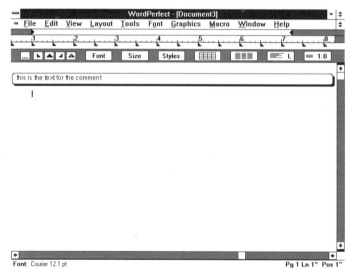

Figure 45. After clicking on *OK* in the Figure 44 *Create Comment* dialog box, you see the comment text appear in the document. The comment appears in the document at the cursor location.

If you place the cursor after the comment code, then it is possible to edit it by selecting the *Edit* command from the *Comment* sub-menu of Figure 43. The *Convert to Text* command will convert the comment to normal WordPerfect text. This is the only way a comment can be printed in WordPerfect.

LINE DRAW

Figure 46. The *Line Draw* command in the **Tools** menu activates the *Line Draw* dialog box of Figure 47.

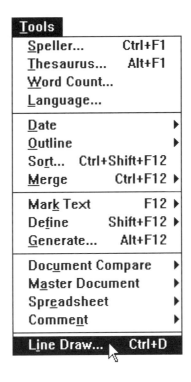

Figure 47. Through this dialog box it is possible to create lines in your document using the directional arrow keys on the keyboard. Select a line drawing option from the *Characters* section of the dialog box. You also must select an option from the *Mode* section of the dialog box.

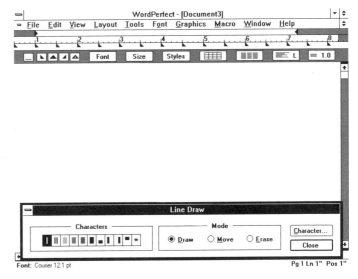

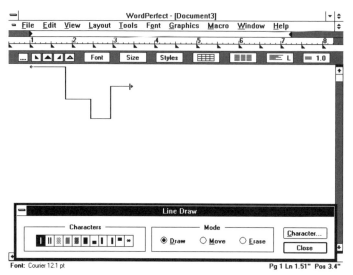

Figure 48. Select the *Draw* option from the *Mode* section and start using the arrow keys. A line will appear in the document in the direction corresponding to the arrow key(s) you are using.

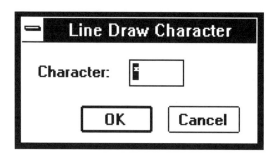

Figure 49. If you click on the *Character* button in the *Line Draw* dialog box, you activate the *Line Draw Character* dialog box. Here you can key in your own character from the keyboard and click on *OK.* This character takes the place of the last option in the *Characters* section of the *Line Draw* dialog box. This character can then be used to create a line.

Note: To print properly, lines drawn with the Line Draw feature must be printed in a fixed pitch font, such as Courier. The font code must appear in your document before the area drawn with Line Draw.

DIALOG BOXES

LOCATING DIALOG BOXES

Many WordPerfect menu commands activate dialog boxes. The following pages provide a quick visual summary of how to access these dialog boxes.

THE FILE MENU

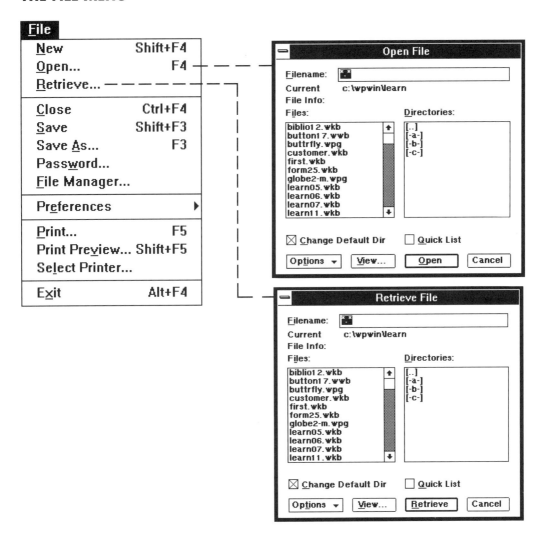

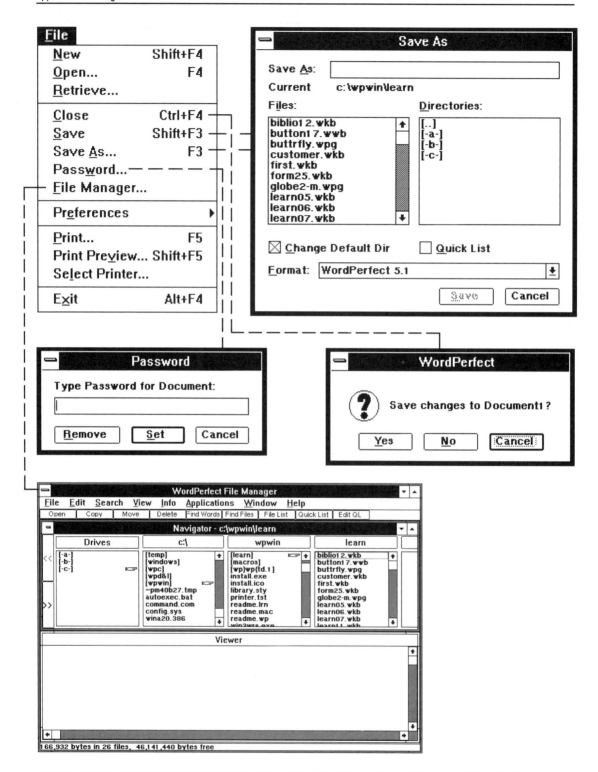

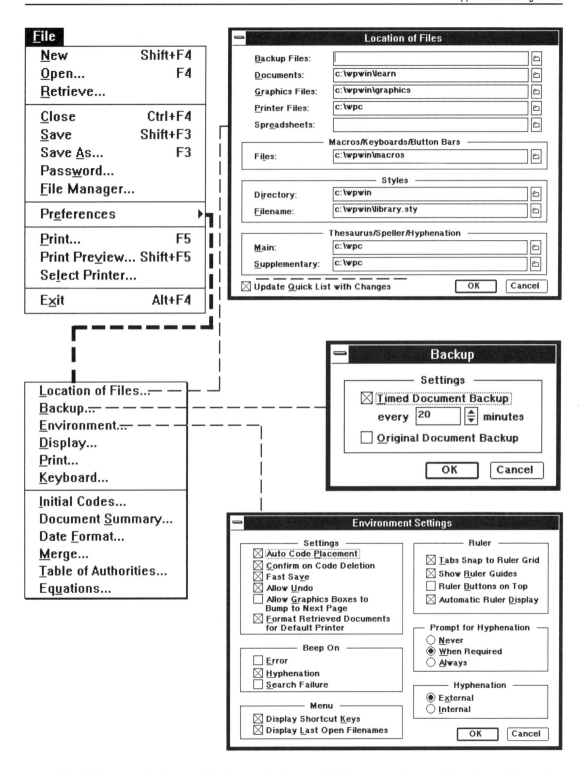

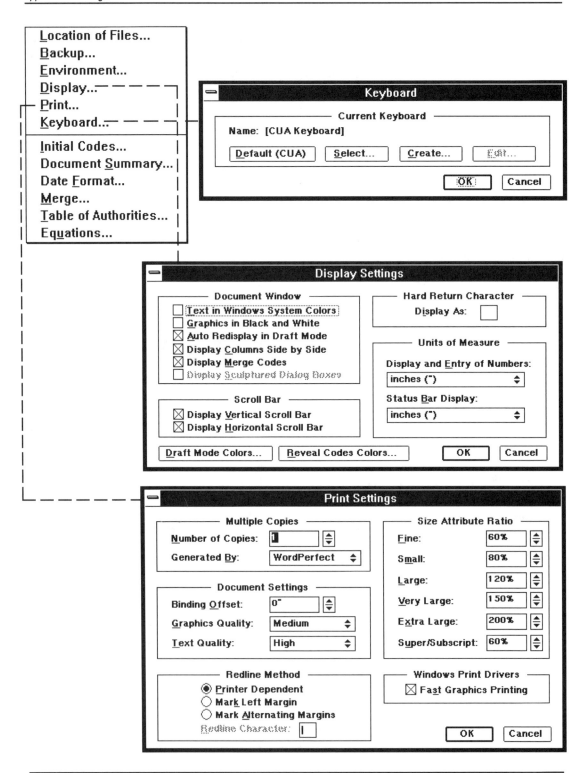

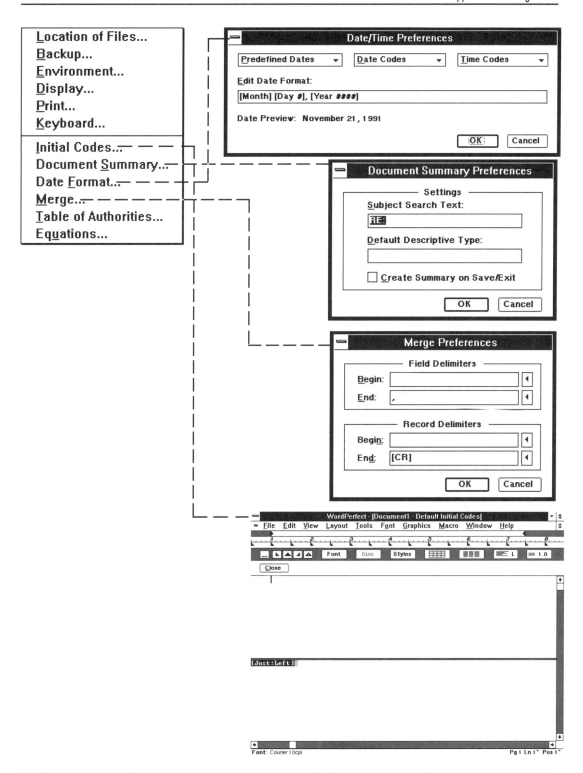

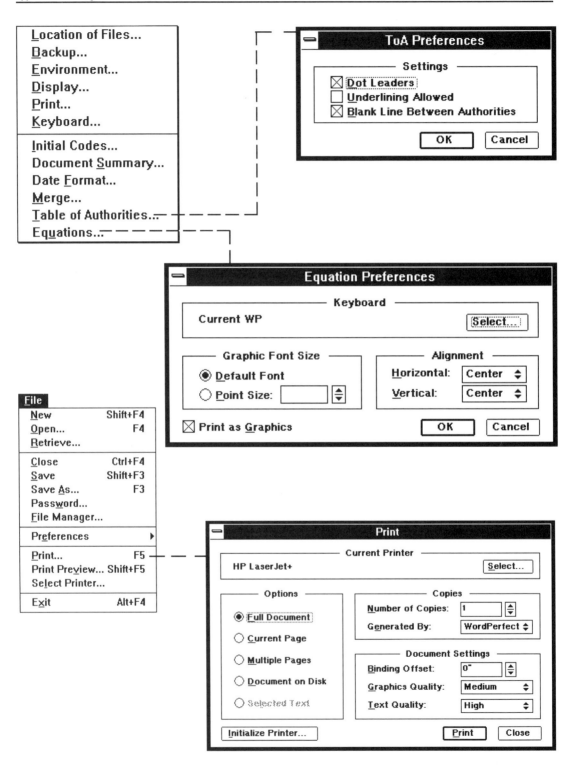

Location of Files...
Backup...
Environment...
Display...
Print...
Keyboard...

Initial Codes...
Document Summary...
Date Format...
Merge...
Table of Authorities...
Equations...

ToA Preferences

Settings
☒ Dot Leaders
☐ Underlining Allowed
☒ Blank Line Between Authorities

OK   Cancel

Equation Preferences

Keyboard
Current WP   Select...

Graphic Font Size
◉ Default Font
◯ Point Size:

Alignment
Horizontal: Center ⬍
Vertical: Center ⬍

☒ Print as Graphics   OK   Cancel

File
New   Shift+F4
Open...   F4
Retrieve...

Close   Ctrl+F4
Save   Shift+F3
Save As...   F3
Password...
File Manager...

Preferences   ▶

Print...   F5
Print Preview... Shift+F5
Select Printer...

Exit   Alt+F4

Print

Current Printer
HP LaserJet+   Select...

Options
◉ Full Document
◯ Current Page
◯ Multiple Pages
◯ Document on Disk
◯ Selected Text

Copies
Number of Copies: 1
Generated By: WordPerfect ⬍

Document Settings
Binding Offset: 0"
Graphics Quality: Medium ⬍
Text Quality: High ⬍

Initialize Printer...   Print   Close

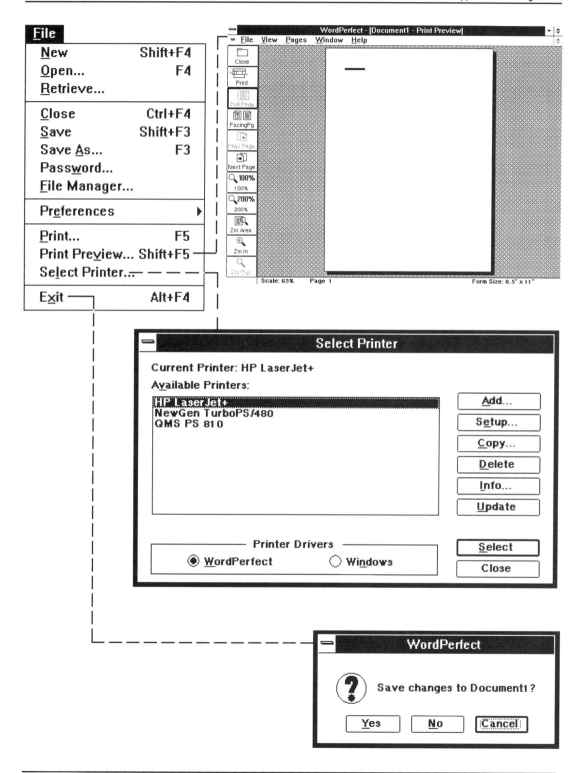

File

New	Shift+F4
Open...	F4
Retrieve...	
Close	Ctrl+F4
Save	Shift+F3
Save As...	F3
Password...	
File Manager...	
Preferences	▶
Print...	F5
Print Preview...	Shift+F5
Select Printer...	
Exit	Alt+F4

WordPerfect - [Document1 - Print Preview]

File   View   Pages   Window   Help

Close
Print
Full Page
FacingPg
Prev Page
Next Page
100%
200%
Zm Area
Zm In
Zm Out

Scale: 65%   Page 1   Form Size: 8.5" x 11"

Select Printer

Current Printer: HP LaserJet+

Available Printers:

HP LaserJet+
NewGen TurboPS/480
QMS PS 810

Add...
Setup...
Copy...
Delete
Info...
Update

Printer Drivers

◉ **WordPerfect**   ○ **Windows**

Select
Close

WordPerfect

? **Save changes to Document1 ?**

Yes   **No**   **Cancel**

THE EDIT MENU

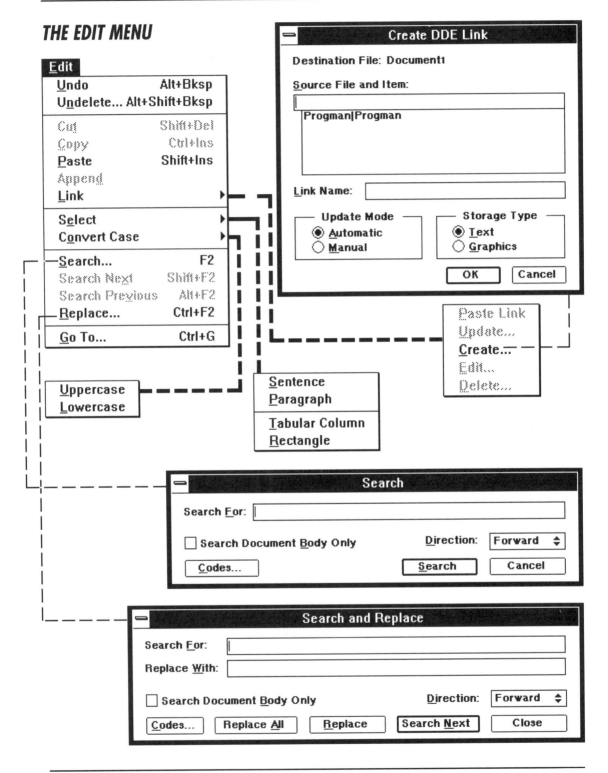

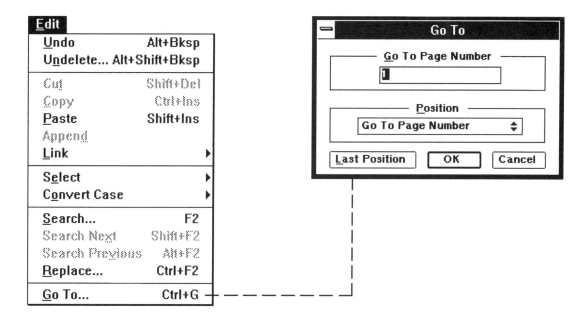

THE VIEW MENU

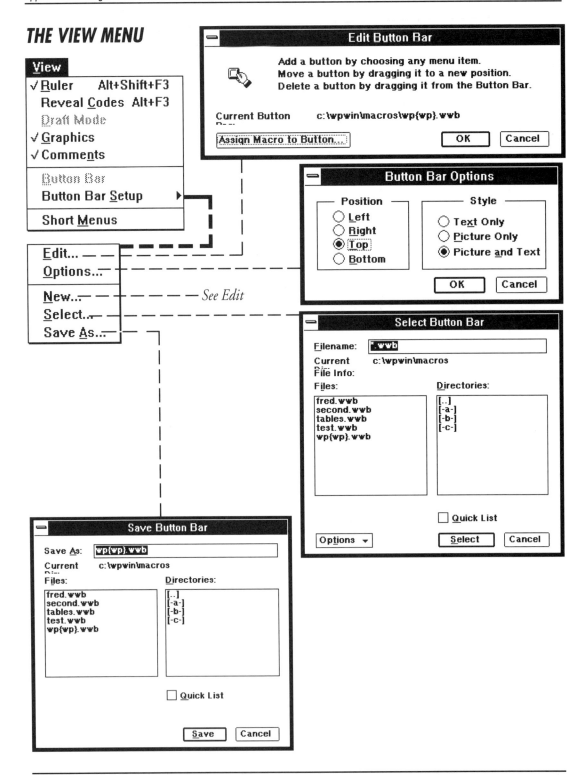

View

√ **Ruler**	Alt+Shift+F3
Reveal Codes	Alt+F3
Draft Mode	
√ **Graphics**	
√ **Comments**	
Button Bar	
Button Bar Setup	▶
Short Menus	

Edit...
Options...
New...
Select...
Save As...

— See Edit

Edit Button Bar

Add a button by choosing any menu item.
Move a button by dragging it to a new position.
Delete a button by dragging it from the Button Bar.

Current Button   c:\wpwin\macros\wp{wp}.wwb

[Assign Macro to Button...]   [OK] [Cancel]

Button Bar Options

Position
- ○ **Left**
- ○ **Right**
- ● **Top**
- ○ **Bottom**

Style
- ○ **Text Only**
- ○ **Picture Only**
- ● **Picture and Text**

[OK] [Cancel]

Select Button Bar

Filename: `*.wwb`
Current Dir: c:\wpwin\macros
File Info:

Files:
fred.wwb
second.wwb
tables.wwb
test.wwb
wp{wp}.wwb

Directories:
[..]
[-a-]
[-b-]
[-c-]

☐ **Quick List**

[Options ▼]   [Select] [Cancel]

Save Button Bar

Save As: `wp{wp}.wwb`
Current Dir: c:\wpwin\macros

Files:
fred.wwb
second.wwb
tables.wwb
test.wwb
wp{wp}.wwb

Directories:
[..]
[-a-]
[-b-]
[-c-]

☐ **Quick List**

[Save] [Cancel]

THE LAYOUT MENU

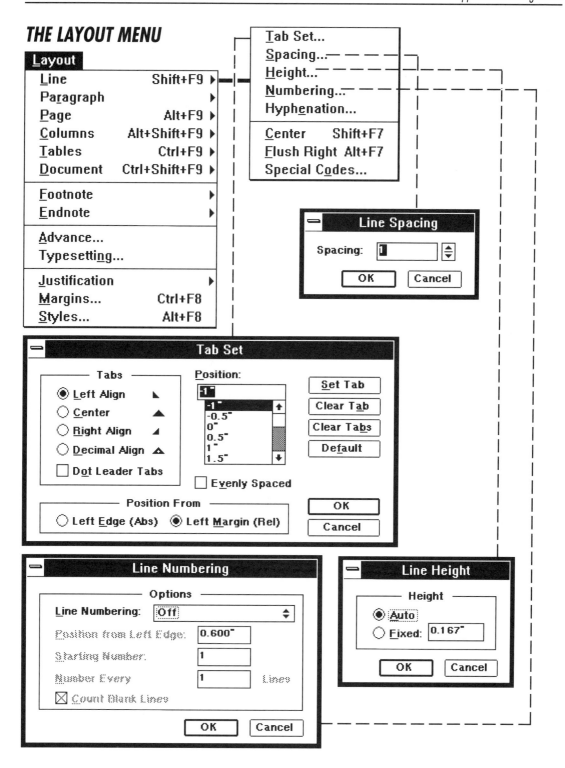

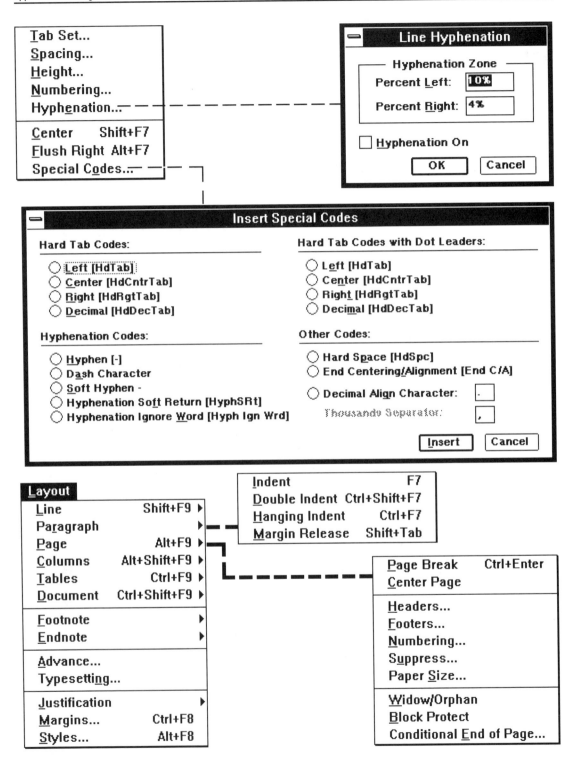

Tab Set...
Spacing...
Height...
Numbering...
Hyphenation...

Center   Shift+F7
Flush Right   Alt+F7
Special Codes...

Line Hyphenation

Hyphenation Zone
Percent Left: **10%**
Percent Right: **4%**

☐ Hyphenation On

[OK]   [Cancel]

Insert Special Codes

Hard Tab Codes:
○ Left [HdTab]
○ Center [HdCntrTab]
○ Right [HdRgtTab]
○ Decimal [HdDecTab]

Hyphenation Codes:
○ Hyphen [-]
○ Dash Character
○ Soft Hyphen -
○ Hyphenation Soft Return [HyphSRt]
○ Hyphenation Ignore Word [Hyph Ign Wrd]

Hard Tab Codes with Dot Leaders:
○ Left [HdTab]
○ Center [HdCntrTab]
○ Right [HdRgtTab]
○ Decimal [HdDecTab]

Other Codes:
○ Hard Space [HdSpc]
○ End Centering/Alignment [End C/A]

○ Decimal Align Character: [.]

   Thousands Separator: [,]

[Insert]   [Cancel]

Layout
Line   Shift+F9 ▶
Paragraph   ▶
Page   Alt+F9 ▶
Columns   Alt+Shift+F9 ▶
Tables   Ctrl+F9 ▶
Document   Ctrl+Shift+F9 ▶

Footnote   ▶
Endnote   ▶

Advance...
Typesetting...

Justification   ▶
Margins...   Ctrl+F8
Styles...   Alt+F8

Indent   F7
Double Indent   Ctrl+Shift+F7
Hanging Indent   Ctrl+F7
Margin Release   Shift+Tab

Page Break   Ctrl+Enter
Center Page

Headers...
Footers...
Numbering...
Suppress...
Paper Size...

Widow/Orphan
Block Protect
Conditional End of Page...

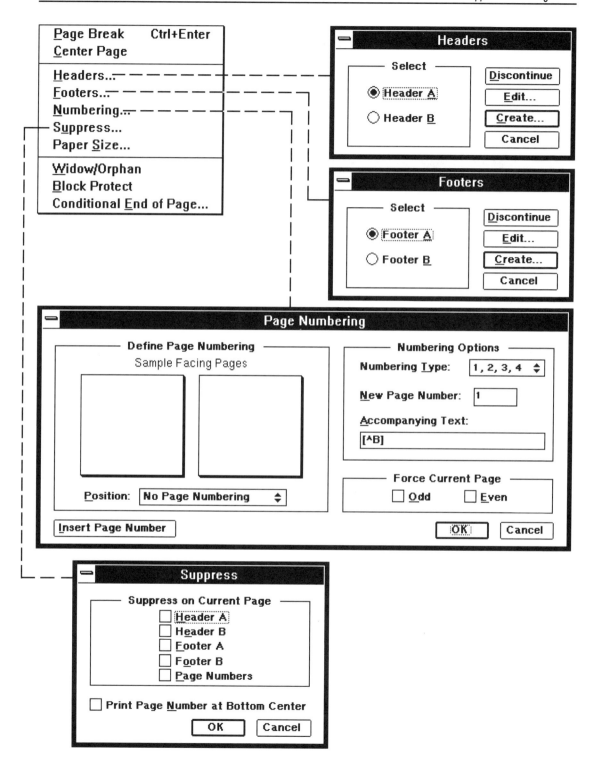

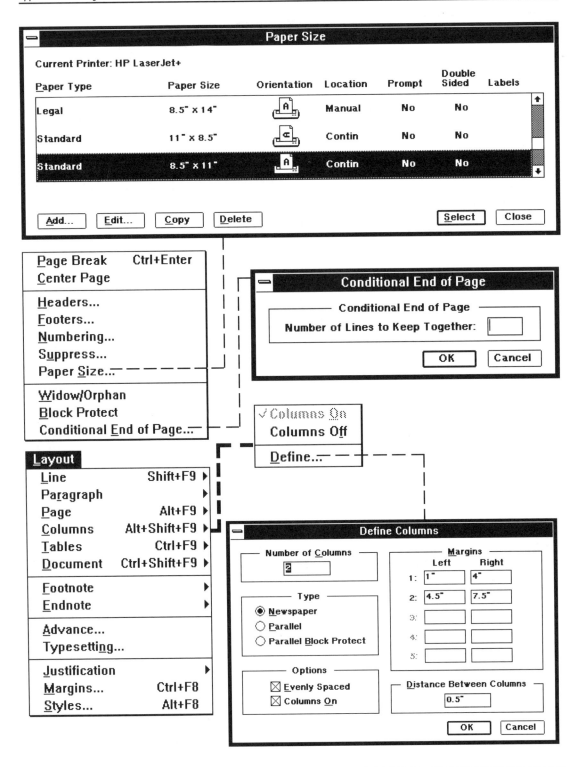

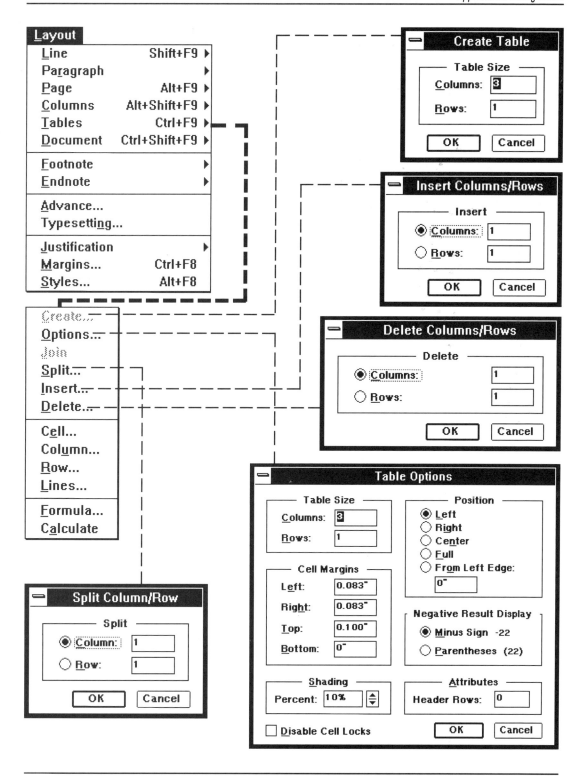

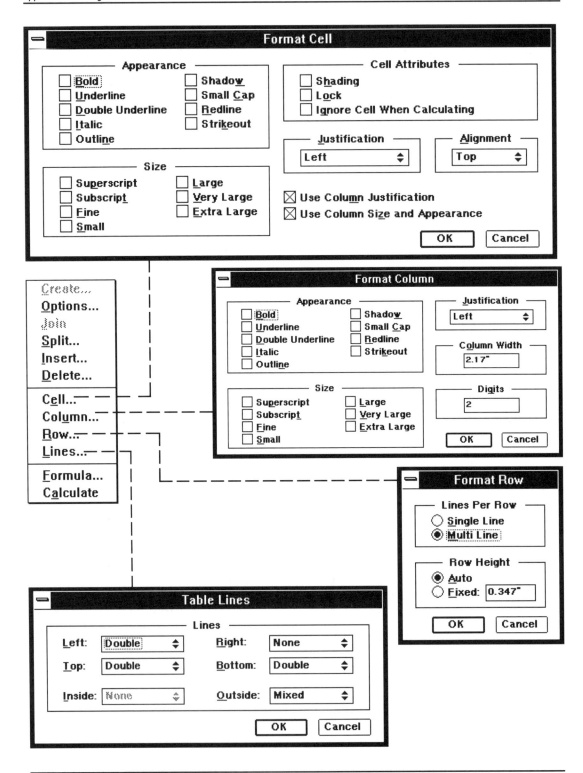

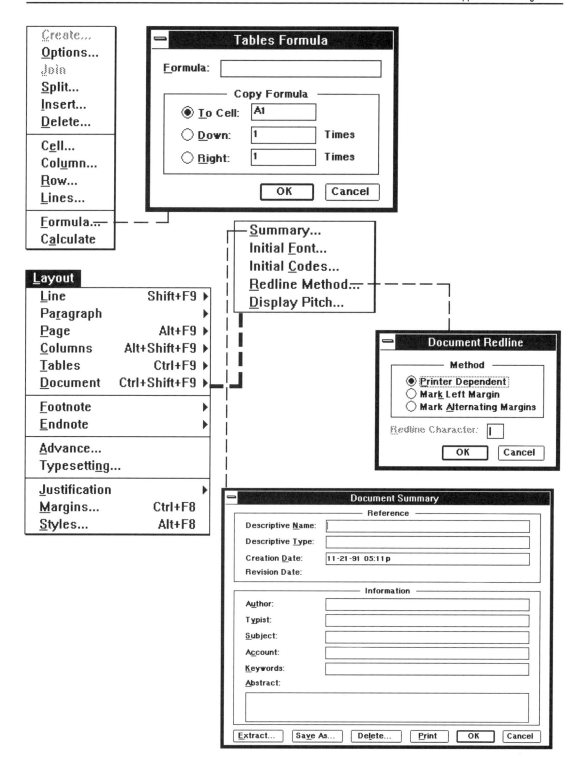

Create...
Options...
Join
Split...
Insert...
Delete...

Cell...
Column...
Row...
Lines...

Formula...
Calculate

Tables Formula

Formula: [   ]

Copy Formula

◉ To Cell: [A1]
○ Down: [1] Times
○ Right: [1] Times

[OK] [Cancel]

Summary...
Initial Font...
Initial Codes...
Redline Method...
Display Pitch...

Layout

Line	Shift+F9 ▶
Paragraph	▶
Page	Alt+F9 ▶
Columns	Alt+Shift+F9 ▶
Tables	Ctrl+F9 ▶
Document	Ctrl+Shift+F9 ▶
Footnote	▶
Endnote	▶
Advance...	
Typesetting...	
Justification	▶
Margins...	Ctrl+F8
Styles...	Alt+F8

Document Redline

Method

◉ Printer Dependent
○ Mark Left Margin
○ Mark Alternating Margins

Redline Character: [ ]

[OK] [Cancel]

Document Summary

Reference

Descriptive Name: [   ]
Descriptive Type: [   ]
Creation Date: [11-21-91 05:11p]
Revision Date:

Information

Author: [   ]
Typist: [   ]
Subject: [   ]
Account: [   ]
Keywords: [   ]
Abstract:
[   ]

[Extract...] [Save As...] [Delete...] [Print] [OK] [Cancel]

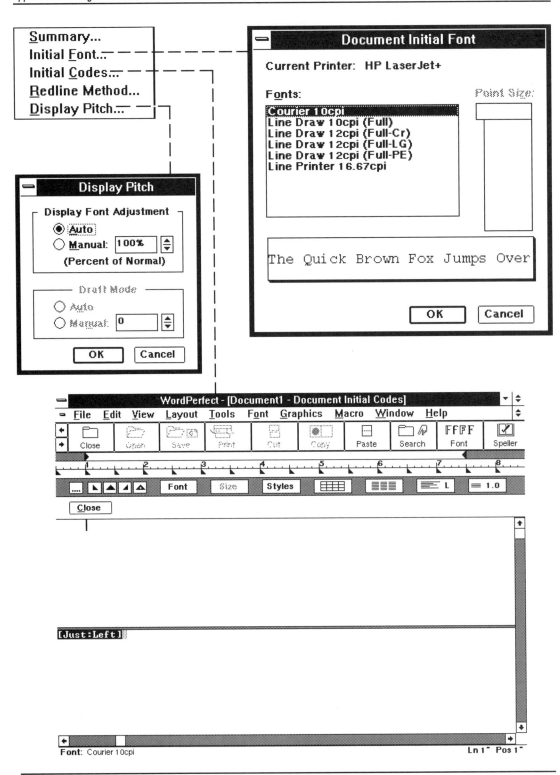

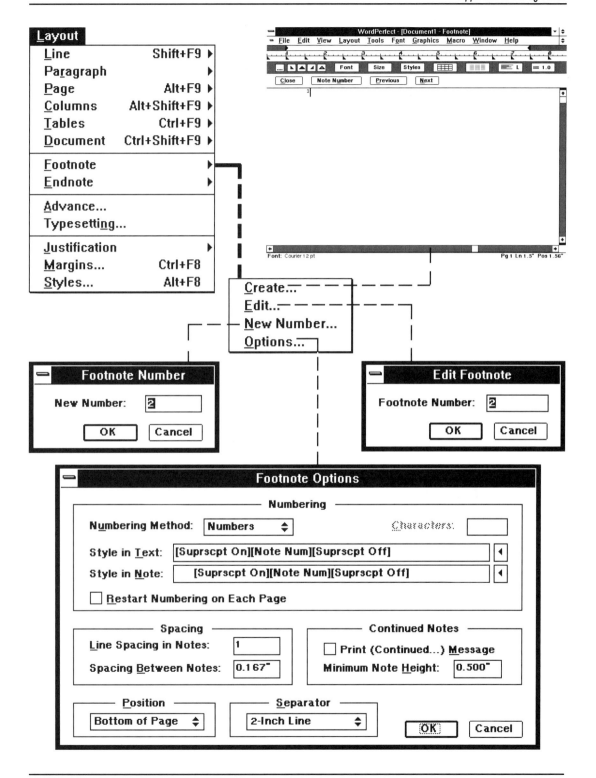

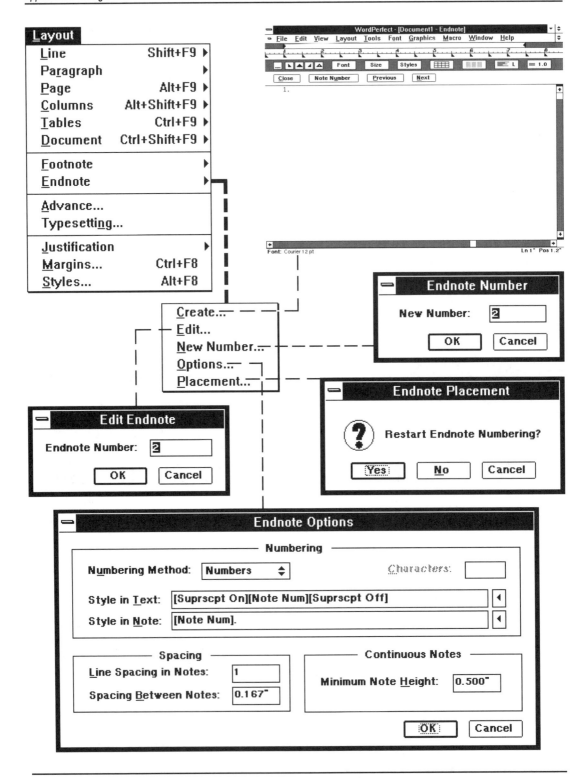

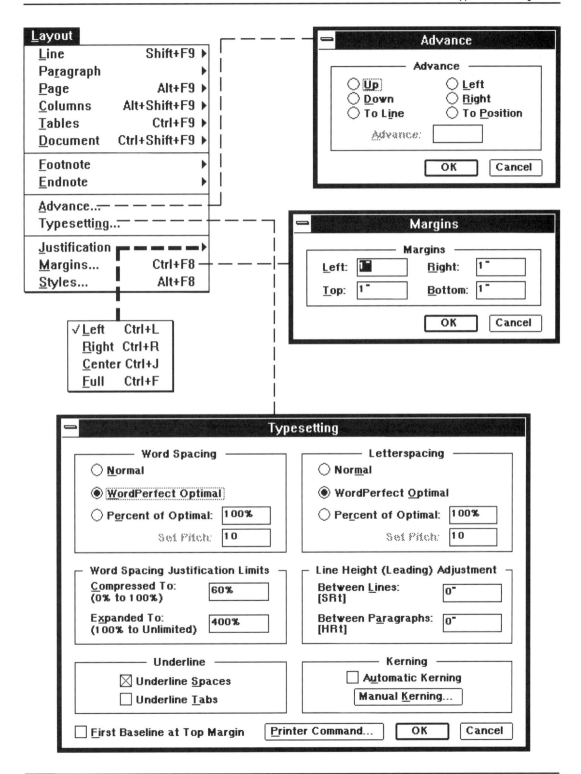

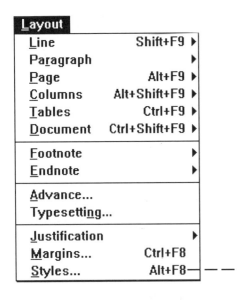

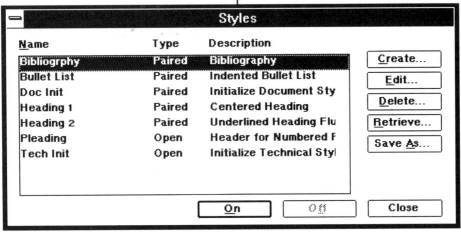

THE TOOLS MENU

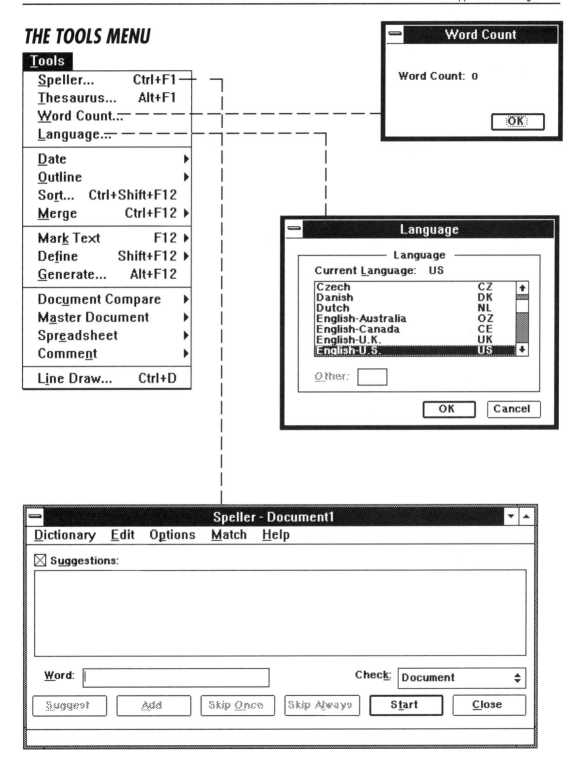

Tools

<u>S</u>peller...	Ctrl+F1
<u>T</u>hesaurus...	Alt+F1
<u>W</u>ord Count...	
<u>L</u>anguage...	
<u>D</u>ate	▶
<u>O</u>utline	▶
So<u>r</u>t...	Ctrl+Shift+F12
<u>M</u>erge	Ctrl+F12 ▶
Mar<u>k</u> Text	F12 ▶
De<u>f</u>ine	Shift+F12 ▶
<u>G</u>enerate...	Alt+F12
Do<u>c</u>ument Compare	▶
M<u>a</u>ster Document	▶
Spr<u>e</u>adsheet	▶
Comme<u>n</u>t	▶
L<u>i</u>ne Draw...	Ctrl+D

Word Count

Word Count: 0

OK

Language

Language

Current Language: US

Czech	CZ
Danish	DK
Dutch	NL
English-Australia	OZ
English-Canada	CE
English-U.K.	UK
English-U.S.	US

Other:

OK   Cancel

Speller - Document1

Dictionary   Edit   Options   Match   Help

⊠ Suggestions:

Word:

Check: Document

Suggest   Add   Skip Once   Skip Always   Start   Close

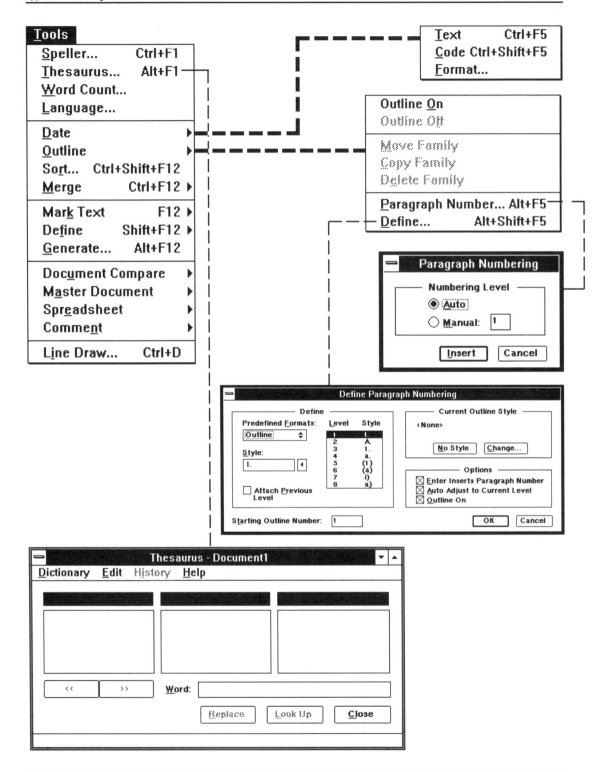

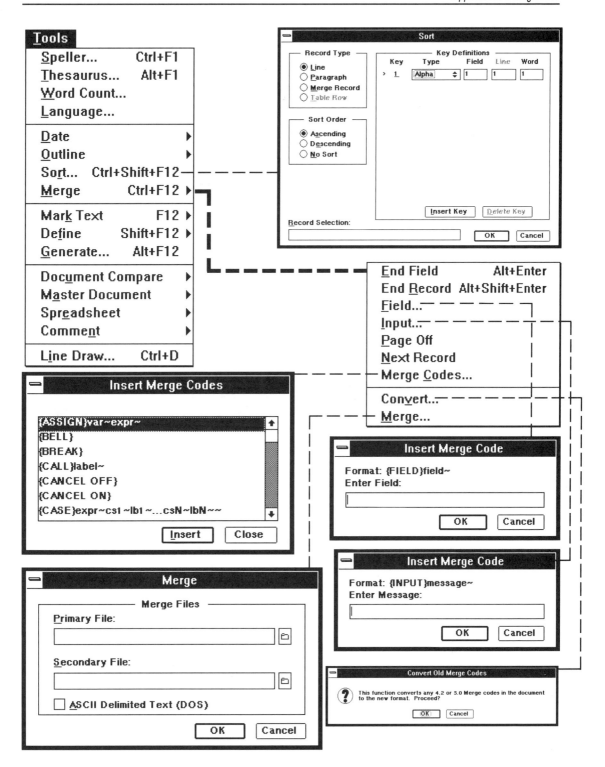

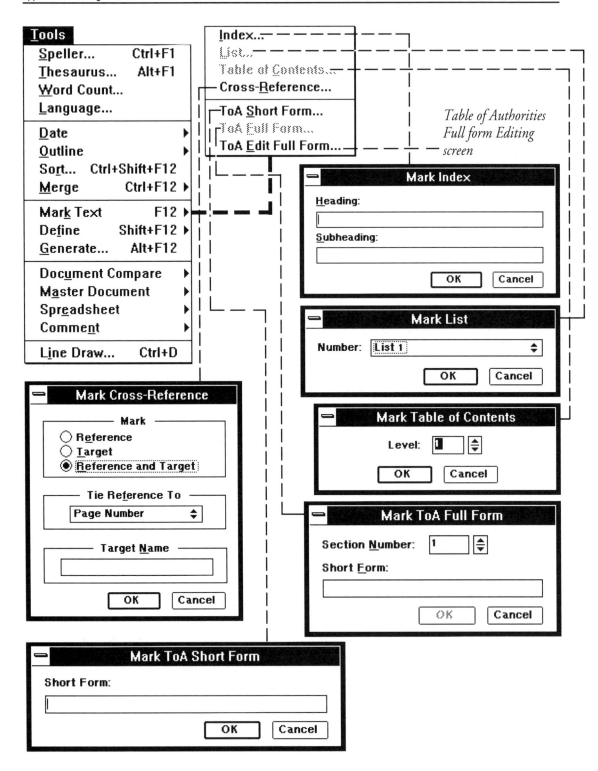

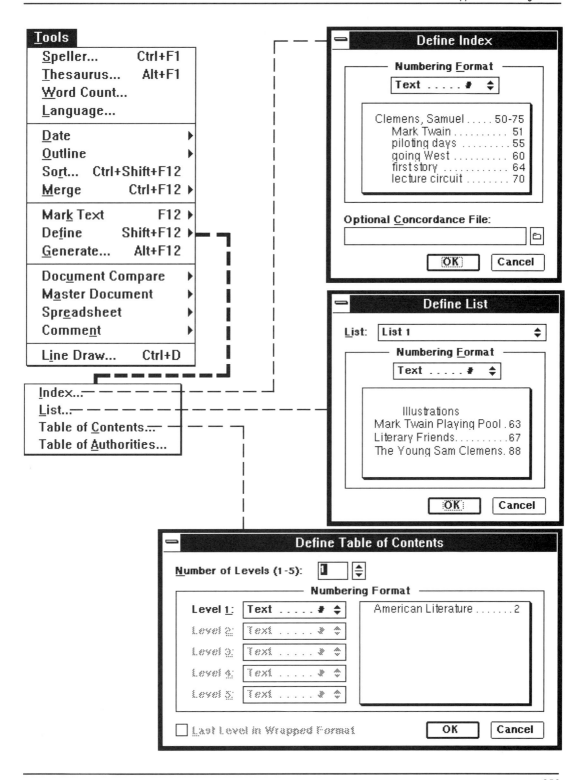

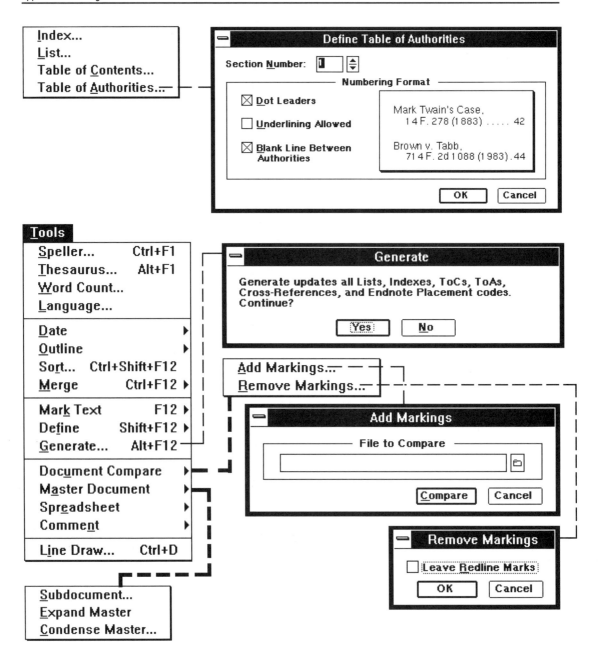

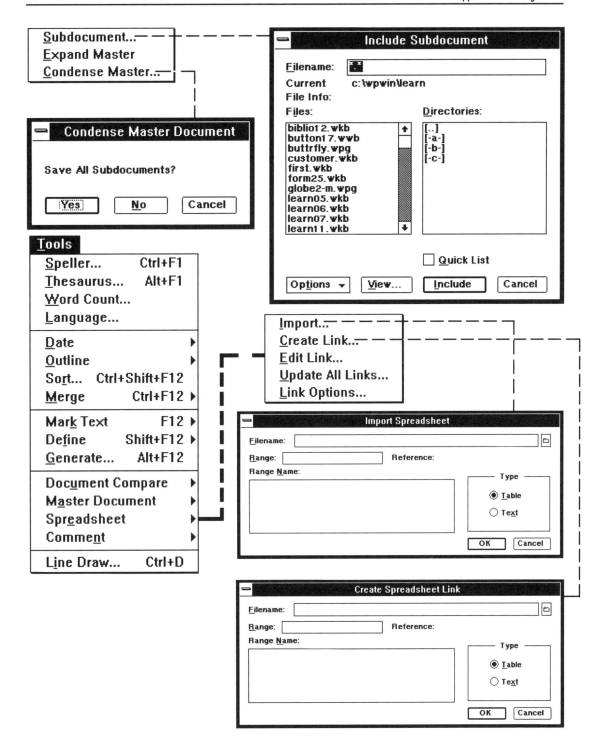

Subdocument...
Expand Master
Condense Master...

Include Subdocument

Filename:
Current   c:\wpwin\learn
File Info:
Files: Directories:
biblio1 2.wkb   [..]
button1 7.wwb   [-a-]
buttrfly.wpg   [-b-]
customer.wkb   [-c-]
first.wkb
form25.wkb
globe2-m.wpg
learn05.wkb
learn06.wkb
learn07.wkb
learn1 1.wkb

☐ Quick List

Options ▾   View...   Include   Cancel

Condense Master Document

Save All Subdocuments?

Yes   No   Cancel

Tools

Speller...   Ctrl+F1
Thesaurus...   Alt+F1
Word Count...
Language...

Date   ▶
Outline   ▶
Sort...   Ctrl+Shift+F12
Merge   Ctrl+F12 ▶

Mark Text   F12 ▶
Define   Shift+F12 ▶
Generate...   Alt+F12

Document Compare   ▶
Master Document   ▶
Spreadsheet   ▶
Comment   ▶

Line Draw...   Ctrl+D

Import...
Create Link...
Edit Link...
Update All Links...
Link Options...

Import Spreadsheet

Filename:
Range: Reference:
Range Name:
                                    Type
                                ⦿ Table
                                ○ Text
                            OK   Cancel

Create Spreadsheet Link

Filename:
Range: Reference:
Range Name:
                                    Type
                                ⦿ Table
                                ○ Text
                            OK   Cancel

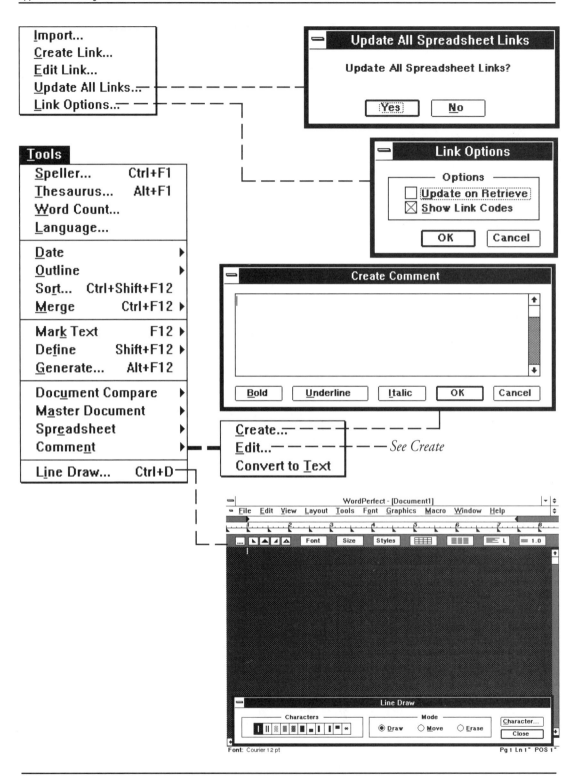

Import...
Create Link...
Edit Link...
Update All Links...
Link Options...

Update All Spreadsheet Links

Update All Spreadsheet Links?

[Yes]   [No]

Link Options

Options
☐ Update on Retrieve
☒ Show Link Codes

[OK]   [Cancel]

Tools

Speller...	Ctrl+F1
Thesaurus...	Alt+F1
Word Count...	
Language...	
Date	▶
Outline	▶
Sort...	Ctrl+Shift+F12
Merge	Ctrl+F12 ▶
Mark Text	F12 ▶
Define	Shift+F12 ▶
Generate...	Alt+F12
Document Compare	▶
Master Document	▶
Spreadsheet	▶
Comment	▶
Line Draw...	Ctrl+D

Create Comment

[Bold] [Underline] [Italic] [OK] [Cancel]

Create...
Edit... — *See Create*
Convert to Text

WordPerfect - [Document1]

File Edit View Layout Tools Font Graphics Macro Window Help

Font Size Styles   L 1.0

Line Draw

Characters
Mode
⦿ Draw ○ Move ○ Erase

[Character...]
[Close]

Font: Courier 12 pt

Pg 1 Ln 1" POS 1"

THE FONT MENU

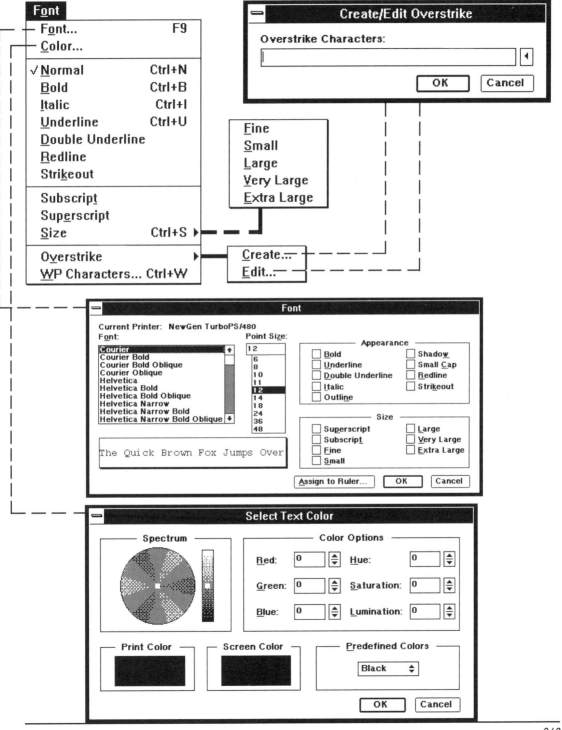

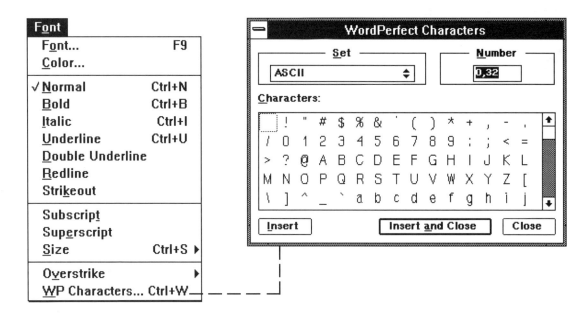

THE GRAPHICS MENU

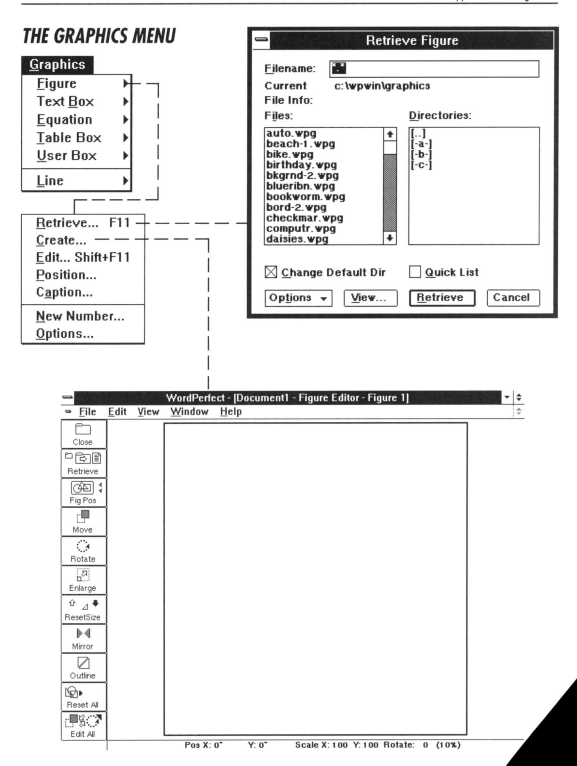

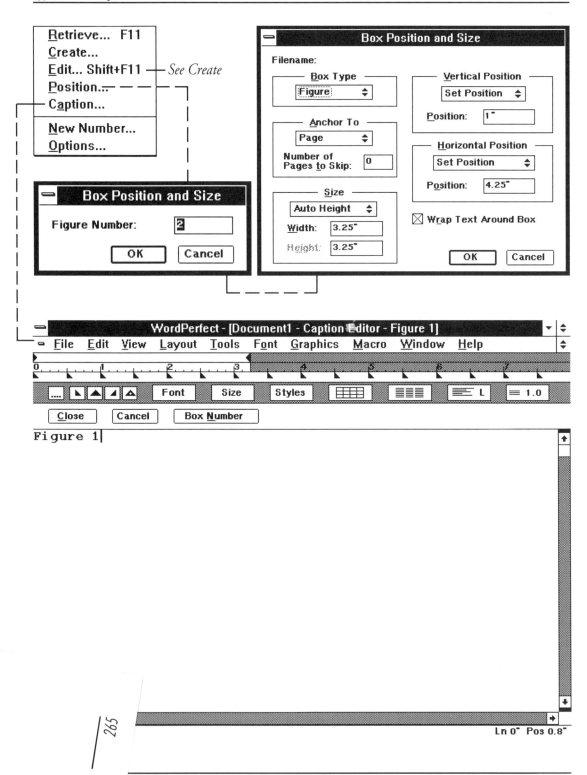

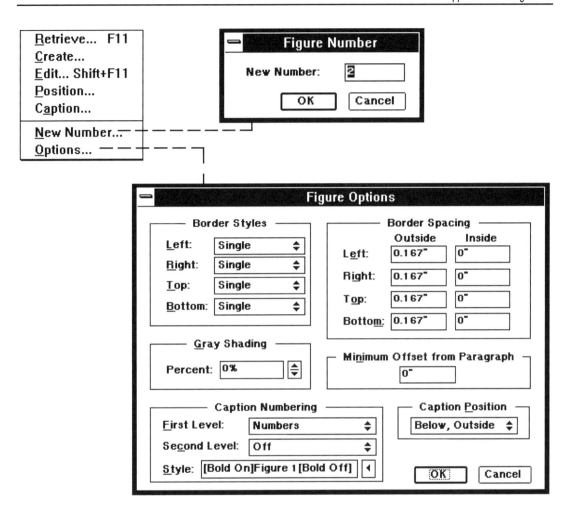

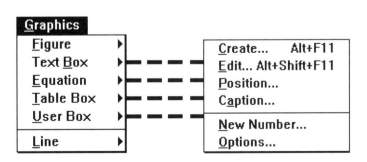

All dialog boxes associated with the *Text Box, Equation, Table Box,* and *User Box* sub-menus are identical to the dialog boxes of the *Figure* sub-menu commands, except for the title bar; we have therefore not displayed them.

In addition, the *Figure* command also includes the *Retrieve* option for importing graphics into WordPerfect.

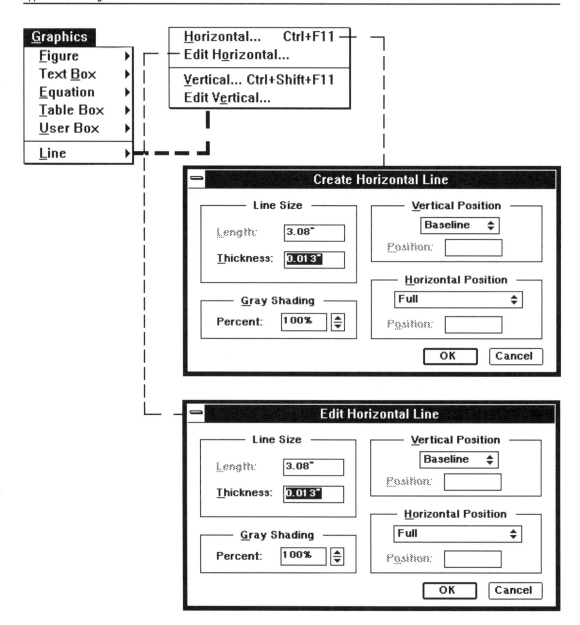

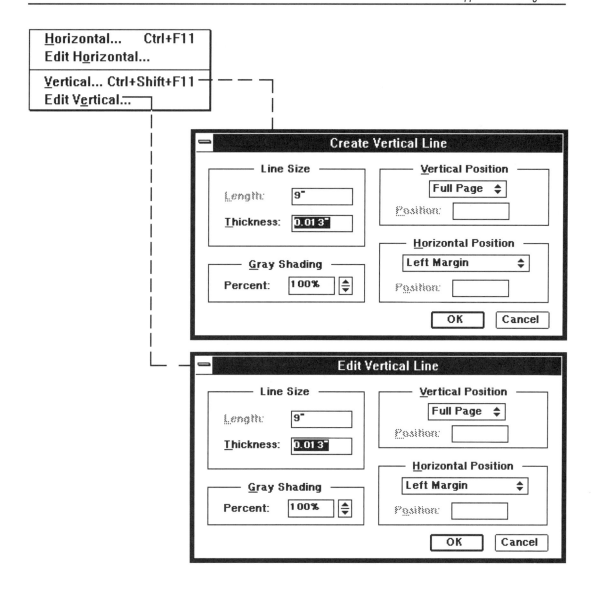

THE MACRO MENU

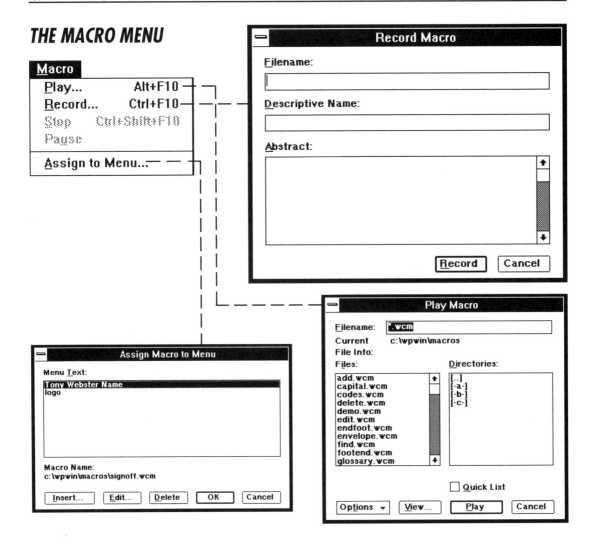

THE WINDOW MENU

Window
Cascade
Tile
√1 Document1

Index